*T*HE volumes of the University of Michigan Studies are published by authority of the Executive Board of the Graduate Department of the University of Michigan. A list of the volumes thus far published or arranged for is given at the end of this volume.

University of Michigan Studies
HUMANISTIC SERIES

VOLUME V

SOURCES OF THE SYNOPTIC
GOSPELS

THE MACMILLAN COMPANY
NEW YORK · BOSTON · CHICAGO
ATLANTA · SAN FRANCISCO

MACMILLAN & CO., Limited
LONDON · BOMBAY · CALCUTTA
MELBOURNE

THE MACMILLAN CO. OF CANADA, Ltd.
TORONTO

SOURCES

OF THE

SYNOPTIC GOSPELS

BY

CARL S. PATTON

FIRST CONGREGATIONAL CHURCH
COLUMBUS, OHIO

New York
THE MACMILLAN COMPANY
LONDON: MACMILLAN & COMPANY, LIMITED
1915

All Rights Reserved

Copyright 1915 By
Carl S. Patton

Printed August, 1915

Composed and Printed By
The University of Chicago Press
Chicago, Illinois, U.S.A.

Paperback ISBN: 978-0-472-75187-7

PREFACE

The purpose of this study is twofold: first, to give some account of the investigations recently made in the Synoptic Problem, and the present status of scholarly opinion concerning it; secondly, upon the basis of such established results, to push the inquiry into certain items a step farther.

The first part of the work, including pages 3–120, tho largely occupied with results reached by many different scholars, and bringing the matter up to where the writer adds his own more personal contribution, is yet not a mere survey of results attained. The writer has expressed his own judgment freely thruout it, as to the merits of arguments of others, and as to the points involved in the discussion. But his more personal contribution lies in the analysis of the groundwork Q into the two recensions, Q Mt and Q Lk.

The one book constantly in the writer's hands during the preparation of this study was A. Huck's *Synopse der drei ersten Evangelien*.[1] Without some such parallel edition of the Greek Gospels constantly open before him, one can neither write nor read profitably upon the Synoptic Question. The question of originality, and of giving credit for arguments and suggestions derived from other students, in a study of this sort, is extremely difficult. In the minute comparison of passages in one Gospel with passages in another, many of the differences and resemblances noted are part of the working material

[1] Mohr, Tübingen, 1906, 3d ed. A fourth edition of this valuable book appeared in 1911, but without important changes.

of most writers upon the Synoptic Problem; when one has worked thru the analyses of other students, has made their results his own, and has also made his own observations upon the basis of them, it becomes almost impossible for him to say what part of the total result is due to himself and for what part he is indebted to others. The writer is more deeply indebted to Paul Wernle, Sir John Hawkins, and the authors of the *Oxford Studies*, than to anyone else. The latter book came out after this study had been completed but the results have been revised somewhat under its influence. I have attempted to give credit in footnotes for suggestions received from many sources, but many must have gone unnoticed.

I am under deep obligation to the kind friends who have encouraged and made possible the publication of this Study, particularly to Mr. William H. Murphy, of Detroit.

CARL S. PATTON

FIRST CONGREGATIONAL CHURCH
COLUMBUS, OHIO
August, 1914

CONTENTS

PART I: GENERALLY ACCEPTED RESULTS OF SYNOPTIC STUDY

CHAPTER I: THE DEPENDENCE OF MATTHEW AND LUKE UPON MARK

	PAGE
THE FRAMEWORK OF MARK IN MATTHEW AND LUKE	3
Up to Luke's "Great Omission"	3
Luke's "Great Omission" and Beyond	7
Luke's "Great Interpolation": Its Content	8
The Jerusalem Narrative	10
The Story of the Passion	12
THE PRIORITY OF MARK	13
Luke's Great Interpolation: Its Non-Use of Mark	16

CHAPTER II: THE ORDER OF MARK'S GOSPEL COMPARED WITH THAT OF MATTHEW AND THAT OF LUKE

ORDER OF MARK IN MATTHEW AND LUKE	19
Table I: Showing Changes Made by Matthew and Luke in the Order of Marcan Material	24
Deductions from the Table	28

CHAPTER III: THE OMISSIONS OF MATTHEW AND LUKE IN THE MARCAN NARRATIVE

OMISSIONS OF MATTHEW AND LUKE IN MARK	30
Omissions Made by Both Matthew and Luke	30
Omissions Made by Matthew in the Marcan Narrative	31
Omissions Made by Luke in the Marcan Narrative	32

CHAPTER IV: THE CHANGES OF MATTHEW AND LUKE IN THE NARRATIVE OF MARK

CHANGES OF MATTHEW AND LUKE IN MARK	37
The Baptism of Jesus	37
The Calling of the First Disciples	38
Jesus in the Synagogue at Capernaum	38
The Healing of Peter's Mother-in-Law	38
The Healing in the Evening	39
The Retirement of Jesus	39
The Calling of Peter	40
The Healing of the Leper	41
The Healing of the Paralytic	41
The Calling of Levi (Matthew)	42

	PAGE
CHANGES OF MATTHEW AND LUKE IN MARK—*continued*	
The Question about Fasting	42
The Walk Through the Corn	43
The Man with the Withered Hand	44
The Crowd and the Healings	44
The Calling of the Twelve	44
The Pharisaic Accusation and Jesus' Defense	45
The True Brotherhood of Jesus; the Parable of the Sower; the Purpose of the Parables	45
The Interpretation of the Parable of the Sower	46
A Group of Detached Sayings	47
The Parable of the Mustard Seed	47
The Storm on the Lake	47
The Gadarene Demoniac	48
The Daughter of Jairus and the Woman with the Issue of Blood	49
The Initial Preaching in Nazareth	51
The Sending out of the Disciples	51
The Judgment of Herod concerning Jesus	52
The Death of the Baptist	53
The Return of the Disciples and the Feeding of the Five Thousand	54
The Walking on the Sea	55
The Return to Gennesaret	56
About the Things That Defile	56
The Canaanitish Woman	57
The Feeding of the Four Thousand	57
The Demand for a Sign	57
The Saying about Yeast	57
The Confession of Peter, and the First Prediction of Sufferings	58
The Demands of Discipleship	58
The Transfiguration	59
The Discussion about Elijah	59
The Healing of the Epileptic Boy	60
The Second Prediction of Sufferings	60
The Strife about Rank	61
Minor Passages	61
SUMMARY OF MATTHEW'S AND LUKE'S TREATMENT OF THE MARCAN NARRATIVE	70

CHAPTER V: HAVE WE THE GOSPEL OF MARK IN ITS ORIGINAL FORM?

HAVE WE MARK IN ITS ORIGINAL FORM?	72
Discussion of the Analysis of Mark by Wendling and von Soden	74
Conclusions of von Soden and Wendling Compared	83
Matthew and Luke Used Our Mark as a Source	88
The Hypothesis of a Primitive Mark Superfluous; Simpler Explanations	88
Some Remarkable Verbal Resemblances	93

CONTENTS ix

CHAPTER VI: USE OF A COMMON DOCUMENT BY MATTHEW
AND LUKE

PAGE

USE OF A COMMON DOCUMENT BY MATTHEW AND LUKE . . 97
   A Recent Attempt to Prove Matthew a Source for Luke . 100

CHAPTER VII: THE EXISTENCE AND CONTENT OF Q

EXISTENCE AND CONTENT OF Q 108
   Deductions from the Table 109
   Table II: Material from Q in Matthew 110
   Deductions from Table III 115
   Table III: Material in Luke Taken from Q 116
   The Necessity for a Further Extension of Q 120

PART II: ANALYSIS OF Q INTO QMt AND QLk

CHAPTER I: ANALYSIS OF Q

ANALYSIS OF Q 123
   Q Originally an Aramaic Document, Used in Greek
      Translations by Matthew and Luke 123
   The Analysis of Q into QMt and QLk 126

CHAPTER II: Q, QMt, AND QLk, IN THE DOUBLE TRADITION
OF MATTHEW AND LUKE

Q, QMt, AND QLk IN MATTHEW AND LUKE 129
   The Preaching of John the Baptist 129
   The Messianic Proclamation of the Baptist 130
   The Temptation 130
   "Blessed Are the Poor" 131
   "Blessed Are They That Mourn" 132
   "Blessed Are They That Hunger" 132
   "Blessed Are The Persecuted" 132
   A Saying about Salt 133
   A Saying about Light 133
   A Saying about the Law 135
   "Agree with Thine Adversary" 135
   About Non-Resistance and Love of Enemies 135
   The Lord's Prayer 136
   A Saying about Treasures 137
   A Saying about the Eye 137
   About Double Service 138
   About Care 138
   About Judging 139
   The Beam and the Mote 139
   About Seeking and Finding 139
   The Golden Rule 140
   The Narrow Gate 140
   The Tree and Its Fruits 141
   Warning against Self-Deception 141
   The Two Houses 143

CONTENTS

Q, QMT, AND QLK IN MATTHEW AND LUKE—*continued*

	PAGE
The Centurion's Son	143
"Many Shall Come from East and West"	145
Two Men Would Follow Jesus	146
"The Harvest Is Great"	146
"The Laborer Is Worthy of His Hire"	146
"Greet the House"	147
"More Tolerable for Sodom"	147
"Sheep among Wolves"	148
How to Act under Persecution	148
The Disciple and His Teacher	148
Exhortation to Fearless Confession	149
Strife among Relatives	150
Conditions of Discipleship	150
"He That Receiveth You"	151
The Question of the Baptist and Jesus' Answer	152
The Woe upon the Galilean Cities	152
"I Thank Thee, O Father"	152
Jesus' Defense against the Pharisees	153
"He That Is Not with Me"	153
Jonah and the Ninevites	153
A Speech about Backsliding	154
"Blessed Are the Eyes That See"	154
The Parable of the Yeast	154
The Blind Leading the Blind	155
A Saying about Faith	155
A Saying about Offenses	156
The Stray Sheep	156
About Forgiveness	157
Rewards for Discipleship	157
Against the Pharisees	157
"Whoso Humbles Himself"	158
Against the Pharisees	158
A Woe upon the Scribes	159
"I Send unto You Prophets"	160
The Lament over Jerusalem	161
The Day of the Son of Man	161
The Body and the Eagles	161
The Days of Noah	161
The One Taken, the Other Left	162
The Watching Servant	162
The True and False Servants	162
Results of the Preceding Investigation	162

CHAPTER III: Q IN THE SINGLE TRADITION OF MATTHEW (QMT)

Q IN THE SINGLE TRADITION OF MATTHEW	166
Two Beatitudes	167
Four More Beatitudes	167
"Ye Are the Light of the World"	169
"Let Your Light Shine"	169
Various Sayings from the Sermon on the Mount	170
A Saying about Offenses	171

Contents

Q in the Single Tradition of Matthew—*continued*

	PAGE
The Commandment about Divorce	171
About Oaths	172
The Second Mile	172
Another Old Testament Commandment	173
About Alms-Giving	173
About Prayer	174
About Fasting	175
Pearls before Swine	175
The False Prophets	176
A Saying about Trees	177
"By Their Fruits"	177
An Oft-Repeated Formula	177
The Conclusion of the Story of the Centurion's Servant	178
"I Will Have Mercy and Not Sacrifice"	179
The Healing of Two Blind Men	179
The Healing of a Dumb Man	180
Instructions to the Disciples	180
Further Instructions to the Disciples	180
A Saying about Elijah	181
"He That Hath Ears, Let Him Hear"	182
The Occasion of Pronouncing Woes upon the Galilean Cities	182
Reason Assigned for the Pronunciation of the Woes	182
"Come unto Me"	183
A Saying about the Law	184
An Old Testament Quotation	184
"Generation of Vipers"	184
A Saying about the Judgment	185
An Interpretation of the Sign of Jonah	185
The Weed in the Field	185
The Parables of the Treasure, the Pearl, the Fish-Net, and the Scribe Instructed in the Kingdom	186
Peter Walking on the Water	187
"To the Lost Sheep of the House of Israel"	187
A Summary of Jesus' Healing Work	188
The Keys of the Kingdom of Heaven	189
An Insertion in the Story of the Transfiguration	189
"Whosoever Humbles Himself as This Little Child"	189
The Unforgiving Servant	190
About Eunuchs	190
The Laborers in the Vineyard	190
The Two Sons	191
The Wedding Feast	191
Against the Pharisees	191
The Parables of the Ten Virgins, the Talents, the Judgment	191
"Twelve Legions of Angels"	192

Chapter IV: Q in the Single Tradition of Luke (QLk)

Q in the Single Tradition of Luke	193
The Preaching of John the Baptist	193
The Initial Preaching of Jesus in Nazareth	194
The Call of Peter	194

Contents

	PAGE
Q IN THE SINGLE TRADITION OF LUKE—*continued*	
The Woes	194
The Reception of John's Preaching	195
The Sinner in Simon's House	195
A Would-Be Follower of Jesus	196
The Return of the Seventy	196
The Great Commandment	197
The Good Samaritan	197
Mary and Martha	197
The Parable of the Friend on a Journey	198
The Mother of Jesus Praised	198
"If Thine Whole Body Is Light"	198
The Parable of the Foolish Rich Man	198
The Exhortation to Watchfulness	198
"To Whom Much Is Given"	199
"I Came to Cast Fire upon the Earth"	199
The Galileans Slain by Herod	199
The Parable of the Fig-Tree	200
"Go Tell That Fox"	200
The Healing of the Dropsical Man	201
About Taking the Less Honorable Seats at the Table	201
Whom to Invite to a Feast	202
The Parable of the Dinner and the Invited Guests	202
Conditions of Discipleship	203
The Lost Sheep	203
The Lost Coin and the Prodigal Son	203
The Unjust Steward	203
A Criticism of the Pharisees	204
The Rich Man and Lazarus	205
"Unprofitable Servants" and the Healing of the Ten Lepers	205
About the Coming of the Kingdom of God	205
Matter Peculiar to Matthew or to Luke	206
Matter Peculiar to Luke	210
Did Luke's Great Interpolation Originally Exist as a Separate Documentary Source?	214
Other Possible Sources for Material Peculiar to Luke	217
Conclusions Regarding Q Material in the Single Traditions of Matthew and Luke	218

CHAPTER V: REVIEW OF Q MATERIAL IN MATTHEW, LUKE, AND MARK

REVIEW OF Q IN MATTHEW, LUKE, AND MARK	221
Considerations Favoring Analysis of Q into QMt and QLk	221
Table IV: Contents of Q Material in Matthew	222
Table V: Contents of Q Material in Luke	224
Passages Closely Similar, Yet With Divergences Too Great to Be Accounted for upon the Hypothesis of an Undifferentiated Q	226
With Matthew's Q before Him, Luke Would Not Have Omitted So Much of It	227
The "Secondary Traits" Are in QMt and QLk, Not in Q	230

CONTENTS xiii

PAGE

CHAPTER VI: DID MARK ALSO USE Q?

DID MARK ALSO USE Q? 234
    What Material Did Mark Take from Q? 236
    The Messianic Announcement of the Baptist 237
    The Baptism of Jesus 237
    The Temptation of Jesus 238
    The Beelzebul Controversy 238
    Five Detached Sayings 239
    The Parable of the Mustard Seed 240
    The Sending Out of the Twelve 241
    A Sign Refused 241
    "Whosoever Will Follow Me" 241
    "Whosoever Is Ashamed of Me" 242
    About Offenses 242
    About Salt 243
    About Divorce 243
    The First Who Shall Be Last 243
    True Greatness 244
    About Faith 244
    Against the Pharisees 244
    The Holy Spirit Speaking in the Disciples 244
    Other Marcan Passages Considered, But Rejected . . 244
    Table VI: Contents of Q Material in Mark 246
    Do the Vocabulary and Style of Mark and Q, Respectively, Throw Any Light upon Their Literary Relationship? 246
    Conclusions as to Mark's Dependence upon Q . . . 248

CHAPTER VII: THE ORIGINAL ORDER OF Q

ORIGINAL ORDER OF Q 249
    Table VII 250
    Table VIII 250
    Table IX 251
    Table X 252

CHAPTER VIII: SUMMARY AND CONCLUSIONS

PART I

ACCEPTED RESULTS OF SYNOPTIC STUDY

CHAPTER I

THE DEPENDENCE OF MATTHEW AND LUKE UPON MARK

The one universally accepted result of modern study of the synoptic problem is the dependence of Matthew and Luke upon the Gospel of Mark.

Tho it is no longer necessary to demonstrate this use of Mark by Matthew and Luke, the relation among the three Gospels is not to be dismissed with a simple statement of this dependence. The Gospel of Mark is the one document possessed by us in substantially the same form in which it was used by Matthew and Luke. A consideration of how Matthew and Luke treated the sources which we no longer have before us will be influenced by the treatment which they accorded to this one source which we have. Our first work, therefore, is to observe, with some thoroness, the manner in which Matthew and Luke use the Gospel of Mark. If any proof is still required that Matthew and Luke did employ this Gospel, it will appear in the discussion.

FRAMEWORK OF MARK'S GOSPEL IN MATTHEW AND LUKE— UP TO LUKE'S "GREAT OMISSION"

Matthew and Luke begin with introductory matter of their own, occupying the first two chapters of their Gospels. With the appearance of John the Baptist their narrative begins to coincide with that of Mark. Luke in a manner characteristic of his Gospel attempts to supply historical details. Mark (i, 6) gives a fuller description of the personal habits and appearance of the Baptist; the others omit this, and pass to a description of his preaching (Mt iii, 7–10; Lk iii, 7–9). Luke adds a brief section (iii, 10–14) on this subject derived from some source of his own.

After these insertions of non-Marcan material, Matthew and Luke come back to the narrative of Mark, and recount (Mk i, 7–8; Mt iii, 11–12; Lk iii, 15–18) the messianic prediction of the Baptist, the baptism of Jesus (Mk i, 9–11; Mt iii, 13–17; Lk iii, 21–22), the temptation (Mk i, 12–13; Mt iv, 1–11; Lk iv, 1–13), and the initial appearance of Jesus in Galilee (Mk i, 14–15; Mt iv, 12–17; Lk iv, 14–15). Between the messianic preaching of the Baptist and the baptism of Jesus, Luke has inserted a notice of the arrest and imprisonment of John, and between the baptism and the temptation, his table of the ancestors of Jesus.[1] The large amount of closely parallel matter in Matthew and Luke, especially in their account of the Baptist's preaching and their narrative of the temptation, shows their use of a common non-Marcan source; but the order of their narrative, as well as its wording, shows their use of Mark also. To his account of the initial appearance of Jesus in Galilee, Luke adds (iv, 16–30) an account of Jesus' first preaching in Nazareth.

Matthew proceeds to tell with Mark (Mt iv, 18–22; Mk i, 16–20) of the calling of the first disciples. Luke postpones this, having a more detailed and interesting account of the call of Peter which he will introduce later (Lk v, 1–11). Mark (i, 21–28) then tells of Jesus' preaching in a synagogue at Capernaum. This Matthew omits, but Luke (iv, 31–37) gives the story as Mark has it. Matthew

---

[1] Cf. Sanders, *Journal of Biblical Literature*, XXXII, 184 ff., for evidence that this did not stand in the original text of Luke.

here inserts his Sermon on the Mount and the healing of the nobleman's daughter (Mt v, 1—viii, 13); he then comes back to the narrative of Mark, and with Luke tells (Mk i, 29-31; Mt viii, 14-15; Lk iv, 38-39) of the healing of Peter's mother-in-law. The three evangelists then relate together (Mk i, 32-34; Mt viii, 16-17; Lk iv, 40-41), the story of the healings at evening. Luke and Mark add the story of Jesus' retirement into a desert place (Mk i, 35-38; Lk iv, 42-43), which Matthew omits. Mark and Luke then add a brief statement of a preaching tour thru Galilee (Mk i, 39; Lk iv, 44); Matthew has already utilized this statement, somewhat enlarged, as introductory to his Sermon on the Mount (Mt iv, 23-25). Luke inserts (Lk v, 1-11) his account of the calling of Peter, postponed from its earlier position in Mark. The three then tell together the story of the healing of the leper and the paralytic, the call of Levi (called Matthew in Matthew), and the discussion about fasting (Mk i, 40—ii, 22; Mt viii, 1-4; ix, 1-17; Lk v, 12-39). Matthew (ix, 35—x, 16) inserts his account of the sending out of the twelve, which Mark and Luke give later. After this he comes back into agreement with the other two, and all three relate the incident of Jesus' walking thru the corn on the Sabbath (Mk ii, 23-28; Mt xii, 1-8; Lk vi, 1-5), the healing of the withered hand (Mk iii, 1-6; Mt xii, 9-14; Lk vi, 6-11), and the healings in the crowd (Mk iii, 7-12; Mt xii, 15-21; Lk vi, 17-19).

At this point Luke has transposed two brief sections of Mark, because, it is evident, by so doing he secures a better introduction to his Sermon on the Level Place, which he now (Lk vi, 20-49) proceeds to give. By placing the account of the calling of the twelve (Mk iii, 13-19; Lk vi, 12-16) just before the account of the gathering of the throng (Mk iii, 7–12; Lk vi, 17–19) he secures his audience for his Sermon on the Plain; if the narrative had been given in reverse order, as by Mark, the sermon might appear to have been addressed to the twelve alone. After his Sermon on the Plain (Lk vi, 20–49) Luke adds the story of the widow's son, the anointing in Simon's house, and the ministering women (vii, 11–17, 36–50; viii, 1–3), not found in either Mark or Matthew, after which the three take up the same story again in the accusation of the scribes and the speech about Beelzebub, tho Luke's order is here not that of the other two (Mk iii, 20–30; Mt xii, 22–37; Lk xi, 14–23). After the insertion of non-Marcan material by both Matthew and Luke, both return to Mark's narrative in the story of the family of Jesus who had come to take him home (Mk iii, 31–35; Mt xii, 46–50; Lk viii, 19–21), the parable of the Sower, the speech about the purpose of the parables, the interpretation of the parable of the Sower, and the group of detached sayings (Mk iv, 1–25; Mt xiii, 1–23; Lk viii, 4–18); Matthew, however, omits three out of the four sayings at this point, because he has already incorporated them in his Sermon on the Mount.

Then follows in Mark alone (Mk iv, 26–29) the parable of the Seed that grew of itself, the only section of Marcan material thus far omitted by both Matthew and Luke. Then the parable of the Seed-Corn, which Luke omits but Matthew gives (Mk iv, 30–32; Mt xiii, 31–32).[1] Then come the storm on the lake, the story of the Gadarene demoniac, the healing of Jairus' daughter, with the interpolation of the story of the woman with the hemorrhage

---

[1] This statement may be questioned, as Lk xiii, 18–19 may be considered parallel to Mk iv, 30–32. At all events Matthew has the passage with Mark. The matter is complicated by the fact that the parable apparently stood in both Mark and Q.

(Mk iv, 35—v, 43; Mt viii, 23-34; ix, 18-26; Lk viii, 22-56), all in the same order. Then follows the rejection in Nazareth (Mk vi, 1-6; Mt xiii, 53-58); Matthew follows Mark in it, but Luke omits it because he has related a similar incident in his fourth chapter. Luke then follows Mark in relating the incident of the sending out of the twelve (Mk vi, 6-13; Lk ix, 1-6); Matthew has given it in an earlier location. The judgment of Herod concerning Jesus is then given by all three (Mk vi, 14-16; Mt xiv, 1-2; Lk ix, 7-9). Matthew gives with Mark (Mk vi, 17-29; Mt xiv, 3-12) the story of the Baptist's death; Luke omits it, having concluded his story of John in connection with his account of the baptism of Jesus (Lk iii, 19-20). Then follow in all three the return of the disciples and the feeding of the five thousand (Mk vi, 30-44; Mt xiv, 13-21; Lk ix, 10-17). Thus far, several items of Mark's narrative have been omitted now by Matthew and now by Luke, but only one fragment, the parable of the Seed Growing of Itself (Mk iv, 26-29), by both Matthew and Luke.

LUKE'S "GREAT OMISSION," AND BEYOND

With Mk vi, 45, begins a section extending to Mk viii, 26, in which Matthew follows Mark closely, both in wording and in order (Mt xiv, 22—xvi, 12), except that Matthew omits Mark's healing of the deaf stammerer (Mk vii, 31-37), inserts (Mt xv, 29-31) a summary of the healing narratives, and omits the healing of the blind man (Mk viii, 22-26). Luke omits the entire section. Luke picks up the thread of Mark's narrative again at Mk viii, 27, and he and Matthew follow it thru the confession of Peter (Mk viii, 27-33; Mt xvi, 13-23; Lk ix, 18-22), the prediction of sufferings for the disciples (Mk viii, 34—ix, 1; Mt xvi, 24-28; Lk ix, 23-27), and the transfiguration (Mk ix, 2-8;

Mt xvii, 1–8; Lk ix, 28–36). Luke omits the question of the scribes concerning Elias, but Matthew follows Mark in it (Mk ix, 9–13; Mt xvii, 9–13). After the omission of these five Marcan verses Luke again continues Mark's narrative, as does Matthew, and the three relate together the healing of the epileptic boy (Mk ix, 14–29; Mt xvii, 14–21; Lk ix, 37–43a), and the second prediction of sufferings (Mk ix, 30–32; Mt xvii, 22–23; Lk ix, 43b–45).

Matthew inserts from another source the passage about the temple-tax (Mt xvii, 24–27), and the three continue together in the passage concerning the strife about precedence (Mk ix, 33–37; Mt xviii, 1–5; Lk ix, 46–48). Matthew then drops out for a few verses, but Luke follows Mark in the story of the unknown exorcist (Mk ix, 38–41; Lk ix, 49–50). Luke omits Mark's saying about offenses, but Matthew follows Mark in it (Mk ix, 42–48; Mt xviii, 6–9). Both Matthew and Luke then forsake Mark for the moment, since they have both given his saying about salt (Mk ix, 49–50) in other connections, their treatment of Mark here being evidently influenced by their use of another source.[1] Matthew then inserts a few sections peculiar to his Gospel (Mt xviii, 10–35), a few verses of which (Mt xviii, 10–14; Lk xv, 3–7; Mt xviii, 15; Lk xvii, 3; Mt xviii, 21–22; Lk xvii, 4) are somewhat loosely paralleled in Luke.

LUKE'S "GREAT INTERPOLATION": ITS CONTENT

Beginning with the 51st verse of his 9th chapter, and extending thru the 14th verse of his 18th chapter, occurs Luke's "Great Interpolation," his account of the journey thru Samaria. Here occur in Luke many of Jesus' sayings

[1] Tho Lk xiv, 34a is apparently taken from Mk ix, 50a, as against Mt v, 13a.

which Matthew has combined into his "Sermon on the Mount"; notably the Lord's Prayer, the speech about backsliding, and the saying "Ask and ye shall receive." Here also is much material peculiar to Luke; notably Jesus' visit to the home of Mary and Martha, the blessing of the woman upon the mother of Jesus, the sending out and return of the seventy disciples, the healing of the ten lepers, and the parables of the Good Samaritan, the Friend Asking for Bread, the Foolish Rich Man, the Lost Sheep, the Lost Coin, the Prodigal Son, Dives and Lazarus, the Unjust Judge, and the Publican and Pharisee in the Temple.

Since the purpose here is merely to indicate the relation of the framework of the Gospels of Matthew and Luke to that of Mark, the full content of this great interpolation of Luke's does not need to be presented. Enough has been given to show how long and important a section it is. Thruout it Luke appears to forsake Mark, tho there seem to be evidences that for some of the material contained in this section and also to be found in Mark, Mark and Luke have been drawing upon a common source.[1]

After forsaking Mark for so long, Luke comes back to him, and to Matthew (who has not made this deviation at the same place), in the blessing of the children (Mk x, 13–16; Mt xix, 13–15; Lk xviii, 15–17), the danger of riches (Mk x, 17–31; Mt xix, 16–30; Lk xviii, 18–30), and the third prediction of sufferings (Mk x, 32–34; Mt xx, 17–19; Lk xviii, 31–34). Matthew has meantime inserted (Mt xx, 1–16) his parable of the Workers in the Vineyard, but has not allowed this insertion to influence his adherence to the Marcan order. Luke then drops out of the triple

[1] For discussion of Luke's non-use of Mark thruout the Great Interpolation, see pp. 16–18; for an elaborate analysis of the sources of the section, see Hawkins, *Oxford Studies in the Synoptic Problem*, pp. 29–59.

tradition in the passage concerning the request of James and John for chief seats in the kingdom, but Matthew continues to follow Mark (Mk x, 35–45; Mt xx, 20–28). After this brief omission of Luke's, the three come together again in the story of the healing of Bartimaeus (Mk x, 46–52; Mt xx, 29–34; Lk, xviii, 35–43). Luke inserts his story of Zaccheus, unknown to the other evangelists (Lk xix, 1–10), and his parable of the Talents (Lk xix, 11–27), more or less closely parallel to Matthew's parable (Mt xxv, 14–30).

THE JERUSALEM NARRATIVE

In their account of the happenings in Jerusalem, the three evangelists start out together in the story of the triumphal entry (Mk xi, 1–11; Mt xxi, 1–11; Lk xix, 28–38). Matthew and Luke then insert some material unknown to Mark (Mt xxi, 14–17; Lk xix, 39–44). Matthew follows Mark in the story of the cursing of the fig tree (Mk xi, 12–14; Mt xxi, 18–19); Luke omits this, perhaps considering it a variant of the parable of the Barren Fig Tree given later by all three. The three continue together in the account of the cleansing of the temple (Mk xi, 15–18; Mt xxi, 12–13; Lk xix, 45–48), and Matthew gives with Mark the speech of Jesus concerning the withered fig tree (Mk xi, 20–26; Mt xxi, 20–22); Luke, having omitted the cursing of the fig tree, omits also this speech concerning it.

The three then give together the Pharisees' question about Jesus' authority for the cleansing of the temple (Mk xi, 27–33; Mt xxi, 23–27; Lk xx, 1–8). Matthew adds his parable of the Dissimilar Sons (Mt xxi, 28–32), and the three relate together the parable of the Evil Husbandmen (Mk xii, 1–12; Mt xxi, 33–46; Lk xx, 9–19). Matthew next gives the parable of the Wedding Feast (Mt xxii, 1–14) which Luke has given earlier, in his Great Interpolation (Lk xiv, 16–24). Matthew and Luke follow Mark again in the question about the tribute money (Mk xii, 13–17; Mt xxii, 15–22; Lk xx, 20–26) and the question of the Sadducees about marriage (Mk xii, 18–27; Mt xxii, 23–33; Lk xx, 27–40). Matthew continues to follow Mark in the question about the great commandment (Mk xii, 28–34; Mt xxii, 34–40); Luke has included this also in his Great Interpolation (Lk x, 25–28); both Matthew and Luke omit the complimentary remarks of the scribe to Jesus given by Mark (Mk xii, 32–34). This omission does not hinder their following Mark in his next sections, the question of David's son, and the speech against the Pharisees (Mk xii, 35–37; Mt xxii, 41–46; Lk xx, 41–44, and Mk xii, 38–40; Mt xxiii, 1–36; Lk xx, 45–47). Matthew's largely expanded form of the latter of these two sections shows him to be here combining some other source with Mark.

Luke's discourse against the Pharisees recorded in this place agrees closely with Mark's, but he has given in his eleventh chapter much of the non-Marcan material which Matthew gives in this place (Lk xi, 39–50). Matthew then inserts the lament over Jerusalem (Mt xxiii, 37–39) which Luke has given at an earlier and less appropriate point (Lk xiii, 34–35). Matthew deserts, but Luke follows, Mark in the story of the widow's mite (Mk xii, 41–44; Lk xxi, 1–4). All three continue together in the prediction of the destruction of the temple (Mk xiii, 1–4; Mt xxiv, 1–3; Lk xxi, 5–7), and in the signs of the parousia (Mk xiii, 5–9; Mt xxiv, 4–8; Lk xxi, 8–11). Thruout the remainder of the "Little Apocalypse" Matthew has an occasional expansion of Marcan material, and Luke makes an occasional omission, but it is obvious that Matthew and Luke are here, in the main, following Mark closely (Mk xiii; Mt xxiv; Lk xxi). There follow in Matthew several sections not duplicated in Mark, as the saying about the days of Noah (Mt xxiv, 37–41), the parables of the Watching Servant (Mt xxiv, 42–44), the True and False Servant (Mt xxiv, 45–51), the Wise Virgins (Mt xxv, 1–13), the Talents (Mt xxv, 14–30), and the parable of the Judgment (Mt xxv, 31–46). Luke has given to the "Little Apocalypse" an ending of his own (Lk xxi, 34–36); the material which Matthew has inserted continuously in his xxiv, 37—xxv, 30, Luke has scattered over his seventeenth, twelfth, and nineteenth chapters; the Matthean parable of the Judgment is duplicated in neither Mark nor Luke. Luke adds a summary of the activity of Jesus in Jerusalem (Lk xxi, 37–38).

THE STORY OF THE PASSION

Here the three evangelists start out together with the machinations of the rulers (Mk xiv, 1–2; Mt xxvi, 1–5; Lk xxii, 1–2). Luke drops out the account of the anointing in Bethany, which Mark and Matthew relate (Mk xiv, 3–9; Mt xxvi, 6–13), Luke having related a similar event in an earlier chapter (Lk vii, 36–50). The three then go on together in the story of the bargain of Judas with the priests (Mk xiv, 10–11; Mt xxvi, 14–16; Lk xxii, 3–6), and the account of the preparation for the Passover (Mk xiv, 12–17; Mt xxvi, 17–20; Lk xxii, 7–14). Luke then brings forward Mark's story of the institution of the Lord's Supper, apparently feeling that it fits better here than as given by Mark; except for the transposition of Luke's xxii, 21–23 (=Mk xiv, 18–21; Mt xxvi, 21–25), the three agree in their account of the prediction of the betrayal and the institution of the Supper. Luke then adds a section of seven verses (Lk xxii, 24–30) on the strife about rank in the coming kingdom, which Mark and Matthew have

DEPENDENCE OF MATTHEW AND LUKE ON MARK   13

given earlier (Mk x, 42-45; Mt xx, 25-28). After this interruption of the common order the three go on with the prediction of the denial by Peter (Mk xiv, 26-31; Mt xxvi, 30-35; Lk xxii, 31-34). Then come, tho interrupted by here and there a slight addition peculiar to Matthew or Luke, and with transpositions of verses or small sections more frequent than in other parts of the Gospels, the scene in Gethsemane, the arrest, trial, execution, and burial of Jesus, and the story of the empty grave (Mk xiv, 32—xvi, 8; Mt xxvi, 36—xxviii, 10; Lk xxii, 39—xxiv, 11); thus bringing us down to the mutilated end of Mark's Gospel.

Matthew and Luke have thus taken, between them, with trifling exceptions, the entire Gospel of Mark. The historical framework of the Synoptic Gospels goes back to Mark.

THE PRIORITY OF MARK

We add here a brief statement of the theory that Mark's Gospel is an abstract of the Gospels of Matthew and Luke. Tho this theory is no longer defended, it may be worth while to summarize the more general considerations which have led to its abandonment.

1. It is impossible, upon this theory, to account for the omission by Mark of so much of the material that stood before him in Matthew and Luke. He has omitted most of the parables and sayings. He has added no narrative. He has therefore made an abstract in which much is omitted, nothing is added, and no improvement is introduced. No reason can be assigned for the making of such a Gospel by abstracting from the fuller and better Gospels of Matthew and Luke. The abstract not only adds nothing of its own, but fails to preserve the distinctive character of either of its exemplars.

2. If Mark had wished to make such an abstract, it is impossible to explain why in practically every instance he follows, as between Matthew and Luke, the longer narrative, while his own narrative is longer than either of those he copied. In the story of the healing of the leper, for example, Matthew (viii, 1–4) has 62 words, Luke (v, 12–16, without his introduction) has 87, and Mark (i, 40–45) has 97. In the healing of the paralytic (Mk ii, 1–12; Mt ix, 1–8; Lk v, 17–26) Matthew has 125 words, Luke 172, and Mark 190. In the calling of Levi (Matthew, in the Gospel of Matthew) Matthew has 92 words, Luke 93, and Mark 110 (Mk ii, 13–17; Mt ix, 9–13; Lk v, 27–32). In the parable of the Sower (Mk iv, 1–9; Mt xiii, 1–9; Lk viii, 4–8) Matthew has 134 words, Luke 90, and Mark 151. In the interpretation of that parable (Mk iv, 13–20; Mt xiii, 18–23; Lk viii, 11–15) Matthew has 128 words, Luke 109, and Mark 147. Many more such instances might be given. In every case the additional words of Mark contain no substantial addition to the narrative. They are mere redundancies, which Matthew and Luke, each in his own way, have eliminated.

3. Mark contains a large number of otherwise unknown or unliterary words and phrases. For example, σχιζομένους, i, 10; ἐν πνεύματι ἀκαθάρτῳ, i, 23; κράβαττος, ii, 4, and in five other places; ἐπιράπτει, ii, 21; θυγάτριον, v, 23; vii, 25; ἐσχάτως ἔχει, v, 23; σπεκουλάτωρ, vi, 27; συμπόσια συμπόσια, vi, 39; εἰσίν τινες ὧδε τῶν ἑστηκότων, ix, 1; εἷς κατὰ εἷς, xiv, 19; ἐκπερισσῶς, xiv, 31. Such expressions might easily have been replaced by Matthew and Luke with the better expressions which they use instead of these; they could hardly have been substituted by Mark for those better expressions.

DEPENDENCE OF MATTHEW AND LUKE ON MARK 15

4. Mark contains many broken or incomplete constructions; as in iii, 16+; iv, 31+; v, 23; vi, 8+; xi, 32; xii, 38–40; xiii, 11, 14, 16, 19; xiv, 49. Such constructions would be easily corrected by Matthew and Luke; they would not easily be inserted into the narratives of Matthew and Luke by Mark.

5. Mark has many double or redundant expressions, of which Matthew has taken a part, Luke sometimes the same part, sometimes another. Such instances may be found in Mark's Gospel at ii, 20, 25; iv, 39; xi, 2; xii, 14; the corresponding passages in Matthew and Luke will show their treatment of these redundancies.[1]

6. Mark uses uniformly καί, where Matthew and Luke have sometimes καί and sometimes δέ. Mark's use shows him to be nearer the Hebrew or Aramaic. No explanation can be given for his substitution of this monotonous conjunction in the place of the two conjunctions used by Matthew and Luke. The variation in Matthew and Luke of Mark's one conjunction is entirely natural.

7. Mark has many Aramaic words, which he translates into Greek; see especially iii, 17; v, 41; vii, 11; vii, 34. It would be easy for these to be dropped out by writers making use of Mark's material for Hellenistic readers; but very unnatural for Mark to have inserted these Aramaic words into the Greek texts of Matthew and Luke.

8. Mark's narrative thruout is more spirited and vivid than either Matthew's or Luke's. It would be much easier for these graphic touches to be omitted for various reasons by Matthew and Luke, even tho they found these before them in their Gospel of Mark, than for Mark to have added these touches in copying the narratives of

[1] See Hawkins, *Horae Synopticae*, pp. 139–41, for other instances.

Matthew and Luke. One may mention especially the details about the appearance and dress of the Baptist (Mk i, 6); the four men carrying the litter (ii, 3); the statement, "He looked around upon them with wrath, being grieved at the hardness of their hearts" (Mk iii, 5); the names of persons, and their relatives, unknown to the other evangelists, the description of the Gadarene demoniac, the additional details of the conversation between Jesus and the parents of the epileptic boy (ix, 20–24), and many similar items.

LUKE'S GREAT INTERPOLATION: ITS NON-USE OF MARK

Thruout this Great Interpolation, Luke entirely forsakes Mark.[1] Out of the two hundred and fifty-two verses of the interpolation, there are about thirty-five which contain material also to be found in Mark. But thirteen of these thirty-five verses are doublets. And of these doublets, the member which appears in the interpolation seems never to agree in its setting with the verse in Mark to which it is parallel, whereas the verse which, outside the interpolation, constitutes the other member of the doublet does so agree. In the case of five of these doublets, the member standing outside the interpolation is also more closely similar to Mark in wording than the half standing in the interpolation. The thirteen verses containing the doublets therefore came apparently from some other source than Mark.

Nine other brief sayings in the interpolation have a parallel in Mark, and also in Matthew. But the similarity in each case is greater between the Marcan and Matthean than between the Lucan and Marcan forms, and thus

[1] For an elaborate analysis of the sources of the material in the Great Interpolation, see Hawkins, *Oxford Studies in the Synoptic Problem*, pp. 29–59.

indicates that these Lucan verses were not drawn from Mark, tho Matthew's parallel verses apparently were.[1] The placing of these nine verses in Luke is unlike that in Mark, but their placing in Matthew is exactly similar to Mark's. In twenty-two out of the thirty-five verses of the Great Interpolation that are paralleled in Mark there are thus but three expressions, at the most, that can possibly be held to indicate that Luke is here following Mark.

Two more such expressions are found in the remaining thirteen verses. Four of these contain the discussion about the Great Commandment, paralleled in Mk xii, 28–34, and Mt xxii, 34–40. The connection is identical in Matthew and Mark, but very different in Luke. The same is true of the introductory question of the scribe. Mark and Matthew assign to the questioner the Old Testament quotation which Luke assigns to Jesus. The commendation of the questioner, common to Mark and Luke, and the addition, also common to them against Matthew, of ἐξ ὅλης τῆς ἰσχύος σου (ἐν ὅλῃ τῇ ἰσχύϊ σου) would naturally point toward a dependence of Luke upon Mark, but are not strong enough to counterbalance so much evidence in the opposite direction.

The next seven verses (xi, 15, 17–23) contain the defense of Jesus against the charge of having a devil. Mark and Luke agree but slightly, Matthew and Luke very closely. Matthew has 136 words, Luke 139, Mark only 98, whereas the narratives which Luke takes from Mark are invariably abbreviated by Luke. Matthew and Luke have the same setting, Mark a different one. Matthew follows Mark against Luke in the little parable of the

[1] An apparent exception is Lk xiv, 34 = Mk ix, 50; no parallel in Matthew. Lk xvii, 2 = Mk ix, 42, and Lk x, 27 = Mk xii, 30 should perhaps be added, but are not so clear.

Strong Man Armed; Luke has no parallel. Matthew has conflated two sources, one of which was Mark, but Luke has forsaken Mark for the other source.

The remaining two verses, the parable of the Mustard Seed (Lk xiii, 18–19; Mk iv, 30+; Mt xiii, 31+) show the same features as those just considered. We conclude that thruout his Great Interpolation, Luke, while having some matter paralleled in Mark, was not following Mark, but some other source.

CHAPTER II

THE ORDER OF MARK'S GOSPEL COMPARED WITH THAT OF MATTHEW AND THAT OF LUKE

In the treatment of the framework of the Synoptics, something has been said of the way in which Matthew and Luke treat the order of the material which they have taken from Mark. The subject, however, calls for a more careful analysis.

At the opening of the 3d chapters of Matthew and Luke, these writers begin their use of Marcan material. Thru the story of John the Baptist, the baptism and temptation of Jesus, and his first preaching in Galilee, Matthew and Luke follow Mark's order, with the trifling exception that Luke has brot forward to his 3d chapter the account of John's imprisonment, which in Mark is not given till his 6th chapter and in Matthew till his 14th, Matthew's order here being the same as Mark's. Luke's insertion of the genealogy of Jesus between the baptism and the temptation of Jesus does not constitute a deviation from the order, but only an addition to the material, of Mark. In Luke's 4th chapter (16–30) he brings forward an incident which Mark relates much later (Mk vi, 1–6), the incident also being much worked over by Luke. Matthew, on the contrary, follows Mark in next relating the call of the first disciples; Luke continues his deviation in order by postponing this till later.[1]

---

[1] Chapter and verse for each of these sections being given in the tabulated arrangement of this same material on pp. 24–27, only such references are given here as are necessary to help the reader to follow the analysis at this point.

Luke then comes back to Mark's order (Mk i, 21–38; Lk iv, 31–43), and follows it thru four sections: the incident in the synagogue at Capernaum, the healing of Peter's wife's mother, the healings in the evening, and the retirement of Jesus. Of these four sections, Matthew omits the first, presumably because he considers himself to have given, in his Sermon on the Mount, a much fuller account of the effect of Jesus' preaching than is conveyed by the words of Mark. The second and third of the four sections Matthew postpones till after his Sermon on the Mount. The last one, about the retirement of Jesus, he omits, because he has no place for it, since he has not recorded the preaching at Capernaum and the incident attached to it, out of which the retirement came.

Luke then inserts (v, 1–11) his account of the calling of Peter. He then returns to Mark's order (Mk i, 40–45; Lk v, 12–16) in the healing of the leper; this incident Matthew has postponed till after his Sermon on the Mount. Matthew again brings forward the account of the storm on the lake and the Gadarene demoniac, which Mark does not relate till his 4th and 5th chapters. But after these deviations he again coincides with Mark and Luke in the healing of the paralytic, the calling of Levi, and the question about fasting. Matthew again forsakes Mark's order by bringing forward the mission of the twelve to a place much earlier than it occupies in Mark's narrative. Having done this he falls again into the Marcan order, which Luke has been still following, and relates in the same order with Mark the walk thru the corn and the healing of the withered hand.

Luke has thus far shown few deviations from Mark's order, Matthew many. These deviations of Matthew's seem mostly to have been occasioned by his insertion of

ORDER OF MARK IN MATTHEW AND LUKE 21

so much non-Marcan material in his Sermon on the Mount. Luke now makes a slight transposition; he relates with Mark the story of the healings and the crowd, and the calling of the twelve, but in the reverse order; he has thus secured a better introduction to his Sermon on the Level Place (beginning Lk vi, 20). After the conclusion of that sermon, and the inclusion of much non-Marcan material, in Luke; and after the Sermon on the Mount in Matthew, and the insertion by him of much Marcan material which in Mark's Gospel comes at later points, Matthew and Luke come back to Mark's order in the Beelzebul controversy. Matthew continues with Mark in the story of the family of Jesus, come to take him home, the parable of the Sower, and the interpretation of that parable. Luke also follows Mark's order thruout these three sections, tho he has placed all three of them at an earlier point in his Gospel, and has transposed the first section.

Beginning again with the storm on the lake and the Gadarene demoniac, Matthew and Luke follow Mark's order thru two long sections. Matthew, in copying Mark's earlier narrative, omitted his healing of the paralytic, his call of Levi (Matthew), and his report of the discussion about fasting, where these occurred in Mark's 2d chapter. He therefore inserts them here in his 9th chapter. After the insertion of these Matthew comes back to the order of Mark in his story of the daughter of Jairus. Luke, having followed Mark's order in the earlier narrative where Matthew deviated from it, follows it here uninterruptedly thru the three sections about the storm on the lake, the Gadarene demoniac, and the daughter of Jairus. After omitting Mk vi, 1–6, the story of the rejection at Nazareth, which Luke has given in an expanded form much earlier, Luke again follows Mark's narrative thru two sections on the sending out of the disciples and the judgment of Herod concerning Jesus. He omits the death of the Baptist, perhaps under the impression that this will be inferred from his leaving him in prison in an earlier chapter, but goes on with Mark again in the account of the return of the disciples and the feeding of the five thousand. Matthew has come back to Mark's order at Mk vi, 14 (Mt xiv, 1), and follows it without deviation or interruption thru about seventy verses; after which, tho omitting several small sections of Marcan material, and inserting some non-Marcan matter, he continues to follow the Marcan order to Mk ix, 48; thus following Mark's order, in spite of additions and omissions, thru more than three of Mark's chapters, without deviation. Luke has fallen out at Mk vi, 45, and takes nothing from Mark again till he reaches Mark's viii, 27; at which point, without having made any insertion of his own peculiar material, he again takes up Mark's narrative, and follows it from Mk viii, 27, to Mk ix, 8 (= Lk ix, 18, to ix, 36); then making another omission of a few Marcan verses, he continues to follow Mark up to Mk ix, 40. In spite of Luke's omission of several brief Marcan sections, and of more than three Marcan chapters at another point, Luke has thus not disturbed the Marcan order from Mk vi, 6, to Mk ix, 40.

Beginning with Mk x, 1, Matthew follows Mark, tho making an insertion of 16 verses, up to Mk xi, 11, at which point he transposes a few verses. Luke has come in at Mk x, 13, and has followed up to Mk x, 34, at which point he makes an omission of ten Marcan verses. Going on with Mark at Mk x, 46, he continues to follow him (tho inserting his story of Zaccheus and his parable of the talents) to Mk xiii, 9, omitting, however, Mark's story of the cursing of the fig tree and the speech of Jesus attached to this incident in Mark's Gospel. After the transposition of a few Marcan verses in Mt xxi, 12–13, Matthew also continues Mark's order, beginning with Mk xi, 20, down to Mk xiii, 9.

From Mk xiii, 9, to xiii, 32, both Matthew and Luke follow Mark's order. At Mk xiii, 33–37, they come upon a section which Matthew postpones and which Luke has previously inserted. After the insertion of some non-Marcan matter common to Matthew and Luke, and of some matter peculiar to each, both Matthew and Luke go on with the Marcan material, beginning where they left off at Mk xiv, 1. Luke omits Mk xiv, 3–9, because of a duplicate or variant of the passage which he has inserted in his 7th chapter; except for this omission (which does not affect Matthew), the three proceed in the same order down to Mk xiv, 17, where Luke again transposes a few verses, but Matthew follows without deviation. From here on to the end of Mark's Gospel, Matthew follows practically without deviation, tho adding much matter of his own. Luke makes a transposition of the story of Peter's denial, and of one or two other items; except for which he also follows Mark's order substantially as he finds it.

This statement of the relative order of Marcan material in the three Synoptic Gospels has been made in a way to facilitate comparison in the large, and give a general idea of how faithfully Matthew and Luke have followed the order of Mark. For purposes of studying the matter in more detail, Table I is appended. The sections are given and numbered as they occur in Mark, and also as they occur in Matthew and Luke.

TABLE I

Showing Changes Made by Matthew and Luke in the Order of Marcan Material

Subject-Matter of Section	Chapter and Verse			Sec. Nos.		
	Mk	Lk	Mt	Mk	Lk	Mt
John the Baptist	i, 1–6	iii, 1–6	iii, 1–12	1	1	1
His messianic announcement	i, 7–8	iii, 15–18	iii, 11–12	2	2	2
Baptism of Jesus	i, 9–11	iii, 21–22	iii, 13–17	3	3	3
Temptation of Jesus	i, 12–13	iv, 1–13	iv, 1–11	4	4	4
Appearance in Galilee	i, 14–15	iv, 14–15	iv, 12–17	5	5	5
Calling first disciples	i, 16–20	v, 1–11	iv, 18–22	6	12	6
In the synagogue	i, 21–28	iv, 31–37		7	7	
Peter's wife's mother	i, 29–31	iv, 38–39	viii, 14–15	8	8	11
Healings in the evening	i, 32–34	iv, 40–41	viii, 16–17	9	9	13
Retirement of Jesus	i, 35–38	iv, 42–43		10	10	14
Preaching tour in Galilee	i, 39	iv, 44		11	11	
Healing of leper	i, 40–45	v, 12–16	viii, 1–4	12	13	7
Healing of paralytic	ii, 1–12	v, 17–26	ix, 1–8	13	14	12
Calling of Levi	ii, 13–17	v, 27–32	ix, 9–13	14	15	17
Question of fasting	ii, 18–22	v, 33–39	ix, 14–17	15	16	18
Walk thru the corn	ii, 23–28	vi, 1–5	xii, 1–8	16	17	19
The withered hand	iii, 1–6	vi, 6–11	xii, 9–14	17	18	25
Crowd and healings	iii, 7–12	vi, 17–19	xii, 15–21	18	20	26
Calling of the twelve	iii, 13–19	vi, 12–16	x, 2–4	19	19	27
The pharisaic accusation	iii, 20–22	xi, 14–16	xii, 22–24	20	43	22
Jesus' defense	iii, 23–30	xi, 17–23	xii, 25–37	21	44	28
Jesus' true kindred	iii, 31–35	viii, 19–21	xii, 46–50	22	28	29
Parable of the Sower	iv, 1–9	viii, 4–8	xiii, 1–9	23	23	30
Purpose of parables	iv, 10–12	viii, 9–10	xiii, 10–15	24	24	31
Interpretation of Sower	iv, 13–20	viii, 11–15	xiii, 18–23	25	25	32
Saying about a light	iv, 21	viii, 16	v, 15	26	26	33
Hidden and revealed	iv, 22	viii, 17	x, 26	27	27	9
Ears to hear	iv, 23	viii, 8; xiv, 35	xi, 15; xiii, 9	28	30	24, 27
The measure	iv, 24	vi, 38	vii, 2	29	21	10
Whoever has	iv, 25	vi, 38	xiii, 12	30	22	32

ORDER OF MARK IN MATTHEW AND LUKE

TABLE I—Continued

Subject-Matter of Section	Chapter and Verse			Sec. Nos.		
	Mk	Lk	Mt	Mk	Lk	Mt
Seed Growing of Itself	iv, 26–29			31		
Mustard Seed	iv, 30–32	xiii, 18–19	xiii, 31–32	32	29	34
Speaking in parables	iv, 33–34		xiii, 34–35	33		35
Storm on the lake	iv, 35–41	viii, 22–25	viii, 23–27	34	30	15
Gadarene demoniac	v, 1–20	viii, 26–39	viii, 28–34	35	31	16
Daughter of Jairus, and woman with issue of blood	v, 21–43	viii, 40–56	ix, 18–26	36	6	20
Rejection in Nazareth	vi, 1–6	iv, 16–30	xiii, 53–58	37	6	36
Sending out disciples	vi, 6–13	ix, 1–6	ix, 35; x, 9–11	38	32	21
Judgment of Herod on Jesus	vi, 14–16	ix, 7–9	xiv, 1–2	39	23	23
Death of the Baptist	vi, 17–29		xiv, 3–12	40		37
Return of disciples and feeding of five thousand	vi, 30–44	ix, 10–17	xiv, 13–21	41	34	38
Walking on the water	vi, 45–52		xiv, 22–33	42		39
Return to Gennesaret	vi, 53–56		xiv, 34–36	43		40
About hand-washing	vii, 1–23		xv, 1–20	44		41
The Canaanitish woman	vii, 24–30		xv, 21–28	45		42
Healing of deaf stammerer	vii, 31–37			46		43
Feeding of four thousand	viii, 1–10		xv, 32–39	47		44
Demand for a sign	viii, 11–13	xi, 29; xii, 54–56	xvi, 1–4	48	45	45
Saying about yeast	viii, 14–21	xii, 1	xvi, 5–12	49	47	46
The blind man of Bethsaida	viii, 22–26			50		
Confession of Peter	viii, 27–33	ix, 18–22	xvi, 13–23	51	35	47
Warnings of persecutions	viii, 34–ix, 1	ix, 23–27	xvi, 24–28	52	36	48
The transfiguration	ix, 2–8	ix, 28–36	xvii, 1–8	53	37	49
Question about Elias	ix, 9–13		xvii, 9–13	54		50
The epileptic boy	ix, 14–29	ix, 37–43a	xvii, 14–21	55	38	51
Prediction of sufferings	ix, 30–32	ix, 43b–45	xvii, 22–23	56	39	52
Strife about rank	ix, 33–37	ix, 46–48	xviii, 1–5	57	40	53
The unknown exorcist	ix, 38–41	ix, 49–50		58	41	
About offenses	ix, 42–48	xvii, 1–2	xviii, 6–9	59	49	54
About salt	ix, 49–50	xiv, 34–35	v, 13	60	48	8

TABLE I—Continued

Subject-Matter of Section	Chapter and Verse			Sec. Nos.		
	Mk	Lk	Mt	Mk	Lk	Mt
Marriage and divorce	x, 1–12	xviii, 15–17	xix, 1–12	61	50	55
Blessing the children	x, 13–16	xviii, 18–30	xix, 13–15	62	51	56
Danger of riches	x, 17–31	xviii, 31–34	xix, 16–30	63	52	57
Prediction of woes	x, 32–34		xx, 17–19	64		58
The request for seats	x, 35–45		xx, 20–28	65		59
Healing of Bartimaeus	x, 46–52	xviii, 35–43	xx, 29–34	66	53	60
Entry into Jerusalem	xi, 1–11	xix, 28–38	xxi, 1–11	67	54	61
Cursing of the fig tree	xi, 12–14		xxi, 18–19	68		62
Cleansing of the temple	xi, 15–19	xix, 45–48	xxi, 12–13	69	55	63
About the fig tree	xi, 20–26		xxi, 20–22	70		64
Question about authority	xi, 27–33	xx, 1–8	xxi, 23–27	71	56	65
Parable of the Vineyard	xii, 1–12	xx, 9–19	xxi, 33–46	72	57	66
Question of Pharisees	xii, 13–17	xx, 20–26	xxii, 15–22	73	58	67
Question of Sadducees	xii, 18–27	xx, 27–40	xxii, 23–33	74	59	68
The great commandment	xii, 28–34	xx, 25–28	xxii, 34–40	75	42	69
The Son of David	xii, 35–37	xx, 41–44	xxii, 41–46	76	60	70
Against the Pharisees	xii, 38–40	xx, 45–47	xxiii, 1–36	77	61	71
Prediction about temple	xiii, 1–4	xxi, 5–7	xxiv, 1–3	78	62	72
Signs of the parousia	xiii, 5–9a	xxi, 8–11	xxiv, 4–8	79	63	73
Warnings of troubles	xiii, 9b–13	xxi, 12–19	xxiv, 9–14; x, 17–21	80	64	74
Anguish in Judaea	xiii, 14–20	xxi, 20–24	xxiv, 15–22	81	65	75
The crisis	xiii, 21–23		xxiv, 23–25	82		76
The parousia	xiii, 24–27	xxi, 25–28	xxiv, 29–31	83	66	77
Parable of Fig Tree	xiii, 28–29	xxi, 29–31	xxiv, 32–33	84	67	78
The "when" of the parousia	xiii, 30–32	xxi, 32–33	xxiv, 34–36	85	68	79
Conclusion of speech	xiii, 33–37			86	69	
The plot against Jesus	xiv, 1–2	xxii, 1–2	xxvi, 1–5	87	70	80
Anointing at Bethany	xiv, 3–9		xxvi, 6–13	88		81
Treachery of Judas	xiv, 10–11	xxii, 3–6	xxvi, 14–16	89	71	82
Preparation for Passover	xiv, 12–17	xxii, 7–14	xxvi, 17–20	90	72	83
Prediction of betrayal	xiv, 18–21	xxii, 21–23	xxvi, 21–25	91	74	84

ORDER OF MARK IN MATTHEW AND LUKE

TABLE 1—*Continued*

Subject-Matter of Section	Chapter and Verse			Sec. Nos.		
	Mk	Lk	Mt	Mk	Lk	Mt
Institution of Supper	xiv, 22–25	xxii, 15–20	xxvi, 26–29	92	73	85
Prediction of Peter's fall	xiv, 26–31	xxii, 31–34	xxvi, 30–35	93	75	86
In Gethsemane	xiv, 32–42	xxii, 39–46	xxvi, 36–46	94	76	87
The arrest	xiv, 43–54	xxii, 47–55	xxvi, 47–58	95	77	88
Trial before Sanhedrim	xiv, 55–65	xxii, 63–71	xxvi, 59–68	96	79	89
Denial of Peter	xiv, 66–72	xxii, 56–62	xxvi, 69–75	97	78	90
Delivery to Pilate	xv, 1	xxiii, 1	xxvii, 1–2	98	80	91
Examination before Pilate	xv, 2–5	xxiii, 2–5	xxvii, 11–14	99	81	92
The condemnation of Jesus	xv, 6–15	xxiii, 18–25	xxvii, 15–26	100	82	93
The mocking of Jesus	xv, 16–20		xxvii, 27–31	101		94
The death journey	xv, 21	xxiii, 26–32	xxvii, 32	102	83	95
The crucifixion	xv, 22–32	xxiii, 33–43	xxvii, 33–44	103	84	96
The death of Jesus	xv, 33–41	xxiii, 44–49	xxvii, 45–56	104	85	97
The burial	xv, 42–47	xxiii, 50–56	xxvii, 57–61	105	86	98
The empty grave	xvi, 1–8	xxiv, 1–12	xxviii, 1–10	106	87	99

A comparison of the number in the Table which a given section bears respectively in Matthew and Mark or Luke and Mark will show the number and extent of the changes which Matthew and Luke have permitted themselves in their disposition of Marcan material.

DEDUCTIONS FROM THE TABLE

An examination of the preceding table will show how generally both Matthew and Luke have followed the order of Mark.

Of the 87 Marcan sections retained by Luke, only 11 sections (Nos. 6, 12, 21, 22, 23, 42–47) are seriously misplaced. From sec. 35 to the end, the order is particularly well preserved, the only changes being in the placing of 49 before 48, and 74 before 73. Luke's displacements are usually made in the interest of a better historical or literary sequence; some of them may also be occasioned by his large omissions of Marcan material and his large insertions of peculiar matter.

Matthew has made rather a larger number of changes in the order of his Marcan material; due perhaps to his habit of combining his Marcan and his other matter, and to his wish to present most of his sayings-material in one block (chaps. v–vii). His notable transpositions occur near the beginning of his Gospel, just before or after the insertion of his Sermon on the Mount, and in that section (the sending out of the twelve) where he has made his most obvious conflation of Marcan and other matter. From sec. 37 to the end, however, changes in order are extremely few. The insertion of 8 between 54 and 55 may be only an apparent dislocation, since the saying about salt may here not have been derived from Mark but from Q. The placing of the cleansing of the temple

Order of Mark in Matthew and Luke 29

before the cursing of the fig tree (secs. 62, 63) may be due to his wish to bring the cursing of the fig tree into immediate connection with the remarks to which it gave rise; the transposition is an improvement. From here on to the end the sections occur precisely as in Mark, except that 21 is inserted between 74 and 75; apparently owing to the influence of Q. The table will also show that Matthew and Luke practically never concur in forsaking the order of Mark. It also warrants the assertion often made of late years that Matthew is more faithful to the content of Mark, permitting himself fewer omissions, but Luke is more faithful to his order.

CHAPTER III

THE OMISSIONS OF MATTHEW AND LUKE IN THE MARCAN NARRATIVE[1]

OMISSIONS MADE BY BOTH MATTHEW AND LUKE

The omission of the stories of the healing of the deaf-and-dumb man and the blind man (Mk vii, 31–37; viii, 22–26), is sufficiently accounted for by the character of those accounts. The crassness of the means used and the apparent difficulty of the cures offended the growing sense of the dignity of Jesus.

The exceedingly patronizing answer of the scribe to Jesus in Mk xii, 32–34 is probably omitted by Matthew and Luke for the same reason. The parable of the Seed Growing of Itself (Mk iv, 26–29) may have been omitted because it so closely duplicated other material in both Matthew and Luke;[2] it has been suggested also that it might have a discouraging effect, or at least not a stimulating one, upon the missionary activities of the early church.

The first visit of Jesus to the temple (Mk xi, 11) is mentioned by Mark in three words only. No incident is connected with it, but Jesus is said to have looked about and, as it was late, to have gone back to Bethany. The incident may have dropped out because unsupported by any events or sayings; or the three words εἰς τὸ ἱερόν

---

[1] We do not include here the omission of single words or phrases, or even occasionally of an entire verse, where it is plain that this is in the interest of some change or condensation.

[2] See especially the parable of the Weed in the Field (Mt xiii, 24–30), the Mustard Seed (Mk iv, 30–32; Mt xiii, 31–32; Lk xiii, 18–19), the Sower (Mt xiii, 1–9; Lk viii, 4–8).

may have crept into the text of Mark after its use by Matthew and Luke (the sense is equally good without them).

The mention of the man in the linen garment (Mk xiv, 51) and the names of Alexander and Rufus (Mk xv, 21) may have been omitted because neither Matthew nor Luke nor their readers would be acquainted with these persons.

OMISSIONS MADE BY MATTHEW IN THE MARCAN NARRATIVE

Matthew omits the account of the preaching of Jesus in the synagogue at Capernaum (Mk i, 21-28) because he wished to give a much more detailed account of Jesus' preaching, in his Sermon on the Mount. This explanation becomes a practical certainty when we observe that the statement which Mark and Luke make concerning the effect of the sermon in the synagogue, "They were astonished at his doctrine, for he taught them as one having authority and not as the scribes," is used by Matthew to describe the effect of the Sermon on the Mount.

Matthew's omission of the flight of Jesus (Mk i, 35-38) is probably due to its failure to fit into his story, as this has been changed on account of the insertion of the Sermon on the Mount. The retirement takes place from Capernaum, as a result of the enthusiasm aroused by Jesus' preaching there. Matthew does not represent Jesus as preaching in Capernaum. He brings Jesus to Capernaum in chaps. 8 and 9, not however to preach, but to work miracles. Jesus closes this series of healings with the statement (Mt ix, 37-38), "The harvest is great but the laborers are few. Pray ye therefore the lord of the harvest that he send forth laborers into his vineyard."

The retirement does not follow naturally upon this series of healings, much less upon these words, and so is omitted.

The omission of the story of the unknown exorcist (Mk ix, 38–41), as Wernle remarks,[1] is not so easy to explain. It may be observed, however, that by its omission Matthew secures a better connection between the two sayings of Jesus which are thus brought into succession: "He that receiveth one such little one in my name receiveth me," and "but he that causeth one of these little ones that believe in me to stumble, it is better for him," etc. (Mt xviii, 5, 6).

The story of the widow's mite (Mk xii, 41–44) Matthew may have omitted because he lacks the connection for it which is supplied in the Gospel of Mark. Mark makes Jesus speak of the Pharisees who "devour widow's houses," and immediately after this introduces the incident of the widow's self-sacrifice. Matthew has omitted the incident because he has not the proper occasion for it.[2]

Matthew's other omissions have been accounted for under the omissions common to him with Luke. The sum total of them is very small and in general they are easily accounted for.

OMISSIONS MADE BY LUKE IN THE MARCAN NARRATIVE[3]

Luke omits the circumstantial account of the death of the Baptist (Mk vi, 17–29); he has long ago inserted the account of his imprisonment (Lk iii, 19–20), wishing to finish with John before beginning with Jesus. "But the circumstantial account did not fit in that place."[4]

[1] Wernle, *Synoptische Frage*, p. 126.

[2] Thruout this discussion I am greatly indebted to Wernle, as anyone must be who has read his *Synoptische Frage*.

[3] Wernle includes among these the defense of Jesus in Mk iii, 23–30, practically duplicated in Lk xi, 17–23. Why not a transposition, rather than an omission? So considered here.

[4] Wernle, *op. cit.*, p. 5.

The longest omission of continuous Marcan material is made by Luke in omitting the whole of Mk vi, 45 to viii, 26. This long omission immediately precedes the long insertion of special Lucan material, indicating a possible difficulty in combining the two sources at this point. Quite without this, however, there are more or less obvious reasons for Luke's omission of every section in this long passage. He avoids[1] the repetition of the same story, and may have regarded Mark's feeding of the four thousand (Mk viii, 1–10) as a repetition of the feeding of the five thousand which Luke has already copied from him.

The demand for a sign is a doublet in Matthew; Luke has taken it once with Matthew from Q and therefore does not care to take it with him here again from Mark (Mk viii, 11–13). The dispute about things that defile (Mk vii, 1–23) had no significance for a gentile writer or his gentile readers. As early as his 4th chapter, Luke has represented Jesus as turning from the Jews, who had rejected him, to the gentiles; he cannot therefore use Mark's story of the Canaanitish woman, (Mk vii, 24–30), with its apparently narrow national outlook: "It is not meet to take the children's bread and throw it to the dogs."[2] The crossing of the lake to Gennesaret has in Mark (vi, 53–56) no particular incident connected with it, merely the statement that many people came to Jesus and were healed. It may have been omitted by Luke because he has a duplicate in viii, 22–25.

[1] Yet not always. Cf. his two bands of teachers, his healing of ten lepers and of one, his two disputes about priority among the disciples, his three predictions of the passion and two of the resurrection. But cf. his omission of anointing at Bethany, the barren fig tree, the mocking by Pilate's soldiers, because of their duplications of his material already used. See Hawkins, *op. cit.*, 69.

[2] Matthew takes no offense at this; for he even adds to it, "I am not sent except to the lost sheep of the house of Israel."

The omission of this item was no particular loss to Luke's account; but with its omission the incident of the walking on the water also fell out. The latter may have been omitted also because of its implied aspersion upon the disciples. Luke may have been the more ready to drop this, as his interest in the miracles of Jesus is confined more largely to the healings, the miracles peculiar to Luke being entirely of this kind.

Luke omitted the discussion of Jesus with the Pharisees about Elias (Mk ix, 9–13) because it had no interest for his gentile readers. The omission of the saying about offenses (Mk ix, 42–48) is accounted for by Luke's having a parallel for the first part of it in another connection; the last part, about cutting off the hand or the foot, may have seemed to him, with his Greek taste, too harsh a saying to be attributed to Jesus.

Luke omitted the journey thru Judaea (Mk x, 1) (or Perea) because in its place he has given a long account (Lk ix, 51—xviii, 14) (again his great interpolation) of the journey thru Samaria. The terminus of both journeys and their place in the story are the same. The question about marriage and divorce (Mk x, 2–12) is again connected with a Pharisaic dispute; Luke has also given his own briefer version of the same item (xvi, 18); for either or both of these reasons he omits it here. The request of James and John for chief seats in the kingdom (Mk x, 35–45) Luke omits because it reflects upon the motives of those disciples; Matthew perceives the same objection to it, but, more faithful to his sources he gets over the difficulty by attributing the request to the mother, instead of to the disciples. Mark's discussion about the disciples' failure to bring bread (Mk viii, 14–21) Luke may have omitted because of its implication of carelessness on the part of the disciples. Luke also uniformly avoids any implication of lack of knowledge on the part of Jesus, and this incident includes one such.[1]

The question about the great commandment (Mk xii, 28–34) Luke may have omitted because it also is connected with a dispute with a scribe. Or if Luke's passage (x, 25–28) be considered a parallel to it, this is enough to account for its omission here. On this latter supposition, Luke has used the saying as an introduction to his story of the Good Samaritan. The cursing of the fig tree (Mk xi, 12–14) Luke apparently regarded as a misunderstanding of the parable of the Fig Tree, which he gives. Whether so or not, it is of the same kind as the other miracles which Luke omits, in that it is not a miracle of healing. The anointing in Bethany (Mk xiv, 3–9) has a parallel in the anointing (both in the "house of Simon") by the sinful woman, which Luke has related in his 7th chapter (vss. 36–50). "The second session of the sanhedrim he has combined with the first."[2]

Concerning the great omission of Luke (Mk vi, 45— viii, 26), it should be added that his Gospel is now considerably longer than Mark's and even than Matthew's. He had much material of his own to incorporate. Rolls of papyrus were of an average length, and not capable of indefinite extension. Luke could not include all Mark's material without omitting much that he has derived elsewhere. If it was necessary or convenient for him to make an omission amounting in length to the matter he has passed over in Mark, it was much easier and simpler for him to omit an entire section of that length, than to

---

[1] Hawkins, *op. cit.*, p. 71. It seems strange that Hawkins' discussion of the "great omission" contains no reference to Wernle's treatment of the same subject.

[2] Wernle, *op. cit.*, p. 6.

go here and there thru Mark to make his necessary total of eliminations. This consideration, with the character of the material omitted, sufficiently accounts for the "great omission."[1]

[1] On the size of ancient books, see Sanday, *Oxford Studies*, pp. 25–26; cf. Birt, *Das antike Buchwesen*.

CHAPTER IV

THE CHANGES OF MATTHEW AND LUKE IN THE NARRATIVE OF MARK[1]

THE BAPTISM OF JESUS

(Mk i, 9–11; Mt iii, 13–17; Lk iii, 21–22)

Matthew adds to Mark's account the conversation in which John objects to baptizing Jesus, and Jesus quiets his scruples (Mt iii, 14–15). This reflects the later time, when the superiority of Jesus to John had been historically demonstrated, and when the baptism might have given offense by seeming to imply a need of forgiveness. The item approaches the point of view of the similar addition in the Fourth Gospel. Matthew, who has added this item here, is the only evangelist who says that John's baptism was εἰς μετάνοιαν (iii, 11). Matthew's added conversation appears, still more elaborated, in the Gospel of the Hebrews. Luke (iii, 21) adds that Jesus was praying during his baptism, which may be an accommodation to the custom of the early church. Mark says the voice from the sky was addressed to Jesus; Matthew represents it as addressed to the crowd, perhaps to give more public honor to Jesus. The Gospel of the Ebionites adds to Mark's "in thee I am well pleased," the quotation from the Psalms, "this day have I begotten thee"; and certain MSS contain the same words in the text of Luke, omitting "in thee I am well pleased." These variations show the freedom of the early tradition, but its unanimity

---

[1] For complete and detailed discussion, see Wernle, Wellhausen, Harnack.

in the idea that the baptism was Jesus' messianic consecration. Matthew and Luke replace Mark's σχιζομένους, a word not elsewhere found, with a word common in such connections.

THE CALLING OF THE FIRST DISCIPLES
(Mk i, 16-20; Mt iv, 18-22; Lk v, 1-11)

Luke postpones this account, and in connection with it gives the story of the miraculous draft of fishes, unknown to Mark and Matthew. The reason is not apparent, especially since the transposition involves Luke in some anachronisms. Matthew follows Mark's account closely,[1] retaining even the parenthetical and appended explanation in vs. 16. He omits Mark's words, "with the hired men," perhaps because of his general tendency toward condensation, perhaps because the departure of James and John from their father is rendered less critical by Mark's mention of the hired men.

JESUS IN THE SYNAGOGUE AT CAPERNAUM
(Mk i, 21-28; Mt vii, 28-29; Lk iv, 31-37)

Luke omits "and not as the scribes," because his readers would not understand the allusion. He replaces Mark's awkward phrase ἐν πνεύματι ἀκαθάρτῳ by the good Greek phrase ἔχων πνεῦμα δαιμονίου ἀκαθάρτου. He omits Mark's mention of Galilee at the end of his account, because he has inserted it at the beginning. Matthew's omission of the whole story may be controlled by his unwillingness, elsewhere manifested, to represent the demons as recognizing Jesus as the Messiah.

[1] See pp. 95-96, where the account of the call of the first disciples is further discussed, and printed in heavy-faced type.

THE HEALING OF PETER'S MOTHER-IN-LAW

(Mk i, 29–31; Mt viii, 14–15; Lk iv, 38–39)

Mark calls Peter by the name of Simon, as is uniform with him up to the time Jesus gives him the name of Peter at his calling of the twelve. Matthew calls him Peter, by which name he knows him from the beginning. Luke's displacement of the call of Peter involves him in the anachronism of having the healing take place in his house before he becomes a disciple.

THE HEALINGS IN THE EVENING

(Mk i, 32–34; Mt viii, 16–17; Lk iv, 40–41)

Mark says "In the evening when the sun was set." Matthew has reduced the redundancy of this expression by saying merely "When it was evening." Luke has caught the point of Mark's expression, namely, that the Sabbath was over, and so has reduced the pleonasm by saying only "The sun having set." Mark says they brot all the sick to Jesus and he healed many. Matthew improves this by saying they brot many and he healed all. Luke goes a step farther and says they brot all, and he healed every one. No explanation is necessary for these changes except the natural desire to avoid the implication that there were some whom Jesus did not heal, and to make the statement of his cures as positive and inclusive as possible. Matthew mentions only the possessed, Mark puts the sick and the possessed in the same class, Luke gives a separate paragraph to each. Both Matthew and Luke avoid Mark's irregular and unusual form ἤφιεν.

THE RETIREMENT OF JESUS
(Mk i, 35-38; Lk iv, 42-43)

Matthew omits, for reasons already given.[1] Luke avoids Mark's strange word, κωμοπόλεις. Where Mark says "Simon and those with him," Luke says "the crowd," because in Luke's story Simon is not yet a disciple.

THE CALLING OF PETER
(Lk v, 1-11)

Luke here displays his freedom in working over the story of Mark. He builds upon Mk i, 19, yet instead of saying that the fishermen were mending their nets in their boats, he says they had gone out of their boats and were washing their nets. He has apparently read Mk iv, 1, also, and builds upon this the statement about Jesus' going into the boat to get away from the crowd (which statement he later omits when he comes to it in Mark's parable of the Sower). (There is a reminiscence here also of Mk iii, 9.) After the draft of fishes, when he comes to the words of Jesus to Peter, he picks up again a fragment of Mark's account, tho still with an addition and with a deviation in the wording; Mark says δεῦτε ὀπίσω μου, καὶ ποιήσω ὑμᾶς γενέσθαι ἁλεεῖς ἀνθρώπων; Luke says μὴ φοβοῦ· ἀπὸ τοῦ νῦν ἀνθρώπους ἔσῃ ζωγρῶν. Luke's closing statement, "They left all and followed him" is substantially, tho not quite in wording, the same as Mark's. No example could be more striking, of Luke's freedom in his treatment of Mark. He exercises this freedom, however, in the narratives rather than in the words of Jesus; when he comes to these latter, even in the midst of a narrative which he has largely created out

---
[1] P. 30; see also pp. 95-96, where the account of the calling of the first disciples is printed in heavy-faced type and is further discussed.

of mere fragments of Mark, he follows Mark comparatively closely. In not many narratives does Luke go to quite such lengths in his re-working as in this story and the account of the rejection (initial preaching) at Nazareth. But this is typical of him, as compared with Matthew's treatment of the same source.

THE HEALING OF THE LEPER
(Mk i, 40–45; Mt viii, 1–4; Lk v, 12–16)

Matthew and Luke both omit Mark's ἐμβριμησάμενος, for which they have in this case double ground; it is an unusual word, and it implies that Jesus was angry. Luke avoids Mark's statement that the man directly disobeyed Jesus' command not to tell of his cleansing.

THE HEALING OF THE PARALYTIC
(Mk ii, 1–12; Mt ix, 1–8; Lk v, 17–26)

Both Matthew and Luke have supplied their own introductions. Both substitute εἶπεν for Mark's λέγει (Mk ix, 5) (a correction which Luke invariably makes). Both use substitutes for Mark's κράβαττον. Luke avoids Jesus' address to the man as τέκνον. In the words of Jesus to his critics and to the paralytic, both follow Mark with general fidelity, and tho Mark's vss. 5b–10 appear to interrupt the story, both follow him in their inclusion of these verses. Luke's change of Mark's vs. 7 is a fine example of his ability to make an improvement in the sense with the least possible change in the wording. Mark reads, τί οὗτος οὕτως λαλεῖ; βλασφημεῖ· Luke changes to τίς ἐστιν ὃς λαλεῖ βλασφημίας; The latter fits much better into the question, "Who has power to forgive sins except God?" Mark has made Jesus, in his dispute with his critics, say "Which is easier, to say, ... or to say, rise, take up thy bed and walk?" Matthew and Luke make him leave out the clause "take up thy bed," reserving this for Jesus' actual address to the man a little later, whereas Mark uses it in both places. Luke heightens the effect of his story by saying "He took up that upon which he had been carried," instead of "he took up his bed." This may be a heightening of the contrast, or perhaps a hint that he did not know exactly what Mark's κράβαττον was, tho he has elsewhere replaced it by κλινίδιον.[1]

THE CALLING OF LEVI (MATTHEW)
(Mk ii, 13–17; Mt ix, 9–13; Lk v, 27–32)

Matthew and Luke both correct Mark's unusual if not ungrammatical use of ὅτι in the sense of why. Mark says "Why does *he* eat with publicans and sinners?" Matthew improves by reading, "Why does *your master* eat," etc. Luke improves still more by directing the question to the disciples in such manner as to include Jesus, "Why do *ye* eat," etc.

THE QUESTION ABOUT FASTING
(Mk ii, 18–22; Mt ix, 14–17; Lk v, 33–39)

Matthew and Luke avoid Mark's verb ἐπιράπτει, a word found nowhere but in this verse of Mark's (ix, 21). At the end they avoid Mark's clumsy expression, "The wine and the bottles will be destroyed," and say, "The wine will be spilled and the bottles destroyed."[2] They both omit the last part of Mark's vs. 19, an obvious

---

[1] This latter is not the usual word for "bed," but means a *little* bed—*some* sort of bed.

[2] Agreement of Matthew and Luke in these two corrections is held to show Urmarkus. The need of correction is obvious enough, and the corrections are the natural ones to make. So also Sinaiticus in Mark, with other authorities.

pleonasm and possibly a later insertion. Luke's addition in his vs. 39 does not fit well, but is bracketed by Westcott and Hort and is probably an insertion. More difficult (and so far as I see impossible) to explain is Luke's suggestion that the patch to be put on the old garment is cut out of a new one—an unusual procedure, certainly. He may possibly have been misled into this statement by his desire to heighten the contrast between old and new.

THE WALK THRU THE CORN
(Mk ii, 23–28; Mt xii, 1–8; Lk vi, 1–5)

Matthew and Luke avoid Mark's expression ὁδὸν ποιεῖν, which sounds as if Mark meant to say that Jesus made a new path thru the corn. They add, what Mark forgets to say, that he and his disciples ate the grain. Luke adds that they rubbed it in their hands. They are led to these corrections by the fact that the justification of Jesus by the example of David has to do, not with making a road thru the grain, but with eating on the Sabbath and, perhaps, eating something which it would not ordinarily have been proper for him to eat. Matthew and Luke omit Mark's colorless and unnecessary "when he had need," and his historically difficult reference to Abiathar.[1] All three have the clause, "and to those that were with him," but each in a different place. Luke improves the order of the clauses in Mark's 26th verse. Matthew adds to the words of Jesus the reference to the priests profaning the temple and yet being guiltless. The addition is suggested by David's eating the shewbread, but does not fit the case so closely, since Jesus was not defending himself against the charge of profaning a holy place. Both Matthew and Luke omit Mark's saying that "The Sabbath

[1] Some MSS omit this reference in Mark.

was made for man, not man for the Sabbath." Sir John Hawkins suggests that the saying may have been offensive to Jewish ears. This may account for Matthew's omission of it; and Luke may have omitted it because he and his readers had not much interest in discussions about the Sabbath. But it is perhaps still more likely that the sentence is a later addition to Mark.

THE MAN WITH THE WITHERED HAND
(Mk iii, 1-6; Mt xii, 9-14; Lk vi, 6-11)

Luke changes Mark's σάββασιν to σαββάτῳ, perhaps because he is not acquainted with the Hebrew (Aramaic) usage of the plural of this word in the sense of the singular. Both Matthew and Luke avoid the direct statement of Mark in his 5th verse that Jesus was angry.

THE CROWD AND THE HEALINGS
(Mk iii, 7-12; Mt xii, 15-21; Lk vi, 17-19)

Matthew's treatment of Mark is influenced by the fact that just before his Sermon on the Mount he has, in iv, 25, given a somewhat similar statement. Luke's transposition has been noticed.[1]

THE CALLING OF THE TWELVE
(Mk iii, 13-19; Mt x, 2-4; Lk vi, 12-16)

Characteristic of Luke is his "He was continuing all night in prayer."[2] The addition by Matthew and Luke of the words ὁ ἀδελφὸς αὐτοῦ (τὸν ἀδελφὸν αὐτοῦ) is held by some to indicate their use of a Marcan text different from ours. The order of the names is not the same in any two of the three lists. Both Matthew and Mark avoid an anacoluthon of Mark in his vs. 16, and omit the appel-

[1] P. 21.   [2] See Lk iii, 21; ix, 18, 28, 29; xi, 1.

CHANGES OF MATTHEW AND LUKE IN MARK 45

lative "Boanerges," with its translation. Matthew and Luke follow Mark in naming Matthew, tho in their account of his call in Mt ix, 13, and Lk v, 27, Luke follows Mark in calling him Levi. Luke changes Mark's "Simon the Canaanite" to "Simon the Zealot." Matthew alone gives the name of Lebbaeus, Mark alone says Thaddeus, Luke alone names Judas the son of James. No simple explanation suggests itself as covering all these deviations. Matthew or Luke or both may have been influenced by a similar list of names in Q or some other non-Marcan source; but that both of them are here following Mark is rendered practically certain by their addition of the appended parenthetical statement concerning Judas, with which all three accounts close.

THE PHARISAIC ACCUSATION AND JESUS' DEFENSE
(Mk iii, 20–30; Mt xii, 22–37; Lk xi, 14–23)

The discussion of this section is complicated by the presence of the section in both Mark and Q, and is therefore postponed to a later time.[1]

THE TRUE BROTHERHOOD OF JESUS; THE PARABLE OF THE SOWER; THE PURPOSE OF THE PARABLES
(Mk iii, 31—iv, 12; Mt xii, 46—xiii, 15; Lk viii, 4—10, 19–21)

Luke has done more than Matthew to turn Mark's narrative into good Greek, tho Matthew has also improved it. The agreement of Matthew and Luke in the addition of $αὐτόν$ in Mt xiii, 4, and Lk viii, 5, where it does not occur in their exemplar (Mk iv, 4), is sometimes held to indicate a text of Mark containing this word. The hypothesis of assimilation seems simpler; or in this case even accidental agreement would not be strange. The

[1] See pp. 153, 238–39.

insertion of πάλιν in Mk iv, 1, not in Matthew and Luke, has been suggested by Weiss to be the work of an editor who saw the confused character of the geographical references since Mk iii, 7.[1]

THE INTERPRETATION OF THE PARABLE OF THE SOWER
(Mk iv, 13–20; Mt xiii, 18–23; Lk viii, 11–15)

Matthew changes Mark's Σατανᾶς to ὁ πονηρός. The latter is used by Matthew in this sense five times, and not at all by Mark and Luke. The change may therefore be regarded as stylistic. Luke's addition of "lest they should believe and be saved" sounds like a Christian addition, and may be explained by the development of the Christian doctrine. Mark's loose and unliterary addition of "and the desires for the rest of the things," after the "cares of the world and the deceitfulness of riches," Luke very naturally corrects into "the cares and wealth and pleasures of life." In iv, 19, Mark uses the participle εἰσπορευόμεναι in a somewhat inexact manner: "The cares of the world and the deceitfulness of riches and the desires for the rest of the things, coming in, choke the word." Luke's change may be accounted for by his desire to improve the style; which he does without discarding Mark's misplaced participle. For he says, "And by the cares . . . . as they [i.e., the people who have heard the word] proceed, they are choked and rendered unfruitful." Probably Schmiedel's statement, in his article in the *Encyclopedia Biblica*, that this instance alone would prove literary relation between Mark and Luke is too strong; especially considering the fact that Luke's participle is not precisely the same as Mark's; but the deviation is certainly an interesting one. In the earlier

[1] *Das älteste Evangelium*, p. 165.

part of the passage Matthew and Luke both omit Mark's reference to the dulness of the disciples. The omission is due to their customary deference to the feeling of a later time.

A GROUP OF DETACHED SAYINGS
(Mk iv, 21-25; Mt v, 15; x, 26; vii, 2; xiii, 12; Lk viii, 16-18; vi, 38)

The divergences in wording, the fact that the verses found together in Mark are separated in both Matthew and Luke, and the additional fact of doublets in Matthew or Luke for all but one of Mark's verses, indicate beyond a doubt that these verses stood in both Mark and Q.

THE PARABLE OF THE MUSTARD SEED
(Mk iv, 30-32; Mt xiii, 31-32; Lk xiii, 18-19)

This section also stood in both Mark and Q. Luke is perhaps independent of Mark here, preferring to follow Q. Matthew seems, as often, to try to combine the two sources, showing some resemblances to Mark as against Luke, and others to Luke as against Mark. The passage is narrative only in Mark, parable only in Luke, and a combination of narrative and parable in Matthew. The anacoluthon in Mk iv, 31, is avoided by Matthew and Luke.[1]

THE STORM ON THE LAKE
(Mk iv, 35-41; Mt viii, 23-27; Lk viii, 22-25)

Matthew and Luke omit the statement that other boats accompanied the one in which Jesus sailed. Perhaps, as Hawkins suggests, they wondered how these weathered the storm. Or, since the point of narrating the story has to do only with the boat in which Jesus sailed, they may simply have seen no advantage in relating the

For further discussion of this and the preceding section see pp. 239-40.

circumstance of the other boats. Matthew substitutes the comparatively common word, tho I believe not common in exactly this connection, σεισμὸς, for Mark's rare word λαῖλαψ. Matthew and Luke omit the statement that Jesus was "asleep on the cushion"; it has been suggested that they may have considered the use of the cushion as an effeminacy unworthy of Jesus; or more probably they have omitted it as of no consequence. They both omit the direct address of Jesus to the sea, as they often omit his words of address to the demons. They do not wish to represent the disciples as distrustful; so while Mark says "Master, dost thou not care that we perish?" Matthew says "Save, Lord; we perish," and Luke simply "Master, we perish."

THE GADARENE DEMONIAC
(Mk v, 1–20; Mt viii, 28–34; Lk viii, 26–39)

The name of the locality is different in each account. Some texts, however, make Matthew agree with Mark; others make him agree with Luke; while still other texts do the same for Luke with reference to Mark and Matthew. The exact location, or the proper name for it, may have been in dispute. Matthew shortens Mark's narrative, as almost invariably. Luke shows himself to be no mere copyist; in view of Mark's statement that after the demoniac's cure they found him "clothed," he supplies in his original description of the demoniac the statement which Mark does not have, that the man wore no clothes. Matthew and Luke again omit Jesus' command to the demon to come out of the man. Luke includes Jesus' question, "What is thy name?" But to make it plain that this question is addressed to the man and not to the demon, he changes Mark's statement, "for we are many," into his own editorial explanation, "for many demons had entered into him." Matthew and Luke are involved in a slight difficulty by their abbreviation of Mark. For while Mark makes those who have seen the cure of the demoniac tell their neighbors about him "and about the swine," Matthew and Luke omit this latter item. It therefore appears from Matthew and Luke that the Gadarenes requested Jesus to depart from their coasts lest their demoniacs should be cured; in Mark they asked him to depart because they did not wish their property destroyed. Luke's change of Mark's ὁ κύριος (Mk's vs. 19) into ὁ θεός, is not easily explained if Luke understood Mark to refer to Jesus by his ὁ κύριος. As the latter word, however, is ambiguous, and as Mark seems to use it more often than the other evangelists with reference to God, Luke *may* have so understood his narrative here. But as the man went and told, not what God, but what Jesus, had done for him, Luke can hardly have so misunderstood Mark; and Luke's change may be due to his feeling that Jesus did not call himself κύριος. This indeed seems to be the only place where Mark puts this self-designation into the mouth of Jesus. Matthew and Luke seem consistently to avoid it.

THE DAUGHTER OF JAIRUS AND THE WOMAN WITH THE ISSUE OF BLOOD

(Mk v, 21-43; Mt ix, 18-26; Lk viii, 40-56)

This curious insertion of one miracle within another might be held to be enough in itself to prove the literary dependence of the three synoptists. Luke's change of Mark's vs. 23 is explained by the anacoluthon in Mark. Matthew and Luke naturally avoid Mark's θυγάτριον. Their substitution of the "tassel of his garment" for "his garment" is unusual, since it seems to indicate their closer definition of the kind of cloak worn by Jesus. The change may serve to heighten the appearance of reverence in the woman. Luke substitutes $παραχρῆμα$ for Mark's $εὐθύς$; the latter is Mark's uniform word for "immediately," used by him forty-one times against Matthew's eighteen and Luke's seven; the former is Luke's favorite word, being used ten times by him, twice by Matthew, and never by Mark. Matthew and Luke omit the question of the disciples to Jesus, "Sayest thou, Who touched me?" as possibly implying lack of respect upon their part. They also omit Mark's parenthetical statement that John was the brother of James; this had been mentioned often enough already. Luke's abbreviation of Mark involves him in the difficulty of saying that Jesus allowed nobody to go *into the house* with him, except the three disciples and the parents of the child, whereas Mark expressly says that he allowed only those to go with him *into the death chamber*. Matthew, not mentioning the death chamber, has a reminiscence of it in his participle $εἰσελθών$, coming as it does after the $ἐλθών$ $εἰς τὴν οἰκίαν$ of his previous verse. In this story also Luke has read Mark thru carefully; and finding that Mark inserts "she was twelve years old" after the statement that she arose and walked, prefers to put this into the more appropriate place as part of the introductory narrative; he is thus enabled at the same time to make the connection in the latter part of the story much better by saying that as soon as the girl sat up Jesus commanded her parents to give her something to eat; a command which in Mark follows only after several other items. Luke thus makes the giving of food to the girl a part of the means used for her recovery.

THE INITIAL PREACHING IN NAZARETH
(Mk vi, 1-6; Mt xiii, 53-58; Lk iv, 16-30)

Luke's working over of the account in Mk vi, 1-6, has already been considered.[1] He has preferred to put it at the beginning of Jesus' ministry, as a sort of introductory résumé of the reception which Jesus received at the hands of the Jews, and his consequent turning to the gentiles. The anachronism involved is seen in the fact that Jesus says, "Ye will say to me, ... what we have heard done in Capernaum do also here in thine own town"; whereas, in Luke's own account the wonders in Capernaum have not yet occurred. The words, "No prophet is accepted in his own country," do not fit so well here as where Mark has them (vi, 4) following upon the question, "Is not this the carpenter, ... and are not his sisters here with us?" and where Mark adds to the word "country" the words "and among his own kinsmen and in his own house." Luke does not add that Jesus was not able to do many wonders there, partly because he is speaking of his preaching only, but still more because he always avoids such statements about the inability or limitation of Jesus.

THE SENDING OUT OF THE DISCIPLES
(Mk vi, 6-13; Mt ix, 35; x, 1, 9-11; Lk ix, 1-6)

Luke has a second sending out of disciples in his 10th chapter. Considering his usual avoidance of duplicates, it seems probable that he took one of these accounts from Mark and one from Q, and that the account therefore stood in both Q and Mark. The account in Luke's chap. 10 is closely akin to one part of Matthew's parallel section, and his account in his 9th chapter is more closely akin to other verses of Matthew's account. These latter

[1] P. 19.

verses of Matthew agree more closely with Mark's account than do his other verses. It seems clear therefore that Matthew has combined the account of the sending out of the disciples which he found in Q with that which he found in Mark. This combination of material from his two sources is characteristic of him, as the careful separation of it is characteristic of Luke.[1]

Comparing here the passages of Matthew and Luke which were apparently taken from Mark, Luke and Matthew correct the anacoluthon of Mark's vss. 8 and 9. Matthew and Mark mention the healing but once; Luke three times. Mark says the disciples are to take nothing, except a staff; Luke and Matthew say they are to take nothing, not even a staff. Mark seems to contemplate a mission chiefly to houses, not so much to cities, tho his word τόπος may indicate the latter. The substitution by Matthew and Luke of κονιορτός for Mark's χοῦν, as well as other minor and verbal deviations, may easily be accounted for by their acquaintance with the account in Q. Harnack suggests that Mark's permission of the staff, which is denied in Matthew and Luke, may indicate a relaxation of the rule, arising in actual practice. If so, Matthew and Luke, because they here follow Q, may represent a more original form of the saying.[2]

THE JUDGMENT OF HEROD CONCERNING JESUS
(Mk vi, 14–16; Mt xiv, 1–2; Lk ix, 7–9)

Matthew and Luke correct Mark's "Herod the king" into "Herod the tetrarch," tho Matthew a few verses

[1] Huck's *Synopse*, pp. 80 and 109, will show the verses belonging respectively to the two sources.

[2] It is argued later, pp. 234–48, that Mark also is dependent upon Q, but since he has the Q material in much briefer and more fragmentary form than Matthew and Luke, his use of Q does not preclude Matthew's and Luke's preservation of more primary features of the Q tradition.

later falls back into the error which he has corrected. Mark says that Herod himself surmised that Jesus was John the Baptist risen from the dead (tho some texts read ἔλεγον for ἔλεγεν in vs. 14). Matthew follows Mark in this by saying distinctly that Herod "said to those about him, it is John," etc. Luke says Herod had heard of the things Jesus did, "and was perplexed because *it was said* that John was risen." Luke may here have been following one text of Mark and Matthew another text. The fact that with ἔλεγεν in Mark's vs. 14, his vs. 16 is a mere repetition of this verse (Matthew omits the parallel to Mark's vs. 16), may indicate either that ἔλεγον is the original reading of vs. 14, or that Luke, finding ἔλεγεν there, corrected it into his own statement which upon the face of it is much better. Luke does not represent Herod as personally making any such statement about John, but says merely that when Herod heard of the deeds of Jesus and of the explanation that was popularly given for them, he desired to see Jesus.

THE DEATH OF THE BAPTIST
(Mk vi, 17–29; Mt xiv, 3–12)

Luke has omitted this because he has long ago finished with the Baptist (in iii, 19–20). The passage seems to be parenthetical in Mark, to explain Herod's statement that he has killed John the Baptist. Mark says Herod did *not* wish to kill John, because he regarded him as a just and holy man. Matthew says Herod *wished* to kill John, but *feared the people*, because *they* considered John a prophet. Matthew's difference here may be due to a different tradition which he considered superior to Mark's, or it may be due simply to the abbreviation he has made in Mark's narrative. Mark's account contains the somewhat improbable feature of the daughter of Herodias dancing before the drunken tetrarch and his companions; which Matthew omits. The Latin word σπεκουλάτωρ in Mark (vi, 27) is dropped in Matthew.

THE RETURN OF THE DISCIPLES AND THE FEEDING OF THE FIVE THOUSAND
(Mk vi, 30–44; Mt xiv, 13–21; Lk ix, 10–17)

Matthew assigns as the reason for Jesus' departure in the boat the news of what had happened to John the Baptist. Mark, treating this latter as purely parenthetical, says Jesus and his disciples went away to escape the crowds. Luke, not having related the death of the Baptist, assigns still a different reason for Jesus' withdrawal, saying that "the *apostles*" had returned, and Jesus went aside with them, apparently to hear their report. Luke says they retired to Bethsaida, where it seems out of place that the feeding of the five thousand should occur; this latter event being more appropriately located by Mark and Matthew in a "desert place." Mark and Matthew both say the crowds went on foot; Mark says they preceded Jesus, Matthew and Luke, that they followed him when they knew of his departure. The deviations are easily accounted for by the desire of Matthew and Luke to improve the story of Mark. Luke's mention of Bethsaida is accounted for by his desire to supply exact details wherever possible; perhaps also by the fact that the second feeding, which he omits, was related to have occurred in that place. Luke is apparently unaffected, in his placing of the five thousand in Bethsaida, by the fact that he represents Jesus as saying, "We are here in a desert place." He may also have been misled in his location of the miracle by the mention, in Mark vi, 45 (which Luke omits), of the departure of Jesus and his disciples for Bethsaida. Luke transposes Mark's statement of the numbers fed, to an earlier and presumably better position. Matthew adds, as in the feeding of the four thousand, that the numbers given were exclusive of women and children; apparently from his desire, or the desire of the tradition lying back of him, to heighten the impressiveness of the miracle. Mark's Hebraism, συμπόσια συμπόσια, is omitted by both Matthew and Luke.

THE WALKING ON THE SEA
(Mk vi, 45–52; Mt xiv, 22–33)

Mark's narrative seems to imply (vs. 46) that Jesus "meant to walk past them." Matthew implies, on the contrary, that Jesus was coming to their help. Matthew "spiritualizes" the account by adding the experiment of Peter: "Peter can do it so long as he has faith."[1] It has been observed that in this narrative, as in others which Matthew takes from Mark but which Luke omits, the verbal agreement is considerably closer than in the sections which Matthew and Luke both copy. Schmiedel has suggested that this points to a common document occasionally employed by Matthew and Mark but not by Luke. The hypothesis of a later assimilation of Matthew and Luke seems simpler. At all events, the very close agreement of Matthew and Mark in this narrative, up to the point where Matthew inserts the experiment of Peter, may possibly indicate that this latter is later than the body of Matthew's Gospel. Whether so or not, its presence is easily accounted for by Matthew's ecclesiastical point of view, the primacy of Peter being asserted by him

[1] Wellhausen, *Einleitung*, p. 59.

in one other notable passage which occurs in Matthew alone. Probably Matthew has drawn these special passages about Peter from a source of his own, and, according to his custom, has here combined one of them with a narrative of Mark's.

THE RETURN TO GENNESARET
(Mk vi, 53–56; Mt xiv, 34–36)

This section is omitted by Luke. There are no sayings in it. Matthew's customary abbreviation is shown in his 44 words against Mark's 72; but there is much close verbal correspondence in spite of this.

ABOUT THE THINGS THAT DEFILE
(Mk vii, 1–23; Mt xv, 1–20)

Mark has an editorial comment about the scrupulosity of the Jews. It may be a later addition in his narrative, at least this may be the case with the words καὶ πάντες οἱ Ἰουδαῖοι, which make it apply to the whole people and not simply to the Pharisees; or it may have seemed to Matthew to be somewhat exaggerated and have been omitted by him on that account. Its omission improves the connection in Matthew's narrative, and might be sufficiently accounted for by Matthew's tendency to omit superfluous or negligible portions of Mark's stories. In his vs. 11 (Matthew has transposed several verses) Mark has the Aramaic word κορβᾶν, omitted by Matthew. In Mark's vs. 19 occurs the phrase καθαρίζων πάντα τὰ βρώματα. The construction is loose, the nearest verb with which the participle can be connected being the λέγει of the first part of the preceding verse. This alone might have induced Matthew to omit it; still more, the implication, that Jesus had in this saying abolished the distinction between clean and unclean. Nor is it surprising that Matthew should omit, among Mark's list of the things that come out of a man's heart and "defile him," his mention of the "evil eye."

THE CANAANITISH WOMAN
(Mk vii, 24-30; Mt xv, 21-28)

Matthew omits Mark's statement that Jesus was not able to be hid. It may have seemed to him an unworthy limitation of the power of Jesus. Mark also recounts a clever answer of the woman, "The dogs under the table eat of the children's crumbs"; and Jesus, for the cleverness of her reply, as he says, grants her wish. It is not strange that Matthew replaces this by Jesus' words, "Great is thy faith."

THE FEEDING OF THE FOUR THOUSAND
(Mk viii, 1-10; Mt xv, 32-39)

Matthew follows Mark closely. He seems in vss. 37 and 38 to be quoting from his own account of the previous feeding. This item brings out a tendency of Matthew to repeat in one place phrases which he has used in another.

THE DEMAND FOR A SIGN
(Mk viii, 11-13; Mt xii, 38-39; Mt xvi, 1-4; Lk xi, 29; xii, 54-56)

Doublets in both Matthew and Luke indicate the presence of this section in both Mark and Q.[1]

THE SAYING ABOUT YEAST
(Mk viii, 14-21; Mt xvi, 5-12)

Matthew omits the rebuke to the disciples in Mark (viii, 17, 18). He apparently manufactures a saying of Jesus in his vs. 11, in order to introduce therewith his own editorial statement of vs. 12.

[1] For further discussion see p. 241.

THE CONFESSION OF PETER AND THE FIRST PREDICTION OF SUFFERINGS

(Mk viii, 27–33; Mt xvi, 13–23; Lk ix, 18–22)

Matthew spoils the question of Jesus by obtruding his own estimate of him in the words "The son of man" in vs. 13. Upon Peter's answer, he adds Jesus' words of commendation, and makes Jesus reciprocate by telling Peter who he (Peter) is, and that the church shall be founded upon him. The addition may be later than Matthew. If not, it betrays the ecclesiastical interest, and especially the interest in the primacy of Peter, which comes out elsewhere in Matthew. Matthew and Luke correct Mark's statement, "after three days he shall rise again," to "on the third day," so making the prediction agree more accurately with the facts, and giving a Greek method of reckoning instead of the Hebrew. It is not surprising that Luke omits the rebuke to Peter; Matthew's inclusion of it seems strange. Both omit Mark's statement that "Jesus spoke the word openly," because, as Hawkins suggests,[1] if this meant that he spoke to the crowd, it is contradicted by Mark's vs. 34; if it meant that he told them clearly about the resurrection, it would seem strange that the disciples did not understand.

THE DEMANDS OF DISCIPLESHIP

(Mk viii, 34—ix, 1; Mt xvi, 24–28; Lk ix, 23–27)

Mark's redundant expression ὀπίσω ἀκολουθεῖν is corrected by each of the others, in a different way. The phrase καὶ τοῦ εὐαγγελίου in Mark's vs. 35 sounds like a later addition; it would hardly have been omitted by Matthew and Luke if it had stood in their source.

[1] *Horae Synopticae*, p. 123.

Matthew makes Jesus say that "the son of man is about to come"; Mark and Luke say "when the son of man comes"; Matthew betrays his own attitude, or the attitude of his time, to the long-expected parousia. Mark's extremely awkward order of words, τίνες ὧδε τῶν ἑστηκότων,[1] each of the other evangelists corrects in his own way.

THE TRANSFIGURATION
(Mk ix, 2–8; Mt xvii, 1–8; Lk ix, 28–36)

Mark says "he was changed in form" (μεταμορφώθη), which Luke improves to "the appearance of his countenance was different" (τὸ εἶδος τοῦ προσώπου αὐτοῦ ἕτερον). Both Matthew and Luke change Mark's "Elias and Moses" to the chronological order. Luke adds that these spoke of the approaching entry of Jesus into Jerusalem, and adduces, as an excuse for the disciples' not understanding, or for Peter's apparently foolish remark, that they were heavy with sleep. Matthew and Luke change Mark's Aramaic ῥαββεί into Greek words, Luke using the ἐπιστάτα which is peculiar to him.

THE DISCUSSION ABOUT ELIJAH
(Mk ix, 9–13; Mt xvii, 9–13)

Mark says Elias has come (in the person of John the Baptist), and they have done whatever they would with him, "as it was written of him." Matthew understands, rightly, that this last is a reference to the Old Testament, and not knowing where or what had there been written of the Baptist, omits it. Perhaps the statement is a later addition to Mark.

[1] A note on this passage by Professor H. A. Sanders says that this is Mark's order in B D (k d c) only.

THE HEALING OF THE EPILEPTIC BOY
(Mk ix, 14–29; Mt xvii, 14–21; Lk ix, 37–43a)

Mark says that when the crowd saw Jesus they were amazed. This might seem to be a parallel to the amazement of the Israelites on seeing Moses' countenance when he came down from the mount. But Matthew and Luke have omitted it. They also omit Jesus' direct address to the demon,[1] and Jesus' statement, "This kind cometh not out except with prayer." This may reflect the custom in ecclesiastical exorcisms, and may have been added by a later hand, or omitted by Matthew and Luke because as matter of fact Jesus had not prayed and therefore the saying did not fit the case.

THE SECOND PREDICTION OF SUFFERINGS
(Mk ix, 30–32; Mt xvii, 22–23; Lk ix, 43b–45)

In the second prediction of sufferings Matthew and Luke both avoid Mark's οὐκ ἤθελεν ἵνα τις γνοῖ (Mk ix, 30). It seems to be a part of Mark's *Geheimnis-Theorie;* but since Matthew and Luke both include some of Mark's other references to this theory, this fact is not a sufficient explanation of its omission, which may perhaps be attributed to the growing reverence for Jesus. Luke's vs. 44a, θέσθε ὑμεῖς εἰς τὰ ὦτα ὑμῶν τοὺς λόγους τούτους, is without parallel in Mark (or Matthew). Luke has also omitted a part of Mark's prediction, "and they shall kill him," which he would hardly have done if he were here following Mark, or if the clause had stood in his copy of Mark. These facts may be taken to indicate that Luke is here following another source. The words quoted from vs. 44a would be very unlikely to be added by Luke himself.[2] Matthew seems to follow Mark, making

---
[1] Cf. a similar omission of the address to the waves, p. 48.
[2] See Bartlet, "Sources of St. Luke's Gospel," *Oxford Studies*, p. 321.

his customary abbreviation and changing Mark's "after three days" to "on the third day." In another instance already noticed both Matthew and Luke make the same change in Mark's statement. Luke may here be following Q. But the absence of any agreements between him and Matthew as against Mark would rather indicate his use of a peculiar source. There are no doublets to substantiate the supposition of the use of Q.

THE STRIFE ABOUT RANK
(Mk ix, 33–37; Mt xviii, 1–5; Lk ix, 46–48)

The section on the strife about rank probably stood in both Mark and Q, but the resemblances are too general for one to draw definite conclusions as to the exact source relationship.

MINOR PASSAGES

It will be sufficient if we look with less detail thru a few more passages of the triple tradition, to note the changes made by Matthew and Luke in the text of Mark.

In the case of the unknown exorcist (Mk ix, 38–41; Lk ix, 49–50) Luke says "he followed not with us" instead of "he followed not us"; the assumption of authority upon the part of John is thereby lessened.

In the saying about offenses (Mk ix, 42–48; Mt xviii, 6–9; Lk xvii, 1–2) Matthew has combined Mark's saying about the hand and his separate saying about the foot, into one. The saying stood in Mark and Q. In the discussion about marriage and divorce (Mk x, 11–12; Mt v, 31–32; Lk xvi, 18; xix, 9) Matthew has rearranged the order of Mark, and has added "except for adultery," as he has done in another place; he has omitted Mark's reference to the woman divorcing her husband, as this would mean nothing to his Palestinian readers.

In the blessing of the children (Mk x, 13–16; Mt xix, 13–15; Lk xviii, 15–17) Matthew and Luke omit Mark's statement that Jesus was angry.

In the saying concerning the danger of riches (Mk x, 17–31; Mt xix, 16–30; Lk xviii, 18–30) Mark makes Jesus say, "Why callest thou me good?" Matthew changes this to "Why askest thou me concerning that which is good?" tho his following words, "There is One who is good," betray the fact that he had Mark's reading before him. Matthew shows his Jewish affinities by making Jesus say that the questioner may "enter into life," by keeping the commandments. Both Matthew and Luke omit one commandment which Mark quotes, because it is not found in the Decalogue. Matthew changes Mark's order of the commandments to agree with the Old Testament. Matthew, having called the questioner a youth, omits from his reply to Jesus the words, "from my youth up." Both omit Mark's vs. 24, which is practically a duplicate of the previous verse. Luke, having included the idea of "sisters" in his word for family, omits sisters, but, with his characteristic interest in women, adds "wife."

In the third prediction of sufferings (Mk x, 32–34; Mt xx, 17–19; Lk xviii, 31–34) the agreement between Mark and Matthew is very close throughout. The only agreement of Matthew and Luke against Mark is in their substitution of εἶπεν for λέγει. Both Matthew and Luke change Mark's "after three days" to "on the third day." Three words in Mark's vs. 34 are reproduced in Luke alone; ἀναστήσεται, ἀποκτενοῦσιν, ἐμπτύσουσιν. Matthew has added καὶ σταυρῶσαι.

In the request for seats in the kingdom (Mk x, 35–45; Mt xx, 20–28) Mark makes James and John ask Jesus directly; Luke omits the incident; Matthew puts the burden of the ambitious request upon the mother instead of upon the sons; tho he betrays the fact that he is remaking Mark, by making Jesus direct his reply to the men.

In the healing of Bartimaeus (Mk x, 46–52; Mt xx, 29–34; Lk xviii, 35–43) Mark says "the son of Timaeus," perhaps in explanation of the Aramaic name. Matthew specifies two men instead of one, giving no names; it has been suggested that he may have been misled by Mark's "Bartimaeus" and "the son of Timaeus," tho the Jewish affinity of Matthew's Gospel makes this unlikely. Since "the son of Timaeus" did not serve to identify the man to their readers, Matthew and Luke omit the phrase. Mark's graphic statement that the man threw off his cloak and ran to Jesus was unsuited to the dignity of the Later Gospels. Matthew and Luke again substitute the Greek κύριε for Mark's ῥαββουνί. They omit his ὕπαγε, which seems out of place.[1]

In the preparation for the entry into Jerusalem (Mk xi, 1–11; Mt xxi, 1–11; Lk xix, 28–38) Mark represents Jesus as telling the disciples who go after the colt, to explain that Jesus has need of him and that he will return him soon. Luke omits the latter item; Matthew changes it to mean that when the disciples have explained to the owner that Jesus needs the animal, the owner will quickly send it to Jesus. The growing reverence for Jesus easily explains the change and the omission. Matthew undoubtedly represents Jesus as riding into Jerusalem upon two beasts, the ass and her foal; the strange phenomenon is explained by his attempt to harmonize the event with an Old Testament prophecy. The prophecy, however, for

[1] I am unable to account for Matthew's addition that Jesus touched the man's eyes.

that matter, had only one beast in mind. Mark says Bethany (in some texts Bethany and Bethphage), Matthew Bethphage, and Luke Bethany and Bethphage; the two names in Luke, and in certain texts of Mark, are probably to be explained as the harmonizing effort of some copyist.

In the cursing of the fig tree (Mk xi, 12–14; Mt xxi, 18–19), the statement of Mark, "For it was not the time for figs," may have been omitted by Matthew because seeming to imply an unreasonable expectation on the part of Jesus. Or it may be a later addition to Mark. Matthew says that the disciples noticed "immediately" that the tree had withered, whereas Mark says they observed this the next day. Matthew's change may have been in the interest of heightening the miracle. Upon his observation here he has hung his statement about the wonder of the disciples in his vs. 20. Luke omits this miracle; probably because he considers the parable of the Fig Tree which he gives in xxi, 29–31 (taking it from Mk xiii, 28–29 = Mt xxiv, 32–33) a variant of, or an improvement upon, the same story.

The speech about the withered fig tree (Mk xi, 20–25; Mt xxi, 20–22) Luke omits because he has omitted the miracle upon which it depends. The saying about faith apparently stood in both Mark and Q, since Matthew has a doublet upon it. This may have been an additional reason for Luke's omission of it here, since he has incorporated it in his xvii, 6.[1]

In the question about authority (Mk xi, 27–33; Mt xxi, 23–27; Lk xx, 1–8) the intervention of the fig tree story in Mark (and Matthew) obscures the point of the question about Jesus' authority, which was directed toward his action in cleansing the temple. There is very close agree-

[1] See p. 244 for further discussion of the saying as in Mark and Q.

ment among the three in the question of Jesus to his questioners (Mk xi, 30; Mt xxi, 25; Lk xx, 4), tho both Matthew and Luke avoid Mark's anacoluthon at the beginning of the following verse.

In the parable of the Evil Husbandmen (Mk xii, 1–12; Mt xxi, 33–46; Lk xx, 9–19) Mark says, "They took him and killed him and cast him out"; Matthew and Luke say, "They cast him outside the vineyard and killed him," presumably influenced in this correction by the fact of Jesus' crucifixion outside the city.[1] Matthew puts into the mouth of the questioners one saying which Mark ascribes to Jesus; the questioners are thus convicted by their own testimony.

In the question of the Sadducees about the resurrection (Mk xii, 18–27; Mt xxii, 23–33; Lk xx, 27–40) Mark says, quite correctly, "The Sadducees, who (as is well known) say there is no resurrection";[2] Matthew not so happily represents them as making this statement to Jesus; Luke corrects still further, being apparently unacquainted with the tenets of the Sadducees as a class, and so says, "Certain of the Sadducees came, denying that there is any resurrection." It is one of the instances, perhaps comparatively few, where Mark would better have been left as he was. To make the contrast between this world and the next stronger Luke adds in his vs. 34, "the sons of this world marry and are given in marriage." He also attempts to explain the apparently incomplete statement, "God is not of the dead but of the living," by adding "for all live to him."[3]

[1] No reason can be given, so far as I know, for Luke's addition of his xx, 18. Some texts ascribe the same saying to Matthew also.

[2] I think I owe this suggestion to Wernle, but do not find the passage in his *Synoptische Frage*.

[3] Bacon explains this saying of Mark's to mean that Jahwe is not a god of the underworld, like Pluto (*Beginnings of Gospel Story*).

In the question about the great commandment (Mk xii, 28–34; Mt xxii, 34–40; Lk x, 25–28), Matthew's addition, "Upon these two commandments hang all the law, and the prophets," is perhaps an old Christian formula, which seems to fit remarkably well in this place.

In the question about David's son (Mk xii, 35–37; Mt xxii, 41–46; Lk xx, 41–44), Luke corrects Mark's statement, "David said in the Holy Spirit," with "David says in the book of Psalms"; Mark is nearer to Jesus, Luke writes for the convenience of his readers who might wish to look up the reference.

In the speech against the Pharisees (Mk xii, 38–40; Mt xxiii, 1–7; Lk xx, 45–47), Mark's "Beware of the Pharisees, who love to walk about in robes, and greetings in the market" is not positively ungrammatical, since the infinitive and the noun may both be the object of the verb. But it is a loose construction; Luke corrects it by the insertion of a second verb governing the noun.

In the predictions of distress (Mk xiii, 9–13; Mt xxiv, 9–14; Lk xxi, 12–19), Mark's προμεριμνᾶτε, a word not found elsewhere in the New Testament or Septuagint, is avoided by Matthew and Luke. Matthew's passage (xxiv, 10–12) about the false prophets who shall deceive many, and the love of many growing cold, whether attributed to the evangelist, or to the tradition lying just behind him, reflects the conditions of his times.

In the saying about the distress in Judaea (Mk xiii, 14–20; Mt xxiv, 15–22; Lk xxi, 20–24), Mark's construction of a neuter noun with a masculine participle, a construction according to the sense (βδέλυγμα .... ἑστηκότα), his unusual construction of εἰς τὸν ἀγρὸν meaning "in the field," and his equally strange combination of words ἔσονται γὰρ αἱ ἡμέραι ἐκεῖναι θλίψις, οἵα οὐ γέγονεν τοιαύτη, are all replaced by Matthew and Luke. Luke omits ὁ ἀναγινώσκων νοείτω, because it is not applicable to his readers. He adds "until the times of the nations are fulfilled," apparently upon Paul's hypothesis that the end could not come till the gospel had first been preached to all the nations (Rom xi, 11, 15, 31). This is Luke's substitute for the explanation which Matthew has copied from Mark, that the Lord has shortened the days for the sake of the Christians. In the speech about the parousia (Mk xiii, 24-27; Mt xxiv, 29-31; Lk xxi, 25-28), Matthew has added εὐθέως. This is Mark's favorite adverb, and its addition by Matthew where it is lacking in Mark is hard to understand. Perhaps, as Bacon says, Matthew the Palestinian wishes to encourage the hope of the speedy coming of Jesus, while Mark the Roman wishes to discourage it; but the reasons for this are not perfectly clear. Schmiedel considers the omission of the εὐθέως in Mark as a sign of his secondary character at this point.

In the passage about the time of the parousia (Mk xiii, 30-32; Mt xxiv, 34-36; Lk xxi, 32-33), Luke omits Mark's statement that "the son" does not know the time; because he always avoids any implication of a limitation in the knowledge of Jesus.[1] In the preparation for the Passover (Mk xiv, 12-17; Mt xxvi, 17-20; Lk xxii, 7-14), Luke omits the "my" in the question which Jesus tells the disciples to ask, "Where is my chamber where I shall," etc.; perhaps, as Hawkins[2] suggests, because it may have seemed to him a somewhat harshly expressed claim.

---

[1] Luke (xvii, 34) wishes to suggest that the parousia may occur in the night.

[2] *Horae Synopticae*, p. 120.

In the institution of the Last Supper (Mk xiv, 22–25; Mt xxvi, 26–29; Lk xxii, 15–20), Luke adds (xxii, 19–20) words which seem to be taken from Paul's account in I Cor. xi, 25. Westcott and Hort regard them as interpolated from that epistle. Matthew adds, in his vs. 28, as he has added in his account of the purpose of John's baptism, "for the remission of sins."

In the account of Jesus in Gethsemane (Mk xiv, 32–42; Mt xxvi, 36–46; Lk xxii, 39–46), Luke's vss. 43–44 are lacking in many manuscripts, and are probably a later addition. Luke and Matthew, probably from the growth of the tradition, and from the wish not to omit anything from this solemn scene, represent Jesus as addressing Judas, but do not agree in the words ascribed to him.

In the account of the arrest (Mk xiv, 43–54; Mt xxvi, 47–58; Lk xxii, 47–55) Mark has the words "but that the scriptures might be fulfilled," without attaching the "that" to anything. Matthew fills out his incomplete sentence by writing, "All this happened that the scriptures," etc. Luke omits the flight of the disciples, because the appearances of the risen Jesus which he recounts take place in Jerusalem. Both Matthew and Luke omit the reference to the young man in the linen garment, either because they did not understand it, or knew it would have no meaning for their readers, or both. Mark says the crowd who came to arrest Jesus came "*from* the chief priests"; Luke has apparently overlooked the preposition, and so represents the chief priests themselves as taking part in the arrest.

To Mark's mocking "Prophesy!" addressed to the blindfolded Jesus by the soldiers, Luke and Matthew add the words, clearly explanatory, "Who is he that struck thee?"

In the denial of Peter (Mk xiv, 66–72; Mt xxvi, 69–75; Lk xxii, 56–62), Matthew and Luke omit two obscure and strange words of Mark, προαύλιον in vs. 68 and ἐπιβαλών in vs. 72. In the treatment of Jesus by Pilate, Luke adds the charge that Jesus had stirred up the people not to pay tribute to Caesar; it is probably a reflection of the anarchistic charges made against Christians in Luke's time. Matthew's addition of Pilate's hand-washing is probably due to his desire, or the desire of the tradition back of him, to relieve the Roman authorities of responsibility for the death of Jesus.

In the story of the journey to the crucifixion (Mk xv, 21; Mt xxvii, 32; Lk xxiii, 26–32), the omission of the names of Rufus and Alexander is probably due (as already said) to the fact that these men were unknown to Matthew and Luke and their readers, and added no weight to the testimony of Simon their father. Luke's extremely vivid touch of Jesus' address to the "Daughters of Jerusalem" can be explained only as a part of his special material for this portion of the life of Jesus.

In the story of the crucifixion (Mk xv, 22–32; Mt xxvii, 33–44; Lk xxiii, 33–43), Luke's words, "Father forgive them, for they know not what they do," are omitted in many manuscripts, are bracketed by Westcott and Hort, and are probably a later addition. Matthew corrects Mark, who says a man came with a sponge, saying, "Let him be," etc.; Matthew makes the crowd address the "Let him be" to the man with the sponge.

Luke apparently differs much more than Matthew, from Mark, in his story of the crucifixion, and the events that led up to and followed it. This can be explained by his possession of special sources for these last days of Jesus, and his desire to use material from these sources with his Marcan matter. Transpositions are especially frequent.

In his xxii, 18, e.g., Luke makes a transposition of Mk xiv, 25. This may be taken as typical of his procedure throughout these sections. Mark gives the reference to the approaching betrayal before the institution of the Supper; Luke, after that institution. Mark places the prediction of the denial of Peter after Peter has left the room; Luke, before his leaving. Similar transpositions are made in the story of the rending of the veil. In all, Luke makes some twelve or thirteen such transpositions in Mark's passion narrative. Matthew follows Mark closely, both in matter and in wording.

Comparing Luke's use of Mark in the other parts of his Gospel with his use of him in these last sections, Hawkins[1] finds that "the verbal correspondence with the Marcan source is about twice as great in the Lucan account of the ministry as in the Lucan account of the passion." The amount of actually new material in Luke's passion section is about three times as great as the amount of new material which Luke introduces into any other correspondingly large section of Marcan narrative.

SUMMARY ON MATTHEW'S AND LUKE'S TREATMENT OF THE MARCAN NARRATIVE

The manner in which Matthew and Luke have treated the Gospel of Mark has been brought out in the concrete and detailed examples that have been considered. No single motive, especially no one so-called "tendency" of either writer explains all his modifications of his Marcan source. Both Matthew and Luke omitted what seemed to them superfluous, as well as whatever appeared

[1] See his study, from which these statements are abridged, in *Oxford Studies in the Synoptic Problem*, pp. 76–77.

to them to conflict with the higher veneration for Jesus which had developed in their times. Luke especially omitted what would have no significance or interest for his Greek readers—disputes with the Pharisees, questions of Jewish law, and other Judaistic features. Both Matthew and Luke treated the actual words of Jesus, as recorded in Mark, with great respect. But the narrative, and in a less degree the parables, they felt free to work over as they would. Matthew shows much greater fidelity to his source than Luke. But both of them reconstructed sentences or whole stories, changed bad constructions into good ones, added what material they would, Matthew combining this with his Marcan material while Luke kept it for the most part distinct. Not every change which they made suggests its explanation to us, and we cannot be certain that in most of them we have the actual motive operating in the mind of the evangelist. But the method of their procedure, the kind of motives that influenced them, the degree of freedom which they took in the re-working of their material from Mark, and their habits with reference to the relation of this Marcan material to the other matter which they wished to combine with it, have been sufficiently established.[1]

[1] The fact that Matthew agrees much more closely with Mark, in those sections which are omitted by Luke, is a somewhat curious one, for which I have seen no sufficient explanation offered. A possible explanation might be that in these sections no opportunity was offered to later copyists to assimilate the texts of Matthew and Luke, and thus introduce further changes from Mark. If the extent of such assimilation could be proved to be great enough, this explanation would perhaps be sufficient.

CHAPTER V

HAVE WE THE GOSPEL OF MARK IN ITS ORIGINAL FORM?

The number of instances in which Matthew and Luke agree in their changes of Mark has given rise to the theory that Matthew and Luke did not use our Mark but an earlier form. A certain number of such agreements might be passed over as merely accidental. A certain number more might be assigned to assimilation. But if the agreements of Matthew and Luke in their corrections of Mark are so numerous and so striking as to be quite beyond accounting for in these ways, the assumption would be justified that Matthew and Luke used, not our copy of Mark, but one in which the text ran as it now does in those passages where Matthew and Luke agree against Mark.

There are some indications that we do not have the Gospel of Mark in its original form. The conclusion is lacking. This however throws no light on an Ur-Marcus, since the conclusion was lacking in the Mark used by Matthew and Luke.[1]

There are many signs of apparent transposition in our Mark. The insertion of one miracle into the midst of another, as in the case of Jairus' daughter and the woman with the issue of blood (v, 21–43), might be held to be such a transposition. The incident of the Beelzebul dispute (iii, 20–30) is inserted between the coming of the family of

---

[1] See Goodspeed on "The Original Conclusion of Mark's Gospel," in *American Journal of Theology*, Vol. IX (1905), pp. 484–90; also, Rördam, *Hibbert Journal*, Vol. III, pp. 769–90, "What Was the Lost End of the Gospel of Mark?"

HAVE WE MARK IN ITS ORIGINAL FORM? 73

Jesus (iii, 21) to take him home with them, and Jesus' statement (iii, 31–35), which is the sequel of their coming, about his true brotherhood. The speech about the cursing of the fig tree (xi, 20–26) intervenes between the cleansing of the temple (xi, 15–19) and the demand of the scribes (xi, 27–33) as to the authority by which Jesus has done so unwonted a thing. After this question about authority, and before Jesus' reply to it, or before the description of the discomfiture of the scribes at the reply, seriously interrupting the connection, comes the parable of the Wicked Husbandmen.[1]

After the story of the transfiguration the prediction of Jesus' sufferings comes in between the Scribes' question about Elijah and Jesus' answer to that question (Mk ix, 11–13). Loisy thinks Mk xiv, 28, out of place. It certainly disturbs the connection. Jülicher considers Mk xiv, 25, to be later and less original than its parallel in Mt xxvi, 29. The saying in xiv, 9, about the name of the woman being known wherever the story of Jesus is told has been suggested as the remark of some preacher or commentator à propos of the occurrence, and not a saying of Jesus. Wellhausen has even suggested that the whole story in xiv, 3–9, may be a later addition. The saying, "Ye shall say to this mountain" (xi, 23) should probably be placed in Galilee, presumably at Capernaum, where with a wave of his hand Jesus could point to both mountain and sea—not in Jerusalem where Mark gives it. Schmiedel considers Mk xiv, 58, secondary. It has been argued, or almost assumed, that the second feeding of the multitude could not have been written by the same hand that described the first, nor the events narrated in the first thirty-four verses of chap. iv have been

[1] See Wellhausen, *Einleitung*, p. 56; Loisy, *Gospel and Church*, p. 29.

written in their present order. If one is at liberty to subtract what he will from the Gospel of Mark, and to rearrange its parts somewhat, he can undoubtedly make a much more readable and better arranged Gospel of it than it now is.

DISCUSSION OF THE ANALYSIS OF MARK BY WENDLING AND VON SODEN

Two attempts have recently been made to resolve our Gospel of Mark into its constituent elements, which are sufficiently successful to be noticed here. The first is that of von Soden, in his *Die wichtigsten Fragen im Leben Jesu*, and the second Wendling's *Ur-Marcus*.[1]

Von Soden[2] begins by distinguishing two strands of narrative, easily separable from each other by matter and style. The great differences between these two strands betray two different authors. As the clearest instance of the earlier strand, he takes Mk ii, 1—iii, 6, which he contrasts with iv, 35—v, 43. In the first, all the interest is centered in the words of Jesus; in the second, in the events themselves. "Let one compare the story of the Gadarene demoniac with its twenty verses and the debate about fasting with its five verses, and estimate the weight of the religious value of the thots expressed in the two sections."

Von Soden next separates Mk vii, 32-37, and viii, 22-26 (the healing of the deaf man and the blind man), as quite distinct in character from such stories as those in ii, 1–12, and iii, 1–6. "In the former, the miracle of healing is itself the subject of the representation; in the latter, the miracle is merely a part of the story, whose real subject is Jesus' forgiveness of sins and his violation of the Sabbath laws."

[1] This study of von Soden's and Wendling's treatment of Mark appeared in the *Harvard Theological Review* for April, 1913.
[2] P. 23.

HAVE WE MARK IN ITS ORIGINAL FORM? 75

In this way von Soden picks out his *Kernstücke*. To these *Kernstücke* certainly belong the group of narratives in i, 21–39; ii, 1—iii, 6; xii, 13–44; iii, 20–35; vi, 1–6; iv, 1–8; iv, 26–32; and x, 13–31; perhaps also vii, 24–30; vi, 14–16; i, 4–11. To these narratives which go back to Peter may also belong the brief notices concerning the stages of growth of the apostolic circle, in i, 16–20; iii, 13–19; vi, 7–13; viii, 27—ix, 1; and ix, 33–40.[1] To these passages von Soden adds xiii, 1–6, 28–37. He says that at the basis of the story of the days in Jerusalem, xi, 1—xii, 12, and the passion narrative in chaps. xiv and xv, lie narratives of a similar style; but these latter he does not include in his *Kernstücke*.

Von Soden then prints the passages which he thus refers to Peter (or the Petrine tradition), "undisturbed by all that our Gospel of Mark has interwoven with them."[2] The result presents the Petrine nucleus of the Gospel as follows: John the Baptist and the Baptism of Jesus; a Sabbath in Capernaum; the offense of the Jews at Jesus' forgiving of sins, his association with sinners, his breaking of the Sabbath, and the fact that his disciples do not fast; how the Jews attempt to take him; how Jesus meets the general misunderstanding; parables about the kingdom of God; the question as to who shall enter that kingdom; the development of the apostolic circle; glimpses into the future.

This makes (with the readjustment in the order of some of the sections) a remarkably straightforward and connected narrative. Von Soden's remarks concerning it are well worth quoting:

These narratives are without any embellishment or secondary interest. They are plastic and concrete in every feature. The

[1] P. 24.
[2] For reasons which he does not explain, he rearranges the sections.

76   SOURCES OF THE SYNOPTIC GOSPELS

local coloring is strikingly fresh and yet in no way artificial. No edificatory remarks are inserted, no reflections, only deeds and striking sayings. No story requires its secret meaning to be explained by symbol or allegory. In no one of them does one feel any occasion to inquire for the meaning, which lies clear upon the surface. Situations and words are too original to have been invented. Everything breathes the odor of Palestine. There is no reminiscence of Old Testament stories. Miracles appear only here and there, and incidentally. . . . . The christological or soteriological question never constitutes the motive of a story. Not once is there any expression from the language of the schools, especially from that of Paul. Words and sentences are reminiscent of the Aramaic. The figure of Jesus itself bears in every reference a human outline. He is stirred and astonished, he is angry and trembles, he needs recuperation and feels himself forsaken of God, he will not have the thotless, conventional designation "good" addressed to him, and confesses that he does not know when all which he sees to be approaching shall be fulfilled. His mother and his sisters fear that he may be out of his mind. This and much else is told with the greatest naïveté. So Jesus lived; so he expressed himself; thus they received him; thus the apostolic circle was formed and developed—this is what the writer intends to tell.[1]

These sections of Mark certainly have a very primary character; so far as their contents is concerned, they may well go back to the Petrine tradition.

With these sections von Soden contrasts the remaining parts of the Gospel, in which he finds not only much interruption of the primary narrative, but much interpretation, much allegorizing, much absence of actual situations, much reminiscence of Old Testament stories, much influence from Paul, and many reflections of the experiences of individual Christians and the Christian church.[2] No one can work thru this analysis of von

[1] Von Soden, *Die wichtigsten Fragen*, pp. 38, 39.
[2] *Ibid.*, pp. 39, 40.

Soden's without feeling that it is easy to distinguish between primary and secondary elements in the Gospel of Mark, and that von Soden has at least pointed out many of the junctures between these two.

The attempt of Wendling in his *Ur-Marcus*[1] is still more thorogoing. The basis of his discussion is Mark's 4th chapter, where he considers the two strands most easily separated. To the original belong iv, 1–9, and vss. 26–33. Vss. 10–25 are later; they have been inserted mechanically, yet so as to respect the older text; they have no organic connection with the rest of the chapter, and even contradict its situation. Jesus is teaching from a boat (and other boats are with his); then suddenly, in vss. 10–25, he is alone with his disciples who ask him the meaning of the parable of the Sower. He gives his explanation, and again without any indication of change of situation he is in the boat surrounded by the other boats, with the people still on the shore, and the storm comes up and is stilled.

This little insertion (iv, 10–25) also contains theories of the writer, quite contradictory to those of the writer of other parts of the Gospel. In other places, Jesus speaks to all the people in parables "as they were able to hear him"; he stretches out his hand over the multitude of his disciples and says, "These are my mother and my sisters"; he is the teacher of the crowd, who understand him better than his own family; there is nothing in his parables that needs explaining. But in this insertion (iv, 10–25) the theory of the writer is that the parables are "mysteries," enigmas, which not only need to be explained (by the allegorical method), but which are spoken for the express purpose of preventing the people

[1] And still more in his *Entstehung*, too elaborate to be here considered.

from understanding. Without the key which Jesus gives, even the disciples do not understand them. The section is also marked by Pauline influences.[1]

Two clews are thus given, aside from interruptions in the narrative, by which the work of a second writer may be detected. He has the *Geheimnis-Theorie* of the parables, and he has in thot and vocabulary reminiscences of the Pauline school. Applying these tests to another section which seems to interrupt the narrative where it stands, Wendling adds a second insertion—iii, 22–30. This is the section about the dispute with the Pharisees, which comes in inaptly between the introduction (iii, 20, 21) and the continuation (iii, 31) of the story of Jesus' family who have come to take him home. It seems to have been inserted in this place because the Pharisees also said "he hath a devil." By repeating in vs. 30 the ἔλεγον ὅτι which he found in vs. 21, the redactor preserves for the continuation of the original story precisely the same connection it would have had without his interpolation; and by the use of the same words in vs. 22 he connects the interpolation with the opening narrative. His hand is seen in the superfluous repetition of words, especially of the subject, as in iii, 24, 25.[2]

To these two insertions should be added a third, iii, 6–19. The motives for it seem to be copied from narratives in other chapters. It consists (in part) of generalization and interpretation, both marks of the redactor's work. It also contains his *Geheimnis-Theorie*.

To these should be added i, 34b ("he suffered not the demons to speak, because they knew him"), because of

---

[1] Cf. especially the words μυστήριον, μετὰ χαρᾶς λαμβάνειν, διωγμὸς, ἐπιθυμίαι, καρποφορεῖν, and see Wendling, p. 35, n. 11.

[2] Cf. ii, 20, also the work of the redactor.

the presence in it of this same theory. Nor does i, 45, fit where it is; the connection without it is good; it also contains the favorite theory of the redactor that the more Jesus told people not to proclaim him, the more they did so, and the more he tried to seclude himself the more they found him.

To these again, on somewhat other grounds and not so securely, should be added the little groups of loosely strung logia which are found in vi, 7–11; viii, 34—ix, 1; ix, 40–50; x, 42–45; xi, 23–25; xii, 38–40; xiii, 9–13. The ground for asserting these to be additions is that these logia are not closely connected in the passages in which they occur, and that they share this characteristic with the similar group of disconnected sayings in the first and best attested interpolation, iv, 21–25.

In i, 1–3, 14*b*, 15, the word εὐαγγέλιον arouses a natural suspicion. The same word also occurs in four other places (viii, 35; x, 29; xiii, 10; xiv, 9), all of which are in passages which are suspicious upon other grounds; consequently with the three instances in chap. i, they are ascribed to the redactor.

With the exception of the interpolation in iv, 10–25, the section i, 16—iv, 33, appears to be a unit, and belongs to the oldest stratum. But with iv, 35, says Wendling, begins a new section, easily distinguished from that just mentioned. It copies the motives and the characteristics of other sections.[1] The writer is to be distinguished, however, not merely from the writer of the earliest stratum, but from the author of the insertions already identified. None of the criteria of the latter's manner appear in the section beginning at iv, 35. It shows

[1] Cf. especially v, 2 with i, 23; v, 6, 7, with i, 24; v, 8–13, with i, 25; v. 13, with i, 26; v, 14–17, with i, 27, and see Wendling, p. 11.

no trace of Pauline conceptions, has none of Jesus' prohibitions to the demons, its *Heimlichkeit* is of a different sort, and goes back to Old Testament exemplars. And since the insertion in iv, 10–25, presupposes the story of the storm on the lake in iv, 35—v, 43, this latter is older than the former. The writer of this section (iv, 35—v, 43) therefore stood between the writer of the original strand, and the evangelist or redactor. The last writer (Wendling calls him Ev) worked over the combined work of his two predecessors.

To the author who is intermediate between the first writer and the Evangelist, Wendling assigns twenty-nine different sections, some of considerable length and some of only a verse or part of a verse. They are as follows: i, 4–14a; iv, 35—v, 42; v, 43b; vi, 14, 17–30, 35–44; ix, 2–8, 14–27; x, 46—xi, 10; xiv, 12–20, 26–35a, 36–37, 39–41a, 42, 47, 51–56, 60–62a, 63, 64, 66–72; xv, 16–20, 23, 24b, 25, 29–30, 33, 34b–36, 38, 40–43, 46—xvi, 7a, 8—about two hundred verses or parts of verses in all.

The contributions of the author of the Gospel are more extensive than those of his predecessor. They comprise i, 1–3, 14b–15, 34b, 39b, 45; ii, 15b–16a, 18a, 19b–20; iii, 6–19, 22–30; iv, 10–25, 30–32, 34; v, 43a; vi, 1–13, 15, 16, 30–31, 45—viii, 26, 30b–33a, 33c–35, 38—ix, 1, 9–13, 28–50; x, 2–12, 24, 26–30, 32b–34, 38–40, 45; xi, 11–14, 18–25, 27a; xii, 14b, 32–34a, 38–44; xiii, 3–27, 30–32, 37; xiv, 8, 9, 21, 35b, 38, 41b, 57–59, 62b; xv, 39, 44, 45; xvi, 7b, in all about two hundred and seventy verses or parts of verses.

This leaves to the original writer the following sections: i, 16–34a, 35–39a, 40–44; ii, 1–15a, 16b–17, 18b, 19a, 21—iii, 5, 20, 21, 31—iv, 9, 26–29, 33; vi, 32–34; viii, 27–30a, 33b, 36, 37; x, 1, 13–23, 25, 31–32a, 35–37, 41–44; xi,

15–17, 27b—xii, 14a, 14c–31, 34b–37; xiii, 1–2, 28–29, 33–36; xiv, 1–7, 10, 11, 22–25, 43–46, 48–50, 65; xv, 1–15, 21, 22, 24a, 26–27, 31–32, 34a, 37, in all about two hundred and twelve verses or parts of verses.[1]

Wendling calls the writers of these three strands M1, M2, and Ev. Printing the text of M1 and M2 without rearrangement, but with the omission of all matter assigned to Ev, he finds them to make a continuous story, well connected and without breaks. Whether M1 alone makes such a story, he is in doubt; and therefore as to whether M2 found M1 as a connected discourse, or himself first assembled the sections of it in connection with his own additions, the same doubt exists. The passion-story of M1 by itself seems to be a connected account; it may therefore be assumed that so much of M1 was found by M2 as a whole and in its present order. Further, since the work of Ev in the passion-story is so slight, it is to be assumed that the combination of M1 and M2 in this story was more carefully done than in many other parts, and also that for this part of the gospel history Ev possessed very few traditions which had not already been embodied in M1+M2. This would agree with the natural assumption that the earliest part of the gospel tradition to be carefully treasured would be that relating to Jesus' death, and that it was only later that the attempt was made to preserve with equal care the story of his whole public career.

When one remembers the fine-spun analyses of the historical books of the Old Testament, which, long ridiculed for their elaborateness, have finally been accepted

[1] In *Die Entstehung des Marcus-Evangeliums*, p. 204, Wendling arranges the verses from M1 in chaps. xiii and xiv as follows: xiii, 1–2, 33, 28–29, 34–36; xiv, 1–2, 10–11, 3–7, 22–25, 43–46, 48–50, 65. Some minor differences in analysis, affecting words or clauses, are registered *ibid.*, p. 237.

by most scholars, one hesitates on this account alone to pronounce an adverse judgment upon Wendling's theory. Yet his analysis certainly seems over-elaborate. It is a great advantage to be able to distinguish the more obvious work of the redactor from the earlier document upon which he worked. All students will feel this with reference to chap. iv, and the advantage in chap. iii is perhaps only less great. Still more welcome is the assignment of vi, 45—viii, 27, to the redactor. The great stumbling-block of this section is its feeding of the four thousand, so obviously copied from the feeding of the five thousand. That one and the same author should have written both these accounts has seemed strange to many readers. But this duplication is as easily disposed of upon von Soden's theory as upon Wendling's. Von Soden's analysis into two strata (without the assumption of two writers) is much simpler than Wendling's analysis into three, with three writers. Wendling's theory is more secure where it goes with von Soden's, and less convincing where it goes beyond it.

Some distinction has in any case to be made between the final writer of the Gospel and the earliest tradition upon which he worked; and Wendling has indicated the criteria which such a distinction must employ. Von Soden's division of the Marcan material into a Petrine and a later source amounts to the same thing. The two critics do not differ greatly about the passages they regard as secondary. Von Soden's Petrine narrative does not differ greatly from Wendling's M1+M2. But the line of demarkation between M1 and M2, and Wendling's reasons for drawing this, are not as self-evident as the line which Wendling and von Soden agree in drawing between the earlier document, or source, and the work of the Evangelist.

HAVE WE MARK IN ITS ORIGINAL FORM? 83

CONCLUSIONS OF VON SODEN AND WENDLING COMPARED

A tabulation of the results discloses the following agreements and disagreements between von Soden's Petrine narrative and Wendling's M1+M2.

Von Soden i, 4–11, 16–20, 21–39 ii, 1–28
Wendling i, 4–14a, 16–34a, 35–39a, 40–44 ii, 1–15a, 16b–17, 18b, 19b

Von Soden iii, 1–6, 13–19, 21–35 iv, 1–9, 21–32
Wendling 21–28 iii, 1–5, 20, 21, 31–35 iv, 1–9, 26–29, 33, 35–41

Von Soden vi, 6–16 viii, 27–38
Wendling v, 1–42, 43b vi, 14, 17–30, 33–44 viii, 27–30a, 33b, 36, 37

Von Soden ix, 1 32–40 x, 13–45
Wendling ix, 2–8, 14–27 x, 1, 13–23, 25, 31, 32a, 35–37, 41–52, xi, 1–10

Von Soden xii, 13–44 xiii, 1–6
Wendling 15–17, 27b–33 xii, 1–14a, 14c–31, 34b–37 xiii, 1–2, 28–29

Von Soden 28–37
Wendling 33–36 xiv, 1–7, 10–20, 22–35a, 36–37, 39–41a, 42–56, 60–62a

Von Soden
Wendling 63–72 xv, 1–38, 40–42, 46–47 xvi, 1–7a, 8

The comparison shows Wendling's analysis to be much more complex than von Soden's. This results from his separation of his groundwork into two strands. It also shows that Wendling assigns considerably more to M1 and M2 than von Soden to his Petrine source. This Wendling can afford to do, since he supposes two documents instead of one. The matter assigned by von Soden to the Petrine source is in part assigned by Wendling to M1 and in part to M2. E.g., i, 4–11, is assigned by von Soden to the Petrine source, and by Wendling to M2; but i, 16–39, is assigned to the Petrine source, and (with the exception of two parts of verses) to M1. The passage ii, 1–28, is assigned by von Soden to the Petrine source, by Wendling to M1 (again with exception of a few parts of verses). Of the one hundred and seventy-seven verses assigned by von Soden to his Petrine source, up to and including xiii, 37 (after which he so assigns nothing), Wendling assigns about one hundred and twenty-four to his M1, and only ten to M2. Tho he assigns some verses to M1 which von Soden does not give to the Petrine source, and omits some (assigning them to the redactor) which von Soden does so assign, up to xiii, 37, the M1 of Wendling agrees very closely with the Petrine source of von Soden. The material assigned to M1 and M2 after xiii, 37, is about equally divided between them. Wendling makes no claims for the Petrine origin of his M1 or M2, but after these are subtracted from the whole Gospel there is a smaller amount left for the work of his redactor than remains after the Petrine source is subtracted. Since Wendling distinguishes between two sources and the work of the redactor, and von Soden only between the Petrine tradition and other matter, this result also is what would be expected.

The relatively great agreement of the results of these two investigations seems to prove that it is possible to distinguish an earlier and a later tradition in the Gospel. Beyond this, the difference between von Soden and Wendling is that the former makes no assertions concerning the identity of the final editor with the writer who recorded the Petrine tradition, while the latter asserts that the redactor is quite another person than the writer of either M1 or M2. Is this latter position of Wendling's susceptible of proof or disproof?

Perhaps the simplest criterion, and the one to be most safely applied, is that of vocabulary. Sir John Hawkins compiled a list[1] of forty-one words which he regards as characteristic of Mark. Do these words occur indiscriminately in M1, M2, and Ev, or are they confined some of them to M1, and some to M2, and some to Ev? Or is there sufficient difference in the frequency with which these words occur in the three strata to justify the assumption of three different authors, and especially that Ev was distinct from the writers of the two documents? If not, the division between earlier and later material in Mark may still stand, but it may have been one and the same writer who put the whole Gospel together out of these earlier and later materials.

Characteristic of Mark[2] is the historic present. Hawkins finds one hundred and fifty-one examples of this use in Mark against seventy-eight in Matthew (twenty-one of these taken from Mark),[3] and four in Luke. Of these one hundred and fifty-one historic presents in Mark, forty-nine occur in passages assigned by Wendling to M1, sixty-nine in M2, and thirty-three in Ev.

Of the peculiarly Marcan words, some prove nothing in this connection. Εὐαγγέλιον is used only by Ev (seven times); but since Wendling uses the presence of this word as a criterion of Ev's work in six out of the seven passages where it occurs, this adds nothing to the proof. Ἄλαλος is used once by M1, twice by M2, and not by Ev. But since Ev adds no story of a dumb man, he has no occasion to use the word. (He does add a story of a stammering man, where he uses the word μογιλάλος.) Κλάσμα, used once by M2 and three times by Ev, signifies little; since

---

[1] Hawkins, *Horae Synopticae*, pp. 12–13.

[2] See Hawkins, pp. 144–48.

[3] The seventy-eight does not include parables, where the present is not historic.

the three uses in Ev occur in the same passage, and this passage is a copy of the passage in M2 (the feeding of the multitudes). Στάχυς occurs three times, all in M1, but this also signifies nothing, since no passage in which it could occur is assigned to M2 or Ev. Ἐκπορεύομαι is used twice each by M1 and M2, and seven times by Ev; but since five of these seven occurrences are in the same passage, they cannot establish any particular fondness for this word on the part of Ev as against the other two. Εἰσπορεύομαι looks a little more favorable for Wendling's hypothesis, since it is used once by M1, twice by M2, and five times, in separated passages, by Ev. Ἀκάθαρτος, found three times in M1, four in M2, and three in Ev; ἀπὸ μακρόθεν, three times in M2 and twice in Ev; διδαχή, used three times by M2 and twice by the redactor, and φέρω, five times used by M1, eight times by M2, and twice by Ev, do nothing toward establishing a distinct vocabulary for any one of the three. Only two words, διαστέλλομαι, used four times by the redactor in four different chapters, and not by M1 or M2; and ἐκθαμβοῦμαι, used only by M2, four times in three different chapters, point in the direction of distinct vocabularies. But the absence of the third of these words can certainly, and of the second probably, be accounted for by the subject-matter.

There is here practically no evidence of distinct vocabularies. Even if there were, it would be fully offset by the use of words having no necessary connection with any particular subject-matter, and therefore equally likely to occur in any part of the Gospel. Five such words are the adverbs εὐθύς, πάλιν, πολλά, οὐκέτι, and οὔπω. Of these, the first (Mark's most characteristic word) is used seventeen times by M1, fifteen by M2, and ten by Ev.

Considering the relative amounts of narrative matter ascribed to the three, this usage seems to indicate an equal fondness for this word among them. The second (πάλιν) is used ten times by M1, eight times by M2, and nine times by Ev; the third (πολλά) is used adverbially three times by M1, six times by M2, and three times by Ev; the fourth (οὐκέτι), twice by M1, twice by M2, three times by Ev; the fifth (οὔπω), once by M1 and four times by Ev.

Characteristic of Mark also is his use of the imperfects ἔλεγεν and ἔλεγον. They are found fourteen times in M1, fifteen times in M2, and twenty-one times in the passages ascribed to Ev.

Of the forty-one verses listed on p. 246 as standing in both Mark and Q, thirty-four are in passages assigned by Wendling to Ev. This would seem to tell in Wendling's favor, since the last writer who had a hand in the making of the Gospel of Mark would naturally be the one most likely to make use of Q. Three verses, however, occur in passages assigned to M1, and four in M2. This would indicate that all three writers, besides having the same favorite words, were acquainted with and made some use of Q. The item of the relation of the various writers to Q, however, has little or no significance; since it is the sections having the greatest amount of logian matter and the least narrative, that are assigned to Ev.

The cumulative effect of these considerations is very much to the discredit of Wendling's assumption of three different writers for our Gospel of Mark. It cannot, to be sure, disprove that assumption; but it at least shows a lack of proof where proof would be most easily found and most convincing.

MATTHEW AND LUKE USED OUR MARK AS A SOURCE

Even if Wendling's analysis had been capable of substantiation on linguistic grounds, his division of our Gospel of Mark into three strands from three different authors would not help us toward an Ur-Marcus lying behind our Gospels of Matthew and Luke. For Matthew or Luke or both of them follow Mark in all the transpositions, dislocations, and other misarrangements of his Gospel. Whether these features stood in the original Mark or not, they evidently stood in the Mark used by Matthew and Luke.

Matthew and Luke also used a Mark which contained the story of Jesus in the same order given by our present Mark. Tho both of them deviate from this order for assignable reasons, one or the other of them is found following it all the time. If these deviations go back to an Ur-Marcus, there must have been one Ur-Marcus in the hands of Matthew and another in the hands of Luke.

THE HYPOTHESIS OF A PRIMITIVE MARK SUPERFLUOUS; SIMPLER EXPLANATIONS

Can the verbal agreements of Matthew and Luke as against Mark, or their deviations from him without apparent reason, be explained upon any simpler hypothesis than that of Ur-Marcus? It appears to the writer that they can.

A certain number (tho no one can say exactly what proportion of the whole) of the agreements of Matthew and Luke against Mark may be allowed to be accidental. Many of them, like the substitution of εἶπεν for λέγει, or of an occasional δέ for Mark's invariable and monotonous καί or the substitution of a common for an uncommon word (like κλίνη for κράβαττος) require no explanation.

Agreements of Matthew and Luke *in their omissions* from the Marcan narrative do not stand upon the same plane with the agreements in *substitutions*, and may all be accounted for on the ground of accident, or by the same desire on the part of both writers to be more concise, or to avoid anything derogatory to Jesus or the apostles; or by some other similar motive at work separately in the minds of the two later evangelists. It is only the agreements in corrections and substitutions that require accounting for. I believe these can be explained chiefly on two grounds:

1. It is not necessary to assume that Matthew and Luke both worked upon the same identical copy of our Mark. If they used two copies, these two would not be expected to agree absolutely with each other in the wording of every passage. This would account for some of the slight deviations in the wording of either Matthew or Luke where the other agrees with our present Mark. These two copies that Matthew and Luke used may neither of them have been the original (since in both of them the conclusion at least was gone); or at least not the original in its original form. One of them may have been a copy of the original, and the other a copy of this copy. Or they may both, as Sanday argues, have belonged to a type later, and not earlier, than our present Mark. This would account for the agreements, and for such deviations as have not already been accounted for, or cannot be accounted for, by the known literary peculiarities of Matthew and Luke. Since the text of Mark that has come down to us is more corrupt than that of either Matthew or Luke, various words in which Matthew and Luke now agree against Mark may have stood in the text which both of them used, and may later have dropped out, before the copy was made to which our present texts

go back. Or the two copies of Mark, assumed above, may both have been made from the original copy which Mark made with his own hand. Upon this supposition even, they would not always agree, and so deviations in Matthew and Luke from Mark, and occasional agreements in such deviations, would be explained. Or these agreements may be explained, as is obvious in many instances, by the working of similar motives in the minds of Matthew and Luke, even assuming them to have made their extracts from one and the same copy, or from two practically identical copies, of Mark.

Dr. E. A. Abbott, in his *Corrections of Mark* (London, 1901) gives an exhaustive list of the deviations from Mark in which Matthew and Luke agree. Many of these are such as to suggest that Matthew and Luke used not an Ur-Marcus, but a text of Mark later than the one that has come down to us. E.g., in twelve instances Matthew and Luke agree in supplying the subject or object which our Mark omits. In fifteen, they agree in correcting abrupt constructions, supplying a connecting word. In thirteen (exclusive of λέγει) they agree in correcting Mark's historic present. In twelve they agree in replacing Mark's relative clause or his subjunctive by a participle. In twenty-three they agree in substituting εἶπεν for λέγει. In thirty they agree in the use of δέ for καί. It is not impossible that Matthew and Luke, independently bent on improving Mark's style, have accidentally agreed in making these same improvements in the same places (especially since there are other improvements of the same sort in which they do not agree). But it is a much simpler and more adequate hypothesis, that they both used a text of Mark in which these corrections had already been made.

Yet even of this text they probably did not use the same identical copy. And as the copy used by one or both of them may have been two or three removes from the text from which it started, many changes may have crept into the copy used by one of them, not contained in the copy used by the other. This would account alike for the agreements in deviations from our present Mark, and for the fact that these corrections are not all of them found in both Matthew and Luke. This last item is further accounted for by the freedom of Matthew and Luke in making their own corrections in the copy that lay before them.[1] Allowance should also be made for the fact that we cannot be sure that we have yet recovered the true text of either Matthew or Luke.[2]

2. The agreements of Matthew and Luke against Mark can further be accounted for by the hypothesis of assimilation. Matthew made certain changes of his own in the wording of Mark; Luke apparently made many more. The various texts still extant show many efforts of copyists to bring the deviations of Matthew and Luke in small verbal items into an agreement. If this same process went on during the period covered by our earliest manuscripts, it is probable that it went on to a much greater extent at an earlier date, before our Gospels had acquired the sacredness which they later came to possess. A fine illustration of this process and its results is to be seen in the Matthean and Lucan versions of the Lord's Prayer, in which the probably original "Let thy Holy Spirit come upon us and purify us," of Luke, has been assimilated to "Thy kingdom come," and in many manuscripts also to "Thy will be done as in heaven so upon earth," of

---

[1] See Sanday's essay, in *Oxford Studies*, pp. 21–22.
[2] Turner, *Theological Studies*, January, 1909, p. 175, quoted by Sanday.

Matthew. The extent of this sort of assimilation can never be determined; but it seems quite sufficient to account for agreements of Matthew and Luke against Mark not easily accounted for on other grounds.

A more general reason against the assumption of an Ur-Marcus in the hands of Matthew and Luke is the comparatively small number and importance of their agreements against Mark, as compared with the very large number of the deviations in which they do not agree, and as compared also with the vastly greater number of instances in which both Matthew and Luke follow Mark faithfully. In other words, if Ur-Marcus differed from our Mark only in those words and phrases in which Matthew and Luke agree against our Mark, then Ur-Marcus was at the most not a different Mark from ours, but only a different copy or text of our Mark. The assumption of an Ur-Marcus was a natural one for the explanation of the phenomena in question; but it is a cumbersome hypothesis, and insecure; further study seems to discredit it. Matthew and Luke used our Mark, not another.

It has often been suggested that the Marcan material covered by the "great omission" of Luke (Mk vi, 45—viii, 26) was absent from the copy of Mark used by Luke, tho present in that used by Matthew. Reasons for Luke's omission of this long Marcan section have been given, and seem sufficient without the assumption of its absence from Luke's copy of Mark. But the theory of its absence has also important items directly against it. The section has the general Marcan characteristics. Mark has one hundred and forty-one historic presents; eighteen of them are in this section. He uses εὐθύς thirty-four times, five in this section; πάλιν twenty-six times, five in this section. He is partial to the imperfects ἔλεγεν and ἔλεγον, which he uses fifty times (against Matthew's twenty-three and Luke's nine), six times in this section. The same habit of duplicate expression which occurs in other parts of his Gospel appears here. ὅ ἐστιν in the sense of "i.e.," peculiar to Mark among the evangelists, appears here twice (four times elsewhere in the Gospel). Seven out of the nine sections begin with καί. The section seems to be too homogeneous with the rest of the book to be from a different hand.[1]

The foregoing considerations seem to render the hypothesis of Ur-Marcus superfluous. The phenomena for which it was designed to account are more easily and naturally explained by other suppositions.

SOME REMARKABLE VERBAL RESEMBLANCES

In the preceding pages sufficient consideration has been given not only to the fact, but to the manner, of the use of Mark by Matthew and Luke. Visual illustration, by the printing of a few passages in different kinds of type may serve to enforce some of the more general facts already brot out. The words (or parts of words) common to the three Synoptics, in the following passages, will be printed in heavy-faced typo.

| Mt ix, 5–6: τί γάρ ἐστιν εὐκοπώτερον, εἰπεῖν· ἀφίενταί σου αἱ ἁμαρτίαι, ἢ εἰπεῖν· ἔγειρε καὶ περιπάτει; ἵνα δὲ εἰδῆτε ὅτι ἐξουσίαν ἔχει ὁ υἱὸς τοῦ ἀνθρώ- | Mk ii, 9–10a: τί ἐστιν εὐκοπώτερον, εἰπεῖν τῷ παραλυτικῷ· ἀφίενταί σου αἱ ἁμαρτίαι, ἢ εἰπεῖν· ἔγειρε καὶ ἆρον τὸν κράββατόν σου καὶ ὕπαγε; ἵνα δὲ εἰδῆτε ὅτι ἐξουσίαν ἔχει ὁ υἱὸς τοῦ ἀνθρώ- | Lk v, 23–24: τί ἐστιν εὐκοπώτερον, εἰπεῖν· ἀφέωνταί σοι αἱ ἁμαρτίαι σου ἢ εἰπεῖν· ἔγειρε καὶ περιπάτει; ἵνα δὲ εἰδῆτε ὅτι ὁ υἱὸς τοῦ ἀνθρώπου ἐξουσίαν ἔχει |

---
[1] See Hawkins, *Oxford Studies*, pp. 64–66.

| που ἐπὶ τῆς γῆς ἀφιέν-
αι ἁμαρτίας, τότε λέγει
τῷ παραλυτικῷ
    ἐγερθεὶς ἆρον σου
τὴν κλίνην καὶ ὕπαγε
εἰς τὸν οἶκόν σου. | που ἐπὶ τῆς γῆς ἀφιέν-
αι ἁμαρτίας, λέγει
τῷ παραλυτικῷ· σοὶ λέγ-
ω, ἔγειρε ἆρον τὸν
κράββατόν σου καὶ ὕπαγε
εἰς τὸν οἶκόν σου. | ἐπὶ τῆς γῆς ἀφιέν-
αι ἁμαρτίας, εἶπεν
τῷ παραλελυμένῳ· σοὶ λέγ-
ω, ἔγειρε καὶ ἄρας τὸ
κλινίδιόν σου πορεύου
εἰς τὸν οἶκόν σου. |

Here the evangelists differ each from the other in the words ascribed to Jesus, but when they come to the parenthetic explanation injected into the midst of the sentence, ἵνα δὲ εἰδῆτε, etc., they agree exactly, not only in the wording, but in the awkward placing of the clause. The three accounts agree in the first five lines, except for the presence of γὰρ in Matthew, the insertion of τῷ παραλυτικῷ in Mark, and a slightly different form of the verb ἀφίημι in Luke. In the fourth line Luke also inserts σοι, after which come seven consecutive agreeing words (tho with slight rearrangement in order by Luke). Mark then has a clause of six words which Matthew and Luke omit. The latter agree in substituting περιπάτει for ὕπαγε, and two (different) words from the same root for Mark's κράββατον. Luke has preserved the σοὶ λέγω which Matthew has dropped.

| Mt xii, 3–4: οὐκ
ἀνέγνωτε τί ἐποίησεν
Δαυείδ, ὅτε ἐπείνασεν

οἱ μετ' αὐτοῦ;
πῶς εἰσῆλθεν εἰς τὸν
οἶκον τοῦ θεοῦ

καὶ τοὺς ἄρτους τῆς
προθέσεως
ἔφαγον, ὃ οὐκ ἐξὸν ἦν
αὐτῷ φαγεῖν οὐδὲ τοῖς
μετ' αὐτοῦ, εἰ μὴ
τοῖς ἱερεῦσιν μόνοις; | Mk ii, 25–26: οὐδέποτε
ἀνέγνωτε τί ἐποίησεν
Δαυείδ ὅτε χρείαν ἔσ-
χεν καὶ ἐπείνασεν αὐτὸς καὶ
οἱ μετ' αὐτοῦ;
πῶς εἰσῆλθεν εἰς τὸν
οἶκον τοῦ θεοῦ ἐπὶ
Ἀβιάθαρ ἀρχιερέως
καὶ τοὺς ἄρτους τῆς
προθέσεως
ἔφαγεν, οὓς οὐκ ἔξεσ-
τιν φαγεῖν εἰ μὴ
τοὺς ἱερεῖς, καὶ ἔδ-
ωκεν καὶ τοῖς σὺν
αὐτῷ οὖσιν; | Lk vi, 3–4: οὐδὲ τοῦτο
ἀνέγνωτε ὃ ἐποίησεν
Δαυείδ ὁπότε ἐπείνασεν
αὐτὸς καὶ
οἱ μετ' αὐτοῦ ὄντες;
ὡς εἰσῆλθεν εἰς τὸν
οἶκον τοῦ θεοῦ

καὶ τοὺς ἄρτους τῆς
προθέσεως ἔλαβεν καὶ
ἔφαγεν, καὶ ἔδωκεν καὶ
τοῖς μετ' αὐτοῦ, οὓς οὐκ
ἔξεστιν φαγεῖν εἰ μὴ
μόνους τοὺς ἱερεῖς; |

Few brief passages in the triple tradition will better repay study than this. Note that the three introduce their question with three different particles. Matthew and Luke omit the apparently superfluous words of Mark, χρείαν ἔσχεν, but Luke retains the αὐτός of Mark which Matthew has dropped. Luke adds ὄντες, perhaps in deference to Mark's οὖσιν, used in a similar phrase but different connection. He substitutes ὡς for the πῶς of Mark and Matthew. Mark and Luke both have the statement that David "gave" the bread to those that were with him, Luke adding that he "took" it. All three have in conclusion the phrase "to those with him," but each has inserted it in a different place. Matthew follows Mark more closely than does Luke, the latter transposing one or two clauses. Both Matthew and Luke have omitted the reference to Abiathar, either because they (or Luke at least) had no interest in it, or for its historical difficulty. In spite of these changes there is a most remarkable verbal agreement thruout. Except for Mark's superfluous "had need," and his reference to Abiathar, nothing can be found in either account that is not duplicated, practically word for word and almost letter for letter, in one or both of the others.

| Mt iv, 18–22: Περιπατῶν δὲ **παρὰ τὴν θάλασσαν τῆς Γαλιλαίας εἶδεν** δύο ἀδελφούς, **Σίμωνα** τὸν λεγόμενον Πέτρον **καὶ Ἀνδρέαν τὸν ἀδελφὸν** αὐτοῦ **βάλλοντας** ἀμφίβληστρον εἰς τὴν θάλασσαν· **ἦσαν γὰρ ἁλεεῖς. Καὶ λέγ**ει αὐτοῖς· **δεῦτε ὀπίσω μου, καὶ** ποιήσω ὑμᾶς ἁλεεῖς ἀνθρώπων. οἱ δὲ εὐθέως **ἀφέντες τὰ δίκτυα ἠκολούθησαν αὐτῷ. Καὶ προβὰς** ἐκεῖθεν **εἶδεν** ἄλλους δύο ἀδελφούς, **Ἰάκωβον τὸν τοῦ Ζεβεδαίου καὶ Ἰωάν**- | Mk i, 16–20: Καὶ **παράγων παρὰ τὴν θάλασσαν τῆς Γαλιλαίας εἶδεν Σίμωνα καὶ Ἀνδρέαν τὸν ἀδελφὸν** Σίμωνος ἀμφιβάλλοντας ἐν τῇ θαλάσσῃ· **ἦσαν γὰρ ἁλεεῖς.** καὶ εἶπεν αὐτοῖς· **δεῦτε ὀπίσω μου, καὶ ποιή**σω ὑμᾶς γενέσθαι ἁλεεῖς ἀνθρώπων. καὶ εὐθὺς **ἀφέντες τὰ δίκτυα ἠκολούθησαν αὐτῷ. Καὶ προβὰς** ὀλίγον **εἶδεν Ἰάκωβον τὸν τοῦ Ζεβεδαίου καὶ Ἰωάν**- |

νην τὸν ἀδελφὸν αὐτοῦ, ἐν τῷ πλοίῳ μετὰ Ζεβεδαίου τοῦ πατρὸς αὐτῶν καταρτίζοντας τὰ δίκτυα αὐτῶν · καὶ ἐκάλεσεν αὐτούς. οἱ δὲ (εὐθέως) ἀφέντες τὸ πλοῖον καὶ (τὸν πατέρα αὐτῶν) ἠκολούθησαν αὐτῷ.	νην τὸν ἀδελφὸν αὐτοῦ, καὶ αὐτοὺς ἐν τῷ πλοίῳ καταρτίζοντας τὰ δίκτυα. καὶ (εὐθὺς) ἐκάλεσεν αὐτούς · καὶ ἀφέντες (τὸν πατέρα αὐτῶν) Ζεβεδαῖον ἐν τῷ πλοίῳ μετὰ τῶν μισθωτῶν ἀπῆλθον ὀπίσω αὐτοῦ.

This passage contains the striking addition of the parenthetical explanation ἦσαν γὰρ ἁλεεῖς. That this should occur in a narrative portion, and not in a saying of Jesus, is the more significant. For the rest, the saying ascribed to Jesus runs word for word (tho its brevity in this case robs this fact of any very remarkable significance); in the narrative portion Matthew mentions that Simon was called Peter (a remark which Mark saves till he comes to the formal naming of the twelve), and in the conclusion he says "they left the boat and their father," while Mark says "they left their father in the boat," adding, "with the hired men." Mark says Jesus *called* the two "immediately." Matthew says they *left* "immediately"

CHAPTER VI

USE OF A COMMON DOCUMENT BY MATTHEW AND LUKE

The document used by Matthew and Luke as the source of their common non-Marcan material was for some time generally identified with the "Logia" which Papias says Matthew, the disciple of the Lord, wrote in Hebrew, undoubtedly meaning Aramaic. Until some sufficient justification for this identification has been given, it seems better to refer to the common non-Marcan source of Matthew and Luke under the more colorless symbol Q.

The common non-Marcan tradition of Matthew and Luke consists almost exclusively of logian material. It contains a few parables, brief, and dealing usually with the "kingdom of heaven," and one or two sections (such as that concerning the centurion from Capernaum, and the Temptation) which may quite properly be regarded as narrative, but which also contain large logian content and may have been introduced for the sake of the sayings.

The proof that the source of the common non-Marcan material of Matthew and Luke was a document and not an oral tradition lies in the extent and character of the agreements between the two Gospels; it cannot be summarized in a paragraph, but comes out only in a detailed examination of the double tradition such as is undertaken in the following pages.

Before the theory of a common documentary source for the non-Marcan material in Matthew and Luke can be accepted, it must defend itself against two apparently simpler hypotheses, viz., that Matthew copied from Luke or Luke from Matthew.

Did Matthew copy from Luke? His genealogical tree does not agree with Luke's.[1] He betrays in his story of the birth at Bethlehem no knowledge of the fact that Joseph's home was originally at Nazareth. This latter place he first mentions in ii, 23, as the place to which Joseph went upon his return from Egypt. Matthew has a greater interest in John the Baptist than has Luke, as is indicated by his fuller treatment of the fact and circumstances of his death, contrasted with Luke's leaving him in prison undisposed of. Yet Matthew does not employ the material concerning the preaching of John, which Luke has embodied in his iii, 10–14. Matthew makes a specialty of the sayings of Jesus, yet omits many that Luke contains. In short, the reason for denying that Matthew copied from Luke is the impossibility, upon that hypothesis, of explaining the omissions of Lucan material from Matthew's Gospel, and the very great divergences between the two Gospels where such divergences would not be expected with either one using the other as an exemplar.

The same argument which refutes Matthew's use of Luke refutes Luke's use of Matthew.

But it may be added, that upon either of these hypotheses it becomes impossible to explain the changes which appear to have been made by both Matthew and Luke in the material common to them, both in its wording and its order. If Matthew copied from Luke, he would

---

[1] Both genealogies may easily be suspected of being later additions. If Luke's genealogy is a gloss there is no apparent reason why it should not have been inserted in the appropriate place; cf. Sanders, *Journal of Biblical Literature*, XXX, 11.

naturally have followed his order, which he does not do. Or, deviating from that order for obvious reasons, he would naturally return to it when those reasons no longer prevailed, which he does not do. Or if Luke copied from Matthew, he could hardly have inserted a genealogical tree which is at variance with Matthew's, in the unnatural place where it now is, as against the natural place in which he found it in Matthew. Nor could he, when he had the Sermon on the Mount before him in the form in which Matthew gives it, break it up into little pieces and scatter it up and down thruout his Gospel. Moreover, in the sayings common to Matthew and Luke it is now one and now the other who preserves what we must consider the most original reading; as when Matthew says, "Cleanse first the inside of the cup," and Luke in place of this says, "Give alms of that which is within." But again it is not Matthew but Luke who gives the more original form of a saying; as when Luke says "Blessed are ye poor," and Matthew says, "Blessed are the poor in spirit."

The phenomena of peculiar words, ninety-five characteristic of Matthew and one hundred and fifty-one characteristic of Luke, is also impossible of explanation upon the theory that either writer copied from the other. If either one were copying from the other, they would certainly agree against Mark in some really important matter, and not merely in an occasional word or phrase. If Luke were copying from Matthew, he would certainly have incorporated some one of those numerous additions which Matthew makes to the narratives of Mark.[1]

In addition to any of the more general considerations which have suggested the possible use of Matthew by

[1] E.g., the verses on Peter and the keys, or on Peter walking on the water, or the conversation of Jesus with John the Baptist at the time of Jesus' baptism.

Luke, a recent writer has evolved an ingenious and somewhat elaborate proof for this use, which it may be well to consider in some detail.

A RECENT ATTEMPT TO PROVE MATTHEW A SOURCE FOR LUKE

Mr. Robinson Smith[1] attempts to dispose both of Ur-Marcus and Q by maintaining that Luke copied from Matthew. His argument rests upon the deviations which Matthew and Luke make, respectively, in their common abbreviations of certain of Mark's narratives. "Where a choice from two or more Marcan expressions has been made, the first choice falls to Matthew and the second to Luke."

As examples of these first choices by Matthew and second choices by Luke, Mr. Smith instances (with the parallel passages in Matthew and Luke) Mk i, 32; iii, 7, 8; x, 29, 33, 34; xii, 3; xiv, 1, 12, 65; xv, 42. The argument seems to be that Luke having both Mark and Matthew before him, and seeing that in each of these instances Matthew has chosen a certain part of Mark's phrase and rejected the rest, himself avoids using that part of the phrase which Matthew has chosen, restricting himself to the part which Matthew has left unused. We will take up first the particular instances, and see whether other, perhaps simpler, reasons suggest themselves for these deviations; after that we will consider the general argument.

Mk i, 32 (Mt viii, 16; Lk iv, 40): Mark's phrase runs Ὀψίας δὲ γενομένης, ὅτε ἔδυ ὁ ἥλιος. Of this phrase, Matthew takes the first three words as they stand. Luke appropriates the remainder, changing into Δύνοντος

[1] In the *Hibbert Journal*, No. 39, April, 1912, pp. 615–25.

USE OF DOCUMENT BY MATTHEW AND LUKE 101

δὲ τοῦ ἡλίου. Mark's phrase is here redundant, and Matthew and Luke (as usual) both reduce the redundancy. But Matthew has omitted the point of Mark's phrase, since in Matthew's account the events described did not happen on the Sabbath. Luke has retained the essential part of the phrase.[1]

Mk iii, 7, 8 (Mt iv, 25; Lk vi, 17): "Mark gives in order and by name six districts from which the multitudes came. Matthew mentions all save the last, Tyre and Sidon. Luke omits the first, fourth, and fifth, but does mention the last, Tyre and Sidon." The changes in these lists seem to be more various than Mr. Smith suggests. Matthew adds Decapolis and omits Idumaea.[2] The thing hard to account for in Luke's list is his omission of Galilee, not his inclusion of Tyre and Sidon. These latter regions would interest him especially, with his universalistic tendency; we should hardly have been surprised to find him adding them if he had not found them in Mark. A simple explanation of the changes made by both Matthew and Luke may perhaps be seen in Matthew's Judaistic tendency, which led him to omit Tyre and Sidon, and in Luke's universalistic tendency which made him include them. To make Mr. Smith's argument hold in this case, Luke should certainly have come much closer than he does, to preserving the parts which Matthew rejects, and rejecting the parts which he retains. It appears that Luke has no great knowledge of nor interest in Palestinian geography, but Tyre and Sidon suited his purpose.

Mk x, 29 (Mt xix, 29; Lk xviii, 29): Mark here has ἕνεκεν ἐμοῦ καὶ ἕνεκεν τοῦ εὐαγγελίου. Matthew has ἕνεκα

[1] This passage has been already treated in a different connection on p. 39.
[2] Omitted in some manuscripts of Mark.

τοῦ ἐμοῦ ὀνόματος, and Luke εἵνεκεν τῆς βασιλείας τοῦ θεοῦ. But Matthew's "my name's sake" is not the same as Mark's "my sake," and seems to bespeak Matthew's later date of writing. Luke's "for the sake of the kingdom of God" has a more primitive sound than the latter part of Mark's phrase. It probably represents the original words of Jesus which Matthew has everywhere changed into the "kingdom of heaven." Since all the passages in Mark where the word εὐαγγέλιον occurs are on independent grounds suspected of being later additions, it seems probable that the reading of Mark which Matthew and Luke had before them here was merely ἕνεκεν ἐμοῦ, that both Matthew and Luke changed this phrase as they would, and that the ἕνεκεν τοῦ εὐαγγελίου of Mark is later than either Matthew or Luke. At all events, it does not seem to be true in this instance that Matthew takes the first part of Mark's phrase and Luke the last.

Mk xii, 3 (Mt xxi, 35; Lk xx, 10): Matthew's account here is quite different from Mark's (which is followed much more closely by Luke). According to Mark, only one servant was sent, whom the vineyard-keepers "caught and beat and sent away empty." According to Matthew several servants were sent; the vineyard-keepers caught them, beat one, killed one, and stoned another. This form of the story indicates the times of persecution in which it was worked over by Matthew—when more than one man had suffered more than one kind of indignity. Luke sticks close to the story of Mark, and merely omits the λαβόντες which Matthew retains. Perhaps Luke had reflected that the servant had to be caught if he was to be beaten, and so regarded the item as superfluous. It does happen to come before the items that Luke retains, but there is no reason to suppose Luke would have had any greater antipathy to omitting it if it had stood last or if Matthew had also omitted it. It is not only hard to detect any influence of Matthew upon Luke here, but much harder to see, if Luke were copying Matthew, why he should not have preferred his several servants to Mark's one. Later in the same story, Luke again omits Mark's λαβόντες where Matthew retains it (Mk xii, 8), tho here both Matthew and Luke change the order of the incidents in the verse, probably to make them conform more exactly to the experience of Jesus. The omission of the participle by Luke and its inclusion by Matthew is most simply explained by Luke's greater interest in stylistic improvement. The instance seems to be barren for Mr. Smith's purpose.

Mk xiv, 1 (Mt xxvi, 2; Lk xxii, 1): Matthew's account is here very different from Mark's. He introduces it with the words, "And it came to pass when he had ended these sayings." This is a formula which Matthew uses five times,[1] and which is found in Matthew alone. Since the construction ἐγένετο followed by a finite verb is found in these five passages alone in Matthew, the formula appears to have stood (once, at least, if not in all five instances) in Q.[2] It also seems to be used by Matthew to mark his transition from one of his sources to the other.[3] The remark which Mark here makes about the approach of the passover, Matthew puts into the mouth of Jesus as a part of the speech which Mark does not have. Luke follows Mark in making the statement a part of his narrative and in omitting the speech which Matthew gives.

[1] vii, 28; xi, 1; xiii, 53; xix, 1; xxvi, 1.
[2] Hawkins, *Horae Synopticae*, p. 165.
[3] Wernle, p. 110.

These facts would seem to indicate that Matthew is here following Q, while Luke follows Mark. Luke's looser statement (omitting the μετὰ δύο ἡμέρας, and substituting his own favorite ἤγγιζεν,[1] and adding his ἡ λεγομένη πάσχα) would seem to go back to his desire not to trouble his Greek reader with too exact details, and yet to supply him with a little information about the Jewish feast. Here again, as in the last instance, it seems especially strange to suggest Matthew as a source of Luke where he shows such an absence of any influence from him.

Mk xiv, 12 (Mt xxvi, 17; Lk xxii, 7): Here, says Mr. Smith, Matthew gives the first and second parts of Mark's phrase, Luke the second and third parts. The fact seems to be that Matthew here, with his usual habit of condensing Mark's narrative, omits (what his Jewish readers would know without his stating it) the statement that on the first day of the feast of unleavened bread they "killed the passover." Luke changes this from a particular to a general statement, so (as above) conveying to his Greek reader some information about the custom of the occasion (ἔδει θύεσθαι τὸ πάσχα). Luke here shows the influence of Mark and not of Matthew; since he follows Mark (Mk xiv, 13; Lk xxii, 10) in including eleven words which he copies very closely and which Matthew omits. He also agrees with Mark in the ascription of supernatural knowledge to Jesus upon this occasion, whereas Matthew's narrative does not carry this implication.

Mk xiv, 65 (Mt xxvi, 67, 68; Lk xxii, 63, 64): Mr. Smith finds the influence of Matthew upon Luke in this passage, in the fact that while Mark says that they "spat

---

[1] Luke uses it twenty-four times against Matthew's seven and Mark's four.

upon Jesus, blindfolded him and smote him, Matthew records the first and third of these actions, Luke the second and third."[1] Why Luke omits the spitting, may not be easy (or necessary) to say. But that Luke here shows the reverse of any influence from Matthew is indicated in the fact that whereas Matthew follows Mark in relating, first the examination of Jesus, then the mockery, and third the denials of Peter, Luke rearranges the Marcan narrative to make it run, first the denials, second the mockery, and third the examination. He has received his suggestion for this rearrangement from the fact that Mark, just before he begins the story of the mockery, has mentioned that Peter was outside the hall, warming himself by the fire.[2] It has seemed (quite naturally) to Luke that this is the place where the story of the denials should be related, tho Mark inserts the story of the mockery before he goes on[3] with the denials. In a passage where Luke has so thoroughly rearranged Mark it seems unnecessary to account for his omission of one word, especially by such a remote theory as that of Mr. Smith; and in a passage, too, where his rearrangement of Marcan material contradicts Matthew's slavish following of it.

Mk xv, 42 (Mt xxvii, 57; Lk xxiii, 54): "Where Mark says, 'When the even was come because it was the preparation, that is the day before the Sabbath,' Matthew says, 'When even was come,' and Luke 'the rest.'"[4] But Luke does not quite say "the rest." He says,[5] "It was the day of preparation, and the Sabbath was dawning." And this he says, not in the same connection, nor with the same purpose, as Mark (and Matthew). Mark and Matthew use their statement about the evening having come as an introduction to their story about the request

[1] P. 617. [2] Mk xiv, 54. [3] In xiv, 66. [4] P. 617. [5] Lk xxii, 54.

106   SOURCES OF THE SYNOPTIC GOSPELS

of Joseph of Arimathea. Luke tells his story of Joseph without any such introduction, and mentions the time only after he has finished that story, apparently with reference to the story of the women which follows, rather than to that of Joseph which precedes. The argument of the last paragraph will apply here.

It will not be necessary to go with equal care thru the five other instances in which Mr. Smith detects in a similar way the influence of Matthew upon Luke.[1] He admits "two, or three, or at the most four, cases of Marcan expressions" of which (without explanation) it might appear that Luke uses the first part and Matthew the last. His willingness to push his theory to the extreme may be inferred from his general estimate of the character of Luke as a writer: "He blurs, obliterates, blunders, fabricates, falsifies, flattens out, mutilates, murders."[2]

The secondary interest of the writer would also seem to have influenced his work somewhat too strongly. That interest is indicated in the following statements: "If Acts was written in A.D. 62, ... and Luke was written before Acts, then Matthew, slipping in between Mark and Luke must throw Mark still further back. . . . . We thus would come very close to the resurrection, perhaps to within fifteen years, and the possibility of legendary and controversial elements having entered into the gospel story would accordingly be reduced to a minimum. . . . . With our understanding of Lucan derivations from Matthew, as well as from Mark, the

[1] See his note, p. 618.

[2] P. 621. This judgment upon Luke is in striking contrast to that expressed by Müller, *Zur Synopse*, p. 3: "Wellhausen calls Luke a 'historian.' This judgment rests on excellent grounds. We see this at once in the manner in which Luke has used the text-scaffolding of Mark. Logical, simple, and transparent considerations have moved him," etc. Müller's judgment is decidedly the better.

ghost of a chance of existence belonging to postulated common sources, such as an earlier or a later Mark and a Q is frightened away, and we are left with the Gospels Mark, Matthew, Luke, written in that order," etc.[1]

Passing from the details of Mr. Smith's statement to the general argument upon which they rest, the present writer can see no cogency in that argument. Even if the use of Matthew by Luke were not contradicted by so many characteristics of both those Gospels, the writer cannot see how the choice by Luke of the second part of a phrase of which Matthew has taken the first part should prove the use of Matthew by Luke. Why should not Luke feel free to take precisely that part of a Marcan phrase which Matthew has taken—if he wanted it? Why should his finding it in Matthew make him feel that he was not at liberty to use it? Why, indeed, if Luke was copying Matthew, should he not have *followed* him in his quotation of a certain part of a Marcan phrase, instead of putting himself every time to the trouble of going back to his Mark to pick out that part of the phrase which Matthew had left? It does not quite appear why the facts cited by Mr. Smith (so far as analysis of the passages from which they are cited leaves any of them standing) might not just as well be turned against his theory as for it.

[1] P. 625.

CHAPTER VII

THE EXISTENCE AND CONTENT OF Q

Coming back to the theory that Matthew and Luke used a common document for their sayings-material, we have next to determine what the content of that document was.

A reasonable degree of unanimity prevails among scholars as to this content, or at least as to a considerable part of it. Where students differ is as to the sayings which are not very closely parallel in the two Gospels, or as to sayings that are contained in only one of the two. As to the sayings which are practically identical in the two, or which show such very marked literary agreements as to put different sources out of the question, there is no dispute.

There appears to be a disposition on the part of some scholars to extend Q indefinitely. In his essay in the *Oxford Studies*, Mr. Bartlet seems to use the symbol to cover the general apostolic tradition (it is not always apparent whether he means written or not). Among German scholars, B. Weiss shows the same disposition. Among American scholars, Mr. B. W. Bacon suggests that Q might originally have contained much more and other material than can now be identified for it; as the narrative parts of it, being taken up by Mark, and copied from him by Matthew and Luke, would fail to leave in these latter Gospels any traces of themselves. This is quite true. But if Q, in addition to nearly all the logian material in Matthew and Luke originally contained all the narrative matter of Mark, Q was not only a complete Gospel, but quite as complete a Gospel as that of Matthew or Luke; perhaps more so, since Matthew and Luke may each have omitted something from Q; and no motive remains for the writing of these later Gospels. Mr. Burkitt[1] has maintained that Q very probably contained some references to the passion; but this position has not commended itself to many, if to any, other students.

Q was a collection of sayings. That the content of it, within limits, can be made out with some degree of unanimity is indicated by the following tables. The first represents the content of Q in Matthew, as given by the five scholars whose names head the five columns, with additional statements in the following columns, concerning the amount of agreement or divergence. The second table does the same thing for the Q matter assigned to the Gospel of Luke by the same five investigators.

DEDUCTIONS FROM THE TABLE

In Table II the verses are indicated as they stand in Matthew without their parallels in Luke (which would add nothing for our purpose here), and without indicating the rearrangement of order which most if not all of these scholars attempt at various places. The purpose here is simply to present the content of Q as made out by these different men. Besides showing what each one of them assigns to Q, I have (in the column headed "All Five") tried to show the verses which all these scholars agree in so assigning; and in the next column the verses assigned to Q by three or more out of the five. In the last two columns I have indicated the total number of verses out

---

[1] In his *Gospel History and Its Transmission*, and *Earliest Sources for the Life of Jesus*.

TABLE II
MATERIAL FROM Q IN MATTHEW

Chap.	Harnack	Wellhausen	Hawkins	J. Weiss	Wernle	All Five	Three or More	Total 5	Total 3
iii	5, 7–12	1–12	7–10, 12	7–10	7–12	7–10	7–12	4	6
iv	1–11	1–11	3–11	1–11	3–10	3–10	1–11	8	11
v	1–4, 6, 11, 12, 39–40, 42, 44–48, 15, 25–26, 13, 18, 32	1–12, 38–48	1–4, 6, 11–12, 18, 25–26, 39–40, 42, 44–48	1–6, 10, 13, 15, 18, 20–48	3–48	3, 4, 6, 39–40, 42, 44, 48	1–4, 6, 11, 12, 18, 25–26, 38, 40, 48, 13, 32	11	23
vi	9–13, 22–23, 19–21, 25–33, 24	19–34	9–13, 20–24, 25–33	1–9 (?), 10–15, 19–33	9–13, 19–34	20–33	9–13, 20–33	14	19
vii	12, 1–5, 16–19, 24–27, 28, 7–11, 13–14	1–6, 7–11, 15–27	1–2, 3–5, 7–14, 21–27	1–5, 7–13, 17–22a, 24–28	1–6, 7–11	1–2, 3–5, 7–11	1–5, 7, 11–13, 17–19, 21, 22, 24–27	10	21
viii	5–10, 13, 19–22, 8, 11–12	5–13	5–10, 11, 12, 19–22	5–13, 19–22	5–13, 19–22	5–13	5–13, 19–22	6	10
ix	37–38		37–38	37–38	37–38		37–38		2
x	24, 25, 7, 10, 16a, 12, 13, 10b, 15, 40, 26–28, 33, 34–36, 37, 38, 39	5–15	7, 8a, 10, 11, 13, 15–16a, 24–25a, 26–28, 38, 40	7–8a, 10, 11a, 12–14, 15–16a, 17, 22, 24–25a, 26a–40	5–16, 23–25, 40–42, 26–39	7, 10, 12, 13, 15	7, 10, 12, 13, 15, 16, 24–40	5	22
xi	2–13, 16–19, 21–23, 25–27	1–19, 20–30	2–3, 4–13, 16–19, 21–27	3–9, 11, 16–19, 21–27	33, 20–27, 2–19, 25–27	3–9, 11, 16–19, 21–23, 25–27	2–13, 16–27	18	24
xii	33, 22–23, 25, 27–28, 30, 43–45, 38–39, 41, 42, 32	22–42	22–23, 27–28, 30, 33, 35, 38, 39, 41–45	11, 23–24, 27–28, 33, 35, 38, 39, 41–45b	22–37, 58–59, 38–45	22–23, 27, 28, 38, 39, 41, 42	22–25, 27, 28, 30, 32, 35, 38, 39, 41–45	8	16

EXISTENCE AND CONTENT OF Q

TABLE II—*Continued*

Chap.	Harnack	Wellhausen	Hawkins	J. Weiss	Wernle	All Five	Three or More	Total 5	Total 3
xiii	16, 17, 31–33		16, 17, 33	16, 17, 31–33 (?)	16, 17, 31–33		16–17, 31–33		5
xv	14		14						
xvii	20b		20						
xviii	12, 13, 7, 15, 21, 22		7, 12–14, 15, 21–22	7, 12–13, 15, 22	7, 12–22		7, 12, 13, 15, 21, 22		6
xix	28		28						
xxi				32ab					
xxii		1–14		1–10	1–14		1–10		10
xxiii	4, 13, 23, 25, 27, 29, 30–32, 34–36	13–39	4, 12–14, 23, 25–27, 29–31, 34–39	4, 6–7, 13–15, 23ab, 25, 27, 29–31, 34–39	1–39	13, 23, 25, 27, 29–31, 34–36	13–15, 23, 25–27, 29–32, 34–39	10	17
xxiv	26–28, 37–41	1–51	27–28, 37–41, 43–51a	26–28, 37–41, 42–44 (?) 45–51	26–28, 37–51	27–28, 37–41	26–28, 37–51	7	15
xxv	29	14–30		1–13 (?)	14–30		29		1
Total	190	256	194	248	302	101	208	101	208

of each chapter, assigned to Q by all five, and by three or more, respectively. No attempt was made to select men whose work would have special tendency toward agreement; undoubtedly two investigators[1] might be substituted for Wellhausen and Wernle, whose work would make the total agreement much greater than it is in the present table.

The analysis of Wellhausen is the least elaborate of the five, and that of Wernle is almost as simple. The other three show more disposition to select out the verse or part of the verse which, occuring in the midst of Q material, should nevertheless be assigned to some other source. Weiss adds a question mark to several of his sections, but these have been included in the table. All the students say that not the same certainty attaches to all the sections which they have included. Sir John Hawkins, especially, says he does not consider his work a "reconstruction of Q," which, with Mr. Burkitt, he considers a task beyond the data at our command.

According to these five scholars, Q has furnished a source for Matthew in eleven chapters. According to three out of the five, Q is found in sixteen chapters. Harnack and Hawkins agree in finding one verse each in chaps. xv, xvii, and xix. Weiss alone finds two-thirds of a verse in xxi. Among the five, they find Q in twenty chapters. The only chapters in which Q is not found by any of them are i, ii, xiv, xvi, xx, xxvi, xxvii, and xxviii.

The most conspicuous absences of Q from Matthew are in his first two chapters, in his chapters dealing with the Passion (chaps. xxvi–xxvii), and in his story of the empty grave and the resurrection appearances (chap. xxviii).

---

[1] E.g., Stanton: see his *Gospels as Historical Documents*, Part II; and Robinson: see his *Study of the Gospels*.

Concerning the absence of Q from chaps. xiv, xvi, and xx, and its practically negligible presence in chaps. xv, xvii, xix, and xxi, it will be observed that these chapters do not deal exclusively with narrative material. Their content is, in brief, the death of the Baptist, the return of the disciples, the feeding of the five thousand, the walking on the sea, the dispute about hand-washing, the Canaanitish woman, the feeding of the four thousand, the demand of the Pharisees for a sign, the confession of Peter, the demands for discipleship, the transfiguration, the healing of the epileptic boy, the prediction of Jesus' sufferings, the temple-tax, the strife about rank, the strange exorcist, the speech about offenses and about the rescue of the lost, the rules for reconciliation with a brother and for forgiveness, the parable of the Evil Steward, the dispute about marriage and divorce, the blessing of the children, the danger of riches; the parable of the Laborers in the Vineyard, the second prediction of sufferings, the demand of the sons of Zebedee, the healing of Bartimaeus, the entry into Jerusalem, the offense of the scribes and priests, the cursing of the fig tree, the purification of the temple, the parables of the Dissimilar Sons and the Evil Vineyard-Keepers.

So far as the narrative material in these chapters is concerned, it is derived from Mark. Of the discourse material, some is connected with the narrative in Mark, and taken, like the narrative, from him.[1] Other passages of discourse material, like the demands of discipleship (Mt xvi, 24-28), not closely connected with Marcan narrative, yet apparently taken from Mark, contain verses

[1] Cf. especially the prediction of sufferings connected with the confession of Peter (Mt xvi, 13-23); the speech about Elijah, connected with the transfiguration (Mt xvii, 9-13); the speech about true greatness, connected with the request of the sons of Zebedee (Mt xx, 20-28).

elsewhere duplicated in Matthew. For these verses, some of which Luke takes from Mark, he has duplicates elsewhere. Since these duplicates in both Matthew and Luke are elsewhere closely connected with Q material, and are in their other connections apparently uninfluenced by Mark, it appears that in these chapters, where Matthew forsakes Q, he has nevertheless embodied certain material from Mark which originally stood alike in Mark and Q.

Other instances of this kind occur in Mt xviii, 1–5, the strife about rank; in xviii, 6–9, about offenses; and in xx, 24–28, about true greatness. These verses represent passages in which, according to Sanday's statement,[1] Mark and Q "overlapped"; or, according to other students (notably Mr. Streeter in the same volume), Mark also copied from Q. As we are here interested, not in the relation of Mark to Q, but only in the content of the latter as it is found in Matthew, we may go back to our statement that Matthew has combined his material from Q in his chaps. iii–viii and x–xii, and practically (if not quite) forsaken him in chaps. xiii–xxii.

Going back once more to Table II, the largest content ascribed to Q is given by Wernle: three hundred and two verses (including a few parts of verses). The next largest are from Weiss and Wellhausen, two hundred and forty-eight and two hundred and fifty-six verses respectively. Harnack and Hawkins assign only one hundred and ninety and one hundred and ninety-four.[2] But the facts that out of the largest content ascribed by any one of the five students (three hundred and two by Wernle), two hundred and eight of the same verses are likewise assigned

---

[1] *Oxford Studies*, p. xxii.

[2] Hawkins' list comes from his *Horae Synopticae*. In his essay in *Oxford Studies* he assigns a considerably larger content to Q.

EXISTENCE AND CONTENT OF Q 115

by two others, and that out of the smallest content (one hundred and ninety by Harnack), one hundred and one are likewise assigned by all five, show that as to the nucleus of Q, including more than half of it according to Harnack and one-third of it according to Wernle, there is practically no dispute.

Table III will show the results of the work of the same five scholars as to the Q material in Luke.

DEDUCTIONS FROM TABLE III

Table III, containing the content ascribed to Q as it is found in Luke, by the same five scholars mentioned above, discloses some interesting results when compared with Table II (pp. 110–11). As was the case with Q in Matthew, the smallest total is assigned by Harnack. That he finds one hundred and ninety verses (including a few parts of verses) in both Matthew and Luke indicates that he has limited his Q pretty closely to the duplicate matter in both Gospels. Hawkins' results are very close in this respect to Harnack's (one hundred and ninety-four Q verses in Matthew and one hundred and ninety-two in Luke), and indicate the same basis of computation. Wellhausen finds Q in two hundred and fifty-six verses of Matthew, and in only two hundred and ten of Luke.

Both tables show that Wellhausen's analysis of Q is much less elaborate than that of any of the other students. Since the number of Q verses which he finds in both Matthew and Luke is considerably larger than that which Harnack and Hawkins find, the disparity between his Q matter in Matthew and in Luke may be accounted for by his willingness to go farther beyond the duplicate material in those two Gospels for his Q. His two hundred and ten Q verses ascribed to Luke are not greatly in

TABLE III

MATERIAL IN LUKE TAKEN FROM Q

Chapter	Harnack	Wellhausen	Hawkins	J. Weiss	Wernle	All Five	Three or More	No. in Five	No. in Three
iii.	7–9, 16–17	1–7	7–9, 17	7–9, 17–18	7–9, 16–17	7	7–9, 17	1	4
iv.	1–13	1–15	3–13	1–13	3–12	3–12	1–13	6	13
vi.	17, 20–23, 27–33, 35b–44, 46–49	20–23, 27–49	17, 20–23, 27–49	47–49	20–49	47–49	20–23, 27–49	3	27
vii.	1–10, 18–28, 31–35	1–10, 18–35	1–3, 6–9, 18–19, 22–28, 31–35	1–3, 7–10, 18–26, 28–35	2–10, 18–35	1–3, 6–9, 18, 19, 22–26, 31–35	1–10, 18, 28, 31–35	19	26
ix.	2, 57–60		57–60	57–60	57–62		57–60		4
x.	2–7b, 9, 16, 21–22, 23b, 24	1–24	2–6, 7b–9, 12–16, 21–24	2–3, 13–14, 16, 21–27	1–16, 21–24	2–3, 16, 21–24	2–9, 12–16	7	13
xi.	2–4, 9–14, 16–17, 19, 20, 23–26, 29–35, 39, 40, 42–46, 51, 53, 58–59	9–32, 37–52	2–4, 9–14, 16, 19–20, 23–26, 29, 32, 34–35, 39, 41, 42, 44, 46–51	2–4, 9–11, 15–16, 24, 26, 29–31, 33–35, 39, 52	2–4, 9–26, 29–36, 39, 52	9–11, 16, 24–26, 29, 31, 39, 42, 44, 46–51	19, 20, 23–26, 29–35, 39, 52, 2–4, 9–17	19	39
xii.	2–10, 22–31, 33–34, 39, 40, 42–46, 51, 53, 58–59	22–46	2–9, 22–31, 33b–34, 39, 40, 42, 46, 51–53, 58, 59	2–8, 10–12, 22–31, 33, 34, 39–46, 51–52	2–12, 22–34, 39–46, 51–53, 58–59	22–31, 33–34, 39–40, 42–46	2–10, 22–31, 33–34, 39–46, 51–53, 58–59	19	34
xiii.	18–21, 24, 28–29, 34, 35	34–35	20–21, 23–29, 34–35	18–21, 23–25, 28–30, 34–35	18–21, 28–30, 34–35	34–35	18–21, 24, 28, 29, 34, 35	2	9
xiv.	11, 26–27, 34–35	16–24	11, 26–27	11, 16–23, 26–27, 34, 35	16–24, 26–27		16–23, 26–27		10
xv.	4–7		4, 5, 7	3–5	3–10		4–7		4
xvi.	13, 16–18		13, 16–17	13, 16–18	13, 16–17		13, 16–17		3

EXISTENCE AND CONTENT OF Q

TABLE III—*Continued*

Chapter	Harnack	Wellhausen	Hawkins	J. Weiss	Wernle	All Five	Three or More	No. in Five	No. in Three
xvii....	1, 3–4, 6, 23, 24, 26, 27, 32, 34, 35, 37	20–35	1, 3, 4, 6, 24, 26, 27, 34, 35, 37	1–2, 5–6, 23, 24, 26, 27, 31, 33b–4	1–4, 23–37	24, 26, 27, 34	1, 3, 4, 6, 23, 24, 26, 27, 31–35, 37	4	14
xviii...	26,			13, 15, 16					
xix....	28, 30	11–27	28, 30	22–25	12–27		26		1
xxii...									
Total.	190	210	192	174	255	80	201	80	201

excess of the number ascribed by Harnack and Hawkins to both Luke and Matthew. He gives to Luke twenty more Q verses, and to Matthew sixty-six more, than Harnack. Of these sixty-six, he may consider thirty to be duplicates in Matthew and Luke (since what constitutes derivation from a common source must always be matter of opinion). The other thirty-six verses he assigns to Q in Matthew, tho lacking duplicates in Luke, on the ground of their general characteristics. The habits of Matthew and Luke, respectively, in their treatment of Mark, render it practically certain that Matthew would feel less at liberty to omit Q material than Luke. Wernle's assignments (three hundred and two Q verses to Matthew and two hundred and fifty-five to Luke) may be explained in the same way.

Somewhat more difficult to understand is Weiss's assignment of two hundred and forty-eight Q verses to Matthew against only one hundred and seventy-four to Luke. He has here in common sixteen fewer verses than Harnack and Hawkins assign in common to Matthew and Luke from Q. But he also assigns to Matthew seventy-four Q verses not paralleled in the Q material which he assigns to Luke. The difference goes back again to the difference of opinion as to the degree of literary similarity which must be taken to indicate a common source; as also to Weiss's interest in the special source (S) of Luke. If we deduct from Weiss's Q in Matthew the twenty-eight verses after which he places an interrogation mark, this will leave him with only forty-six Q verses in Matthew unduplicated in Luke. This is only ten more than Wellhausen has.

All five scholars find Q material in nine of Luke's chapters (against eleven of Matthew's). Three find it in fourteen chapters. Chaps. iii and iv in Matthew correspond with the same chapters in Luke. Harnack finds in Matthew's two chapters seventeen Q verses, and in Luke's two chapters, eighteen. Hawkins finds fourteen in Matthew's two, and fifteen in Luke's. Matthew's chaps. v–viii (Sermon on the Mount) contain according to Harnack sixty-six Q verses, according to Hawkins sixty-eight. To these three chapters of Matthew, chap. vi of Luke forms a partial parallel. It contains, according to Harnack, twenty-six, and according to Hawkins twenty-eight Q verses, parallel to that number of Matthew's sixty-six. Of the remaining forty Q verses in Matthew (chaps. v–viii), Luke has in other connections, in chaps. xi, xii, xiii, xiv, and xvi, thirty-four parallel Q verses. All but six of the verses assigned by Hawkins and Harnack to Q in the Sermon on the Mount are therefore paralleled by Q material in Luke. But of this Q material in Luke more than half is scattered about in different chapters, in marked contrast to its concentration in Matthew. This is perhaps the best single illustration of the fact, often mentioned, that Luke blends his Q material with material from other sources, while Matthew inserts it in blocks.

It does not appear upon the surface why the same five investigators should not reach results concerning Q in Luke with the same consensus as concerning Q in Matthew. It is perhaps explained by the fact that Luke's blending of his material from different sources and his freer treatment of it render Q less identifiable with him. If, however, Wernle, Wellhausen, and Weiss be disregarded, and attention be paid only to the lists of Hawkins and Harnack, these latter lists will be found to agree as closely in their identification of Q material in

Luke as in Matthew. This merely shows that we are on firm ground in the identification of Q, so long as we restrict ourselves closely to the duplicate passages in Matthew and Luke, and require a reasonably strict agreement before admitting a common source. It is when we leave this duplicate material, to extend the limits of Q beyond it, that the uncertainties begin.

THE NECESSITY FOR A FURTHER EXTENSION OF Q

Yet the presence in both Matthew and Luke, especially in the former, of much sayings-material which is not only imbedded in Q matter, but has all the characteristics of Q; the presence of "translation variants"; the natural assumption that even if Matthew and Luke had before them the same identical copy of Q, they would not agree entirely in the amount of material they would respectively quote from it; and the desire to assign as much as seems reasonable to this source before positing another, all lead us to the task of a further determination of the content of Q. This further determination issues in an analysis of Q into QMt and QLk.

PART II
ANALYSIS OF Q INTO QM$_T$ AND QL$_K$

CHAPTER I

THE ANALYSIS OF Q

Q ORIGINALLY AN ARAMAIC DOCUMENT, USED IN GREEK
TRANSLATIONS BY MATTHEW AND LUKE

The starting-point of a further determination of the content of Q is the fact that Matthew and Luke seem to have taken their duplicate matter from a Greek document, but that this Greek document was a translation from the Aramaic. If Matthew and Luke had been independently translating from an Aramaic document, they could not have hit so generally upon the same order of words, especially where many other arrangements would have done as well (and occasionally better), nor would they have agreed in the translation of an Aramaic word by the same unusual Greek word, as notably in the ἐπιούσιον of the Lord's Prayer. The Q they used was a Greek document.

But Jesus spoke Aramaic, not Greek; and if Q is Palestinian, and as early as 60–65 or 70, it would be strange for it to have been written in any language except that which Jesus spoke. Mark had an Aramaic tradition; and tho he probably wrote in Greek he preserved many Aramaic words and expressions; Q as found in Matthew and Luke has no Aramaic words; this seems to be explicable only upon the supposition that though the original of it was in Aramaic, Matthew and Luke knew it only in its Greek form.

The hypothesis of an Aramaic original for Q is rendered practically certain by some of the variations that occur between Matthew's and Luke's versions of it. The clearest illustration of this is found in the speech against the Pharisees. Matthew reads, καθάρισον πρῶτον τὸ ἐντὸς τοῦ ποτηρίου. Luke reads, πλὴν τὰ ἐνόντα δότε ἐλεημοσύνην. One of these Greek clauses would be as difficult to derive from the other, or both of them from the same Greek original, as would be the English translation of the words. The meaning of Luke's is far from clear. In an Aramaic original, however, Matthew's verb might have read דכו, while Luke's might have read זכו. A mere stroke of the pen, if the saying originally stood in Aramaic, explains a variation which cannot be explained at all if the saying was originally in Greek. This statement, however, will apply only if the Aramaic was written and not merely spoken; for the two letters so alike in appearance are not particularly similar in sound.

Tho the above is the simplest and clearest instance, others of the same sort are not wanting. In Matthew's Sermon on the Mount Jesus says, "So persecuted they the prophets which were before you"; while in the corresponding passage in Luke's Sermon on the Plain he says, "In the same manner their fathers treated the prophets." Matthew's phrase (v. 12), τοὺς πρὸ ὑμῶν, and Luke's (vi, 23), οἱ πατέρες αὐτῶν, are equivalents, respectively, of the Hebrew or Aramaic phrases for "your ancestors" and "their ancestors." But whereas the two Greek phrases look nothing alike and could not be mistaken for one another, the difference in the Aramaic again reduces itself to the difference in one letter between the endings כם and הן. For Matthew's saying (x, 12), ἀσπάσασθε αὐτήν (τὴν οἰκίαν) Luke reads (x, 5), λέγετε· εἰρήνη τῷ οἴκῳ τούτῳ. Here Luke preserves the wording of the Aramaic greeting, "Peace be unto you," while Matthew says, "Greet the house." The form which Luke gives of the greeting is that which is used in Yiddish at the present time—שָׁלֹ֖ם לְךָ, "Peace to you," equivalent to our "good morning." That this is what underlay the tradition in Matthew is indicated by the fact that he goes on to say, "If the house is worthy, *your peace* shall abide upon it; but if it is unworthy, *your peace* shall return to you."

The very peculiar Greek used by both Matthew and Luke in the saying about excommunication (εἴπωσιν πᾶν πονηρὸν καθ' ὑμῶν in Mt v, 11, and ἐκβάλωσιν τὸ ὄνομα ὑμῶν ὡς πονηρὸν in Lk vi, 22) seems to go back to the one Aramaic phrase for giving one a bad name. In the speech against the Pharisees Matthew (xxiii, 25) says, "Ye cleanse the outside of the cup and dish but inwardly they [the cup and platter] are full of greed and baseness." Luke makes much better sense by reading (xi, 39), "Ye cleanse the outside of cup and platter, but inwardly ye are full of greed," etc. If it be assumed that the present tense of the verb "to cleanse" was represented in Aramaic by the participle (which would be the usual construction), and that the second person pronoun stood with it in the first clause but was not repeated in the second (as would also be natural in the Aramaic), Matthew's change of the verb in the second clause, from the second person to the third, and his consequent use of "cup and dish" as the subject of it, are easily explained; since the participle carries in itself no distinction between second and third person, and the plural form would fit equally the "ye" and the "they." Instances such as these (I owe them all to Wellhausen)[1] seem to prove conclusively (Jülicher says "beyond a doubt") that, not

[1] *Einleitung*, pp. 16–18.

126   SOURCES OF THE SYNOPTIC GOSPELS

merely an Aramaic oral tradition, but an Aramaic document lies behind the Greek Q used by Matthew and Luke.

METHODS OF MATTHEW AND LUKE IN THEIR USE OF Q

Upon the hypothesis that Matthew and Luke used essentially the same text of Q, an elaborate treatment of their respective use of that document is called for to show which of them, in instances where they differ, is to be charged with the alterations, and to assign the reasons for those alterations. Two scholars, Harnack in his *Sayings of Jesus* and Wernle in his *Synoptische Frage*, have made such an analysis, with the thoroness characteristic of them. The writer has studied these analyses carefully, and upon the basis of them and of such study of the texts as they suggested, made his own analysis. But upon the hypothesis of Q as originally an Aramaic document, used by Matthew and Luke in Greek translations going back to different Aramaic texts, such an analysis becomes superfluous, because superseded by the analysis of Q into the two recensions, QMt and QLk.

THE ANALYSIS OF Q INTO QMT AND QLK

If Q was originally an Aramaic document, used by Matthew and Luke in Greek translations going back to different copies of the Aramaic original, it is fair to assume that these two translations would have had different histories. Q would always be growing, by the aid of oral tradition; and if Q was written before Mark, there was ample time, say twenty-five years at least, before it was used by Matthew and Luke, for the two recensions, circulating in different communities and perhaps originally shaped to suit the needs of different readers, to acquire many dissimilar features. Not only would the same saying in many instances become changed to meet the varying need, or to adapt itself to what was considered a better tradition, but many things would be included in either recension which were not included in the other. Matthew will thus have had a recension of Q which we may designate by the sign QMt, and Luke one which we may call QLk.

The following pages represent an attempt to determine the content of Q, as that is represented in both Matthew and Luke.[1] Of the sections of Matthew and Luke examined, some are marked QMt, some QLk, and some merely Q. By this it is not meant that Matthew and Luke each had a document Q, and besides this a document QMt or QLk, and that they took now from one and now from the other. But where the wording of Matthew and Luke is identical, or so closely similar that the variations can be easily explained as changes made by Matthew or Luke, the material is assigned simply to Q. But where the variations are too great, much greater for example than any changes that have been made by Matthew and Luke or by either one of them where they are taking their logian material from Mark, the material is assigned to QMt and QLk. Reasons for the assignment to QMt or to QLk instead of to simple Q are given in each case seeming to require them. The sum of all passages assigned to any form of Q will constitute the total content of Q, so far as it is contained in both Matthew and Luke. This total content will be somewhat larger than the content that could be assigned to Q without the hypothesis of QMt and QLk, since by this hypothesis many sections

---

[1] Effort will be made later to determine the extent of QMt and QLk by themselves.

will be sufficiently alike to be assigned to Q (QMt and QLk) which otherwise would have to be ascribed to different sources.[1]

[1] The writer began the following examination with the intention of assigning to Q only, and rejecting all passages not showing sufficient agreement to warrant such assignment. He found this task so difficult, involving the rejection of so many passages which did not apparently belong to Q but which nevertheless showed unmistakable signs of literary relation, that he adopted the theory (suggested but not worked out in the introduction to Bacon's *Beginnings of Gospel Story*) of QMt and QLk.

CHAPTER II

Q, QMt, AND QLk IN THE DOUBLE TRADITION OF MATTHEW AND LUKE

THE PREACHING OF JOHN THE BAPTIST
(Mt iii, 7b–10; Lk iii, 7b–9)

This section is universally ascribed to Q. In Matthew's Gospel it contains sixty-three words; in Luke's sixty-four. These are identical in the two Gospels, except for Luke's addition of καὶ at the beginning of his 9th verse, his plural (καρποὺς) where Matthew has the singular, and his substitution of ἄρξησθε for Matthew's δόξητε. The parallelism begins in the middle of the 7th verse of each Gospel; the first part of the verse in each case evidently being supplied by the evangelist. Matthew says John's remark was addressed to the Pharisees and Sadducees. With his customary indifference to class distinctions among the Jews, Luke represents the words as being addressed to all those who came for baptism. They do not seem appropriate to candidates for baptism, whether Pharisees, Sadducees, or others. Luke uses some form of the verb ἄρχω with the infinitive λέγειν eight times as against Matthew's twice. As it seems here to have no advantage over δοκέω it might be safe to suppose that the substitution was made unintentionally, and from the influence of the recollection of similar usage in other parts of Luke's Gospel. The first half of vs. 7 in each Gospel should be assigned to the evangelists; the remainder of the section to Q.

THE MESSIANIC PROCLAMATION OF THE BAPTIST
(Mt iii, 11–12; Lk iii, 16–17)

Matthew's vs. 11 and Luke's vs. 16 are closely parallel to Mark i, 7–8. But they are still more closely parallel with each other, and contain common deviations from Mark which cannot be explained upon the supposition that they are taken from the latter. The wording in the two Gospels, for twenty-six consecutive words, is identical, except for Luke's omission of καί in his vs. 17, and his consequent change of verbs from the finite to the infinitive mood. This section is universally assigned to Q.

THE TEMPTATION
(Mt iv, 3–11; Lk iv, 3–13)

The whole story of the temptation as told by Matthew and Luke includes the two verses of each Gospel which immediately precede the section here specified. These verses are not included here because they seem to the writer to be taken by Matthew and Luke from Mark and not from Q. The common avoidance by Matthew and Luke of Mark's statement that Jesus was "with the wild beasts," and their common substitution of διάβολος for Mark's σατανᾶς, would point toward their exclusive use of Q and their avoidance of Mark in these verses. On the other hand, Matthew and Luke use very different phraseology to express their common idea of the hunger of Jesus (Luke saying οὐκ ἔφαγεν οὐδὲν ἐν ταῖς ἡμέραις ἐκείναις, καὶ συντελεσθεισῶν αὐτῶν ἐπείνασεν, while Matthew says καὶ νηστεύσας ἡμέρας τεσσεράκοντα καὶ τεσσεράκοντα νύκτας, ὕστερον ἐπείνασεν). Matthew agrees with Mark in six consecutive words (except for the transposition of two of them) where Luke has a wording of his own. Whereas Mark says that Jesus was tempted forty days, saying nothing about his hunger, Matthew says he fasted for forty days and was tempted at the expiration of this time, and Luke that he fasted forty days and was tempted during that time. The best explanation for these divergences and similarities is that Matthew and Luke take these verses from Mark but correct him freely under the influence of Q. Q also of course contained these verses, and they will be assigned to him when we come to consider the Q material in Mark. In the rest of the temptation narrative, where Mark has no parallel, there is great verbal similarity. The enlargement of the Old Testament quotation may perhaps be ascribed to Matthew. The transposition of Matthew's second temptation to the third place in Luke seems to spoil the climax in the narrative; Mr. Streeter (*Oxford Studies*, p. 152) argues that Luke would not have spoiled so good an arrangement if he had found it in his source. If this argument were allowed, the section would have to be assigned to QMt and QLk. The writer does not feel that the divergences are great enough to necessitate this, and so assigns it to Q.

"BLESSED ARE THE POOR"
(Mt v, 3; Lk vi, 20b)

Matthew's beatitude is in the third person, Luke's in the second. Matthew adds "in spirit." If the beatitude stood alone, the changes in it are not too great to be attributed to Matthew, and the "in spirit" is what might be expected. But taking it in close connection with much material that could not have stood alike in Matthew's source and in Luke's it is better to assign it to QMt and QLk.

"BLESSED ARE THEY THAT MOURN"

(Mt v, 5; Lk vi, 21b)

The wording is not at all similar, μακάριοι being the only word in common. Yet the two beatitudes sound like two versions of the same one. κλαίω is a Lucan word, used eleven times by Luke in his Gospel, against twice by Matthew and three times by Mark. γελάω is used twice in Luke's Gospel, and not elsewhere in the New Testament. Both of these occurrences are in Luke's "Sermon on the Level Place." These facts, with the context, indicate a source in Luke's hands partly like, and partly unlike, the source in Matthew's. The verse is therefore assigned to QMt and QLk.

"BLESSED ARE THEY THAT HUNGER"

(Mt v, 6; Lk vi, 21a)

Matthew's version is again in the third person and Luke's in the second. Luke understands the hunger to be literal. Matthew "spiritualizes" by adding τὴν δικαιοσύνην. Luke adds νῦν, to point the contrast between his beatitude and the corresponding woe, which Matthew does not have. In spite of these differences, out of ten words in Matthew's form and six in Luke's, five words are identical (except for a deviation in personal ending). Except for the context the verse might be assigned simply to Q; but it is better ascribed to QMt and QLk.

"BLESSED ARE THE PERSECUTED"

(Mt v, 11-12; Lk vi, 22-23)

The verbal similarity is close only in a few places; notably in the ὁ μισθὸς ὑμῶν πολὺς ἐν τοῖς οὐρανοῖς (τῷ οὐρανῷ). Out of thirty-five words in Matthew and

Q, QMT, AND QLK IN MATTHEW AND LUKE 133

fifty-one in Luke, only twelve are identical. Two considerations prevent the assignment of these verses to two totally different sources. The first is their contiguity to so much Q material. The second is the presence in them of two translation variants.[1] The second of these two verses, at least, therefore goes back to two different recensions or translations of one original Aramaic document—QMt and QLk.

A SAYING ABOUT SALT
(Mt v, 13; Lk xiv, 34)

This saying evidently stood in both Mark and Q. Luke follows Mark in καλὸν οὖν τὸ ἅλα and Q in the rest of his saying. Matthew's form of the saying, which makes it addressed to the disciples, "Ye are the salt of the earth," involves a much greater change than Matthew ever permits himself when he transcribes the words of Jesus which he finds in Mark. Luke, on the other hand, could scarcely have found the saying in his source with this application to the disciples, and have changed it to its much less pointed and personal form in his own Gospel. The only conclusion possible from a comparison of Matthew and Luke here is that this saying lay in different forms in their sources. But since it occurs in the midst of so much Q material, it is better to assign it to different recensions of Q than to some other unknown source.

A SAYING ABOUT LIGHT
(Mt v, 15; Lk xi, 33)

This is another saying that stood in both Mark and Q. Mark has the saying in Mk iv, 21. His form of it is the

[1] See Wellhausen's *Einleitung*, p. 36, and pp. 124–25 of this book.

apparently less natural one, "Does the lamp come in order that it may be put under a bushel?" etc. Weiss suggests[1] that it has been given this form to make it refer to the coming of Jesus as the light of the world. Neither Matthew nor Luke has copied this feature of Mark's saying. By his context Matthew makes the saying refer, like the saying about salt, directly to the disciples. Luke has the saying twice: in xi, 33 and viii, 16. In both cases his context would indicate that he took the saying to refer to the teaching of Jesus. Matthew says the light is to give light "to all that are in the house." Luke does not mention the house, but implies it in his statement that "those who are entering in see the light," this form being found in both his reports of the saying. Mark says "under the bushel or under the bed"; Matthew, "under the bushel"; Luke once, "in a dish or under the bed," and a second time, "in a cellar or under the bushel." Luke's fondness for the same ending in his two uses of the saying can be explained only by the supposition that it so stood in one of his sources. The same idea in the conclusion of the saying as it appears in Matthew and Luke, and their common avoidance of the opening formula which is peculiar to Mark, would indicate that Matthew and Luke practically forsake Mark in this saying, and follow their other source. Luke, having a doublet for the saying, may be assumed to have taken it once from Mark and once from his other source; but he is evidently much more influenced by his other source than he is by Mark. The non-Marcan source in which the saying was found by Matthew and Luke was evidently an allied, but not an identical, one; the saying is therefore assigned to QMt and QLk.

[1] *Das älteste Evangelium*, p. 175.

A SAYING ABOUT THE LAW
(Mt v, 18; Lk xvi, 17)

There are twenty-seven words in Matthew's form of this saying; fifteen in Luke's. Only nine words show any correspondence. Matthew's "until all be fulfilled" is held by Schmiedel[1] to be a gloss, added, not by the final editor of Matthew, who did not care for Jewish legalism, but by an earlier editor. Harnack maintains that it goes back to Jesus, and does not necessarily mean that the law shall ultimately pass away. In his essay in the *Oxford Studies* Hawkins maintains that the section can be made "very probable" for Q. Considering the wide divergences, the writer would add that this probability can be established only upon the hypothesis of two recensions of Q; upon that hypothesis it would be granted by everyone.

"AGREE WITH THINE ADVERSARY"
(Mt v, 25-26; Lk xii, 58-59)

Luke prefaces this saying with one peculiar to his Gospel: "Why do ye not, of yourselves, judge what is right?" The close connection of this saying with the passage here under consideration, and the verbal resemblances and divergences of the sections in Matthew and Luke—twenty-five identical words out of a total of forty-three in Matthew and forty-nine in Luke—warrant their assignment to QMt and QLk.

ABOUT NON-RESISTANCE AND LOVE OF ENEMIES
(Mt v, 39, 40, 42, 44-48; Lk vi, 27-30, 32, 36)

It is possible to choose out of these verses here and there a few words which, if they stood alone, would be naturally assigned simply to Q. By regarding only the

[1] *Encyclopaedia Biblica*, col. 1864.

words which very closely correspond, this is accomplished, but with the result that the other words, standing in the same context and in closest connection, must be assigned to totally different sources, or ascribed to the invention or alteration of one of the evangelists. The verbal similarity thruout the section is sometimes close, sometimes remote. Transpositions are frequent. Where Matthew has the simile of the rain and sun, Luke has the comparatively weak words "good to the unthankful and evil." This is a substitution that Luke certainly would never have made for the strong words of Matthew if these had stood in his source. The author assigns the section to the two recensions, QMt and QLk.

THE LORD'S PRAYER
(Mt vi, 9–13; Lk xi, 2–4)

This is one of the sections that point most clearly to different recensions of Q in the hands of Matthew and Luke. It is improbable that any collection of the sayings of Jesus should have lacked this prayer. It is equally improbable that Luke could have had it before him in the more elaborated form of Matthew, and have abridged it to suit himself. Matthew's more elaborate form, on the other hand, does not sound like the deliberate alteration of any one author, but like the accumulated liturgical usage of the Christian community. Luke's introduction to the prayer is certainly not his own invention, and is so appropriate that it is hard to believe that Matthew found it in connection with the prayer in his source and deliberately omitted it. Luke's form seems decidedly more primary. The use in both Gospels of the strange word ἐπιούσιον seems to carry the two traditions back to one original; but the variations are certainly greater than can be accounted for by the literary habits of Matthew and Luke, working upon the same original. In other words, that original had passed thru a different history before it reached our two evangelists. The section is assigned to QMt and QLk.

A SAYING ABOUT TREASURES
(Mt vi, 19–21; Lk xii, 33–34)

The verbal similarity is not close. Except for the proximity of other Q material, the section might be assigned to two entirely different sources. There is, especially, a quite different turn given to the saying in Luke, from that which it has in Matthew, by the introduction of the words "Sell your goods and give alms." In spite of Luke's interest in alms-giving, as disclosed in the Book of Acts, it is hard to credit him with such a re-wording of his text without some help from his source. But the last twelve words in the section are identical in the two Gospels, except that Luke uses the plural form of the pronoun where Matthew uses the singular. Largely on account of these last twelve words the section is assigned to QMt and QLk.

A SAYING ABOUT THE EYE
(Mt vi, 22–23; Lk xi, 34–35)

Of forty-four words in Matthew and forty in Luke, thirty-two are identical. The divergences in the use of conjunctions ($\overset{\text{″}}{o}\tau\alpha\nu$ for $\dot{\epsilon}\dot{\alpha}\nu$, e.g.) and the improvement by condensation of the last sentence are such changes as might be easily ascribed to Luke. The section may, with reasonable assurance, be assigned merely to Q.

ABOUT DOUBLE SERVICE
(Mt vi, 24; Lk xvi, 13)

There are twenty-seven words in this saying according to Matthew, twenty-eight according to Luke. Luke appears to have been the innovator; his addition of οἰκέτης improves the sentence in a way often accomplished by him. With the exception of the presence of this word in Luke and its absence in Matthew the saying is identical in the two Gospels. It is therefore assigned simply to Q.

ABOUT CARE
(Mt vi, 25–33; Lk xii, 22–31)

Considering the length of this passage, the verbal similarity is remarkably close. Out of one hundred and sixty words in Luke and one hundred and sixty-six in Matthew, about one hundred and fifteen are identical. Beginning in the middle of Luke's vs. 22, and at the first of Matthew's vs. 25, there are twenty-six words in Luke which are identical with the same number of words arranged in identical order, in Matthew; except that Luke has omitted (or Matthew has supplied) three words, without affecting the meaning of the passage. Beginning with Matthew's vs. 32 and Luke's vs. 30, there are again twenty-one identical words out of twenty-four in Luke and thirty-one in Matthew. Matthew may here easily be credited with the addition of the words which constitute the difference; for his ὁ οὐράνιος and his καὶ τὴν δικαιοσύνην are characteristic of him: the former expression being used by him seven times and not at all by the other evangelists; the latter, seven times by Matthew, once by Luke, and not at all by Mark. His addition of πρῶτον in his vs. 33 has a decidedly secondary sound. The passage may therefore be assigned simply to Q.

ABOUT JUDGING
(Mt vii, 1-2; Lk vi, 37-38)

Between the beginning and the end of this saying, both of which are alike in the two Gospels, Luke has an amplification of some length. It is highly improbable that this amplification is the work of Luke, who is much more inclined to condense than to enlarge. The Q context in both Gospels, and the almost exact agreement of the saying, except for the enlargement in Luke, warrant the assignment to QMt and QLk.

THE BEAM AND THE MOTE
(Mt vii, 3-5; Lk vii, 41-42)

The verbal agreement is very close. Out of sixty-four words in Matthew and sixty-nine in Luke fifty-six are identical, except for deviation in mode or number. The greater condensation seems characteristic of Matthew. The changes do not seem too great to be ascribed to the two evangelists working on the same source, Q.

ABOUT SEEKING AND FINDING
(Mt vii, 7-11; Lk xi, 9-13)

The agreement is close, except where Luke in his vs. 12 adds the item of the egg and the scorpion which has no parallel in Matthew. In spite of the addition of this verse in Luke, out of eighty words in his version and seventy-three in Matthew's sixty-two are still identical. Luke's substitution of "holy spirit" for Matthew's indefinite "good things" is characterized by Schmiedel as a "deliberate divergence." The same phrase would hardly describe the addition of vs. 12. According to the principle here followed, it might seem natural to assign this verse, and so the whole context, to Luke's recension of Q. But in the whole section, aside from this verse, there are so few deviations, and these so easily accounted for on the part either of Matthew or Luke, that the writer inclines to assign the section simply to Q. Luke's vs. 12 would then be regarded as a gloss, or an addition of Luke from some source of his own, perhaps oral. Between this disposal of the matter and the assignment of the entire section to QMt and QLk there is not much to choose.

THE GOLDEN RULE
(Mt vii, 12; Lk vi, 31)

The last clause of Matthew may be his own addition, or perhaps a formula common among the Christians. It may have been a gloss, or may have been found by Matthew in his recension of Q. At all events, it is not like Matthew to have added it himself; his tendency toward condensation is too well known. Except for this addition the section is sufficiently alike in the two Gospels to admit its assignment simply to Q.

THE NARROW GATE
(Mt vii, 13-14; Lk xiii, 23-24)

With much resemblance in meaning there is here very little similarity in wording. Luke's saying is much briefer, and is introduced by a question addressed to Jesus. It sounds almost like an abstract of the saying as it stands in Matthew—if only a precedent could be shown for Luke's making such an abstract. One can hardly speak with any assurance; but considering the difference of setting, the fact that in Luke the verses we are here considering are part of a considerably longer speech, and the slight verbal resemblances, it may be best to assign Matthew's version to Q, and Luke's to some source of his own, whether oral or written. If assignment to QMt and QLk is not impossible, it is certainly difficult.

THE TREE AND ITS FRUITS
(Mt vii, 16–18; Lk vi, 43–44)

For this saying Matthew has a doublet in xii, 33–35. Mt vii, 20, is also an exact reproduction of vii, 16, with the particle ἄραγε prefixed. If Matthew found this saying in two of his sources, it is impossible to say what the second of these was, for it apparently was not Mark. In Matthew's second report of the same saying he has used the words "generation of vipers," which he has in iii, 7, ascribed to John the Baptist. The fact that both speeches in which the phrase occurs have to do with trees, and the fact of the repetition, not only of the saying twice in Matthew, but of the same sentence twice in one report, may perhaps indicate that Matthew found the saying only in his version of Q, and is himself responsible for the repetition. Or the saying may have been recorded twice in Matthew's version of Q, with the variations shown in Matthew's two citations of it. Upon either hypothesis the form of Mt xii, 35, is much nearer to Lk vi, 45, than is Mt vii, 19–20, or vss. 16–18. The writer assigns the section to QMt and QLk.

WARNING AGAINST SELF-DECEPTION
(Mt vii, 21–23; Lk vi, 46; xiii, 26–27)

Of the first of these three verses in each Gospel, Harnack says it is "perhaps not derived from Q." But the verse stands in substantially the same context in both Gospels—in the Sermon on the Mount in Matthew and the Sermon on the Level Place in Luke. In spite of the difference introduced thruout the verse by Matthew's having it in the third person and Luke's giving it in the second, a reminiscence of the same source may be found in the fact that κύριε is used by Matthew in the vocative, where a more strict construction would require the accusative. The last two verses of the section Matthew has combined with the first, whereas in Luke the context for them is quite different. Thru all three verses Luke seems to have the more primary form. Not only the second person of the verbs, and the direct address of Jesus to the crowd, but the words, "we have eaten and drunk in thy presence and thou hast taught in our streets" have an original sound, whereas Matthew's form, "Many shall say to me in that day, Lord, we have preached in thy name and in thy name have cast out demons," would seem rather to come from a time when many men had been preaching in the name of Jesus. Harnack says that the two sayings are "quite independent," but that there is "a common source in the background." This common source in the background might be the undifferentiated Q, and the immediate sources might be the two recensions of that document. The general character of the sayings, and the context, would encourage such an assignment. Since here as in many other places the version of Matthew seems to indicate adaptation to a later time, but since the Gospel of Matthew cannot be shown to be later than the Gospel of Luke, it seems fair to attribute the divergence between the two evangelists here to the different history thru which their two versions of their common source had passed before coming into their hands. The writer therefore assigns the section to QMt and QLk, tho not without admission that it might be as well to assign the section in one Gospel to Q and in the other to some entirely other source.

THE TWO HOUSES
(Mt vii, 24–27; Lk vi, 47–49)

Comparison of these sections shows a much slighter verbal agreement between them than might have been expected from their general agreement in idea. Even in idea the agreement is not extremely close. Matthew's two houses are built, respectively, upon the rock and the sand; Luke's are built, respectively, with and without a foundation, irrespective of the soil. If Matthew's version be here regarded as the more primary, as is warranted by the fact of its greater simplicity (Matthew seems here also to be nearer to the Aramaic, as indicated by his recurrent use of καί at the beginning of a sentence), the reinterpretation and consequent re-wording shown in Luke's version are altogether too great to be ascribed to the hand of Luke himself, working upon a source identical with Matthew's version. Let anyone compare Luke's treatment of the sayings of Jesus in Mark with the treatment of this saying, which would be required upon the hypothesis of an identical source before him and Matthew, and he will feel that that hypothesis cannot be maintained. And yet, in addition to the general similarity in the sections, there is one other thing that argues strongly for their inclusion in some form of Q, viz., their position, as conclusions, respectively, to the Sermon on the Mount, and the Sermon on the Plain. The writer therefore ascribes them to QMt and QLk.

THE CENTURION'S SON
(Mt viii, 5–10; Lk vii, 1–9)

This is the one narrative section almost universally assigned to Q. But in the first part of the story there is wide divergence. Matthew says the centurion himself came to Jesus. Luke not only says he did not come, but explains why he sent messengers instead of coming himself. Burton alleges that Matthew's omission of the item of the messengers is characteristic of him, with his tendency to condensation. But that the messengers were not in the original story, but were added by Luke (or his source) and not omitted by Matthew, is plain from the fact that the conversation, even in Luke, is based upon the supposition that the centurion had made his request in person. In Luke's vss. 3–6, which contain the account of the sending of the messengers, there are at least five Lucan words (ἔντιμος, παραγενόμενοι, σπουδαίως, μακράν, ἀπέχοντος). These occur in the portion of the story unparalleled in Matthew. But there are also three such Lucan words in the two following verses, where the story of Luke runs quite closely parallel to that of Matthew (διό, ἠξίωσα, τασσόμενος). The changing of a detail, even an important detail, in the narrative part of such a section, especially when contrasted with general faithfulness to the source in that part containing the words of Jesus, would be characteristic of Luke. The humility and faith of the centurion are much enhanced by the change. Yet, as Jülicher remarks, Luke probably did not invent this item of his story; he may have imported it from an oral tradition, following Q in the remainder of the story. Even the presence of the "Lucan" words would not prove the Lucan invention of the sending of the messengers, since these words may have come from Luke's special source for this item and not from himself, tho this latter supposition would tell against the assumption that this special source was an oral one. Of these Lucan words, ἔντιμος is used a second time by Luke (xiv, 8) in a passage not paralleled in Matthew; it is not used by him in Acts. Παραγενόμενοι is used once by Mark, three times by Matthew, eight times by Luke in his Gospel, and twenty times in the Book of Acts. Σπουδαίως is found here only in the Gospels, and not in Acts. Μακράν is used once by Matthew, once by Mark, twice by Luke in his Gospel, and three times in Acts. Ἀπέχοντες (in the intransitive sense) occurs twice in Matthew, once in Mark, three times in Luke's Gospel, and not in Acts. Διό occurs once in Mark, once in Matthew, twice in Luke's Gospel, and eight times in Acts. Ἀξιόω is found in Luke only among the Gospels, and twice in Acts. Τάσσω is found in some texts of Matthew in this passage, but has probably been assimilated from Luke. It is found in one other passage in Matthew, in this passage in Luke, not in Mark, and five times in Acts. These facts cannot be said to throw much light on whether Luke is here to be charged with the verses in which these words occur, or whether they may have stood in his source. But considering the extremely close agreement between Luke's vss. 7b–9 and Matthew's vss. 8b–10 (note especially the εἰπὲ λόγῳ, unparalleled elsewhere), the best conclusion may be that the story stood in Q, much as it now stands in Matthew, and that Luke, perhaps having heard this other version of the story, has himself altered the narrative part of it.

"MANY SHALL COME FROM EAST AND WEST"
(Mt viii, 11–12; Lk xiii, 28–29)

In Matthew these words are interpolated into the story of the centurion's son; in Luke they occur as part of an eschatological speech. They seem better in place with Luke than with Matthew. The sentence "There shall be weeping," etc., is transposed by one evangelist or the other; as it is used in five other places by Matthew, and as he has probably imported into the story of the centurion the verses in which it occurs, it is probable that the transposition is due to him. There is sufficient divergence in wording between Matthew and Luke to warrant the assignment of the verses to QMt and QLk.

TWO MEN WHO WOULD FOLLOW JESUS
(Mt viii, 19–22; Lk ix, 57–60)

To these two sayings Matthew and Luke supply respectively their own introductions. In the first saying, after the introduction, thirty-one consecutive words are identical, except for Luke's substitution of εἶπεν for the original λέγει which still appears in Matthew. In the second saying, after the introduction, the verbal resemblance is close, tho not so close as in the first saying. The second half of Luke's vs. 60 has a late sound, and may be attributed either to Luke or his copy of Q. But the resemblance thruout is close enough to warrant the assignment of the section simply to Q.

"THE HARVEST IS GREAT"
(Mt ix, 37–38; Lk x, 2)

This saying occurs in Matthew's sending out of the twelve and in Luke's sending out of the seventy. Twenty-one consecutive words are identical except for the transposition of two words. It is assigned to Q.

"THE LABORER IS WORTHY OF HIS HIRE"
(Mt x, 10c; Lk x, 7b)

Mark and Q both contained accounts of the sending out of the disciples. This is one of the fragments preserved from Q by Matthew and Luke, but not found in Mark. It is identical except for the substitution of μισθοῦ for τροφῆς. The change may be attributed to Luke or his recension of Q; in this case the change is so slight as to be easily chargeable to Luke; it may bespeak a time later than that indicated by Matthew's form— a time when the traveling preachers received not only their food but some slight wage. It stood in Q.

"GREET THE HOUSE"
(Mt x, 11–13; Lk x, 5–8)

This is one of the best illustrations of the advantages of the hypothesis of the two recensions of Q. Matthew says "greet the house." Luke preserves the Aramaic form of that greeting, which was "Peace to this house." But that this, and not Matthew's indefinite form, was what stood in the original Q is shown by the fact that Matthew adds, "If the house is worthy, let your peace come upon it; but if it is unworthy, let your peace return to you."[1] Luke has here the phrase "son of peace," similar to the phrases elsewhere found in his Gospel, "sons of light," "sons of consolation," "sons of this generation," "sons of the resurrection." These phrases have an Aramaic sound which we should expect to encounter in almost any of the Gospels sooner than in Luke's. He certainly never would have invented them. The translation variants stamp the section as belonging to QMt and QLk.

"MORE TOLERABLE FOR SODOM"
(Mt x, 15; Lk x, 12)

The variations are slight. Ἀμὴν might be taken to indicate QMt, but it might also easily have been omitted by Luke because of its Aramaic tone. The section may be safely ascribed to Q.

[1] See also pp. 124–25.

"SHEEP AMONG WOLVES"
(Mt x, 16a; Lk x, 3)

Luke substitutes ἄρνας for Matthew's πρόβατα, thus heightening the contrast. It may be assigned to Q.

HOW TO ACT UNDER PERSECUTION
(Mt x, 19-20; Lk xii, 11-12)

Although there is general similarity in idea, there is very little verbal resemblance here, perhaps not enough to warrant assignment to any common source, even in differing recensions. Yet the proximity of other Q material in both Gospels and the general character of the verses will perhaps make assignment to QMt and QLk more reasonable than any other.

THE DISCIPLE AND HIS TEACHER
(Mt x, 24-25; Lk vi, 40)

The agreement here is close for a part of the saying; but Matthew adds a clause about the servant and his lord, and a reference to the Beelzebul controversy. Whether attributed to Luke or his source, his addition of κατηρτισμένος may indicate the feeling that the statement as to the equality of the disciple and his teacher required some qualification. This would be more strongly felt, however, if Luke had preserved the word κύριος, which would refer more unmistakably to Jesus. In Luke this section occurs in the Sermon on the Plain; since Matthew has put much material in his corresponding Sermon on the Mount which is not in Luke's Sermon on the Plain, even when he has had to bring this from many other connections, it is strange that he has left out of that sermon this saying, which stands in the corresponding discourse in Luke. This is one of the phenomena difficult of explanation upon the simple hypothesis of Q; since upon that hypothesis Matthew should have found this saying in the same connection as that in which Luke found it, and why, so finding it, he not only took pains to add so much to it, but to transpose it upon the opposite principle to that which he has followed in the transposition of most other Q material, is not easy to explain. On these grounds the saying is ascribed to QMt and QLk.

EXHORTATION TO FEARLESS CONFESSION
(Mt x, 26-33; Lk xii, 2-9)

The agreements and variations in this section are precisely such as to indicate an ultimate common source, but immediate different sources. In Matthew's vs. 27 and Luke's vs. 3, with many of the same words retained, the meaning is directly reversed. On the other hand, φοβεῖσθε (φοβηθῆτε) with ἀπὸ is found here only in the New Testament, and not at all in the Septuagint. Unless this be ascribed to assimilation, it is a coincidence too marked to be explained except by the supposition of an ultimate common source. The same thing is to be said of the phrase ὁμολογήσει ἐν in Matthew's vs. 32 and Luke's vs. 8. Yet in the midst of the section there is a passage of twenty or twenty-five words in which there is practically no verbal coincidence, tho the idea is the same. Luke substitutes "have not anything else that they can do," for Matthew's phrase "can not kill the soul"; it has been suggested that this latter was not congenial to Luke's Greek method of thot. Where Matthew mentions the price of sparrows as "two for a farthing," Luke specifies it as "five for two farthings." The section contains no narrative matter. A comparison of the deviations between Matthew and Luke here, with their agreements with each other in sections where they are taking over the discourse material of Jesus from Mark, will show that these deviations are decidedly too great to be ascribed to the agency of either Matthew or Luke. The passage is therefore assigned to QMt and QLk.

STRIFE AMONG RELATIVES
(Mt x, 34–36; Lk xii, 51–53)

Luke's version seems more elaborated and less original than Matthew's. Luke certainly would not have substituted the comparatively colorless word διαμερισμόν for μάχαιραν if this latter had stood in his source. Without the hypothesis of the two recensions this section would have to be assigned to totally different, perhaps oral, sources. διαμερίζω is used once by Mark, and Matthew and Luke have both copied it from him in that connection. Neither Matthew nor Mark uses the word again; Luke uses it in five other places in his Gospel, including the section now under consideration. As he uses it but twice in Acts, it seems more likely to have been found in his source than to have been here inserted by him. This would tell strongly against the supposition that Matthew and Luke are here working over an identical source; in other words, it would remove this section from simple undifferentiated Q. Only the general character of the material, its close resemblance in meaning in the two Gospels, and its proximity in each Gospel to other Q material, can justify its assignment to QMt and QLk— and then, even, with uncertainty.

CONDITIONS OF DISCIPLESHIP
(Mt x, 37–39; Lk xiv, 26–27; xvii, 33)

Luke's statement is much stronger, and so presumably older, than Matthew's. Wellhausen says Matthew has been "refined out of Luke." In Matthew, the two sayings about taking up the cross, and about finding and losing one's life, follow each other; in Luke, at this place, they are separated by more than three chapters. But both Matthew and Luke give both of these sayings a second time, and the second time the two sayings are continuous in both, as they also are in Mark, from whom they are taken. The facts seem therefore to have been that Matthew and Luke each took both of these sayings from two sources; that in Mark the two sayings occurred together; that in Luke's recension of Q (at least), they were separated; that they were probably separated in Matthew's Q also, but he has combined them according to his habit, helped here by the recollection of the continuity of the two sayings in Mark. The substitution of "who seeks to find his soul" for the simpler form "who finds his soul" might easily be ascribed to Luke; it is in the interest of logicality. But it is quite unlike Luke to have added from oral tradition, or to have inserted from any other written source, so much matter of his own as is found in his vs. 26. The section is therefore assigned to QMt and QLk.

"HE THAT RECEIVETH YOU"
(Mt x, 40; Lk x, 16)

Luke has a doublet for this saying in Lk ix, 48, where the form is slightly more like Matthew's than at this point; but ix, 48, appears to be taken from Mark, with reminiscence of Q. The saying is also given twice in the Fourth Gospel, and with the saying just considered constitutes the total of sayings occurring in all four Gospels. Luke has taken the saying once from Mark and once from Q. Considering Matthew's partiality to doublets, the fact that he has the saying only önce might be taken to indicate its absence from his recension of Q. The saying may therefore be assigned to QLk.

THE QUESTION OF THE BAPTIST AND JESUS' ANSWER
(Mt xi, 2–19; Lk vii, 18–35)

With the exception of the introduction in Luke, this long section may safely be assigned to Q. The preceding narrative in Matthew has supplied a warrant for the statement of Jesus about his healings; Luke, not having led up to the conversation by a similar narrative, inserts the statement here that "in that hour he healed many sick," etc. After the introductions, the verbal resemblance is extremely close, considering the length of the section. Of one hundred and ninety-nine words in Matthew and two hundred and three in Luke, about one hundred and sixty-eight are identical.

THE WOE UPON THE GALILEAN CITIES
(Mt xi, 20–24; Lk x, 13–15)

This section is practically identical in both Gospels, except for Matthew's vs. 24 and the last half of vs. 23, which have no parallel in Luke. They are an elaboration upon the words that precede them, and may be ascribed to Matthew or an editor. The section may be assigned to Q.

"I THANK THEE, O FATHER"
(Mt xi, 25–27; Lk x, 21–22)

The introduction, again, has been supplied by each evangelist, tho it is not impossible that the introduction given in Matthew may have been taken from Q. After the introductions, twenty-nine consecutive words are identical. Again, after Luke's insertion of a few transitional words, the saying, "All things are given to me of my

Father," runs almost, tho not quite, word for word in the two Gospels. The connecting words in Luke would seem to indicate that these two sayings were not consecutive in Q. It is not necessary to have recourse to the recensions here.

JESUS' DEFENSE AGAINST THE PHARISEES
(Mt xii, 27–28; Lk xi, 19–20)

These verses occur in the midst of a narrative which Matthew and Luke have taken from Mark. Mark has no parallel for these verses, and the resemblance in Matthew and Luke is very close; the saying is in fact identical except for Luke's use of δακτύλῳ for Matthew's πνεύματι. The fact that in the succeeding verses Matthew follows Mark practically word for word, while Luke has a version entirely his own, may perhaps indicate that the narrative stood in both Mark and Q, Matthew having followed Mark thruout, except for the verses here considered, and Luke having followed chiefly Q, with an occasional deference to Mark. It may safely be assigned to Q.

"HE THAT IS NOT WITH ME"
(Mt xii, 30; Lk xi, 23)

A statement the exact reverse of this occurs in Mk ix, 40, in a different context. The words here are identical in the two Gospels, the order also being the same. It stood in Q.

JONAH AND THE NINEVITES
(Mt xii, 38–42; Lk xi, 29–32)

Each evangelist has supplied his own introduction. Matthew's vs. 40 is probably an interpolation, or at least a late addition. Beginning with Matthew's vs. 41 and Luke's vs. 32 (the order of Luke's verses has been reversed, perhaps by error of a scribe, since no motive appears for the change), there are fifty-three words in Matthew, fifty-five in Luke, and fifty-three of them are identical. The verses are therefore universally assigned to Q.

A SPEECH ABOUT BACKSLIDING
(Mt xii, 43–45; Lk xi, 24–26)

The correspondence here also is very close; out of sixty-two words in Matthew and fifty-five in Luke, fifty-four are identical. Matthew's surplus of eight words is accounted for by the addition of a clause not found in Luke, and probably a later addition in Matthew; it does not disturb the practical identity thruout the rest of the saying. It evidently stood in Q.

"BLESSED ARE THE EYES THAT SEE"
(Mt xiii, 16–17; Lk x, 23–24)

Luke has supplied his own introduction. Matthew has, as parallel to "the eyes that see," "the ears that hear." This may be a later addition in Matthew; or Luke, not caring so much for the Aramaic parallelism as Matthew does, may have omitted it. Luke has "kings" where Matthew has "righteous men"; δίκαιος is a favorite word with Matthew; on the other hand, Luke's use of "kings" may indicate an apologetic intention upon Luke's part. The saying may be assigned to Q, and the variations charged jointly to Matthew and Luke.

THE PARABLE OF THE YEAST
(Mt xiii, 33; Lk xiii, 20–21)

The introductions in the two Gospels are slightly different. After these, fourteen consecutive words are alike, the only deviation being Matthew's use (as always) of τῶν οὐρανῶν where Luke has τοῦ θεοῦ. The parable stood in Q.

THE BLIND LEADING THE BLIND
(Mt xv, 14; Lk vi, 39)

This is another instance of a saying which occurs in Luke's Sermon on the Plain but outside of Matthew's Sermon on the Mount. Matthew has apparently inserted it in the midst of a discourse against the Pharisees, the rest of which he has taken from Mark. The sayings in Matthew and Luke are not identical. If the saying stood in Q, and Matthew removed it from its Lucan connection to its present position in his Gospel, this was certainly a very unusual procedure with him. The saying is given as a "parable" in Luke, and has the brevity of the parables that were given in Q, tho not their usual reference to the kingdom of God. It is hard to think of Matthew, with his fondness for these brief parables, deliberately omitting to call the saying by this name when it was so called in his source. On the whole, however, it seems best to assign the saying to Q, and to charge Matthew with its displacement.

A SAYING ABOUT FAITH
(Mt xvii, 20; Lk xvii, 6)

The parallel here is not close. But Matthew has a doublet in xxi, 21, and Mark a similar saying in xi, 22. The saying seems therefore to have been in both Mark and Q, and was taken by Matthew from both sources and by Luke from one. The connection of the saying in Luke indicates that he took it from Q; yet his saying is not the same as Matthew's, in that he substitutes a sycamore tree for Matthew's mountain, thus greatly weakening the comparison. The two sayings certainly cannot have been derived by Matthew and Luke from an identical source. It is only on the ground of their general logian character that they can be assigned to QMt and QLk.

A SAYING ABOUT OFFENSES
(Mt xviii, 7; Lk xvii, 1)

The comparison here is complicated by the fact that this saying apparently stood in both Mark and Q. It is closely, but in reverse order by the two later evangelists, connected with a saying taken from Mark. It may be assigned to Q.

THE STRAY SHEEP
(Mt xviii, 12–14; Lk xv, 4–7)

There seems here to be little or no literary relationship. The two passages appear to be rather different versions of the same parable, which have come down thru different channels. If it be assumed that Matthew's version is from Q, there is not enough literary agreement between it and Luke's to prove the latter to be from any recension of that document. Considering the larger content of Matthew's recension, and his apparently greater unwillingness to make omissions from it, it might be safe to assign this to QMt, but to leave Luke's source for his version unspecified. At the same time it is well to remember that the parables stand apparently half-way between the narratives and the sayings, as regards the willingness of the evangelists to deviate from the wording found before them. If enough may be allowed for this difference between parables and sayings, the divergence between the two Gospels in this section might not be considered too great to be accounted for by the known habits of Matthew and Luke, working on different recensions of an original Q; and so the passage might be assigned to QMt and QLk—but certainly not with any confidence.

ABOUT FORGIVENESS
(Mt xviii, 21–22; Lk xvii, 4)

These might be considered merely as variants of the same original saying. If the reference to Peter be taken, like some of the other references to him in Matthew, to be later than the saying itself, the insertion of this reference in Matthew, whether by Matthew or his source, may have changed the form of the saying from its original as preserved in Luke. But the very slight verbal agreement makes any specification of a common literary source hazardous.

REWARDS FOR DISCIPLESHIP
(Mt xix, 28; Lk xxii, 28–30)

The first part of this section varies greatly between Matthew and Luke; with strong similarity in idea, there is practically no verbal agreement. The last ten words are almost identical. Matthew inserts the section into a speech the rest of which is taken from Mark. Luke takes the same speech from Mark, without making this insertion. The verses occur with him in quite another context. His vs. 30a is more primary than anything in Matthew's version. The first part of the section contains too little agreement to have been worked out of an identical source; the last part agrees so closely as to indicate an ultimate common source. We therefore assign the section to QMt and QLk.

AGAINST THE PHARISEES
(Mt xxiii, 4; Lk xi, 46)

The agreement is slight, but somewhat significant. $\phi o \rho \tau i o \nu$ is used only thrice in the New Testament outside of this passage. This is the chief linguistic warrant for assigning the passage to QMt and QLk.

"WHOSO HUMBLES HIMSELF"
(Mt xxiii, 12; Lk xiv, 11)

This proverbial saying is used by Luke in this instance as the conclusion of a speech about taking the chief seats at a feast. He also uses it in xviii, 14, as the conclusion to his parable of the Publican and the Pharisee in the temple. Matthew also uses it in two very different contexts; here as part of a speech against the Pharisees, and in xviii, 4, with reference to a child as type of true greatness. Considering these various usages, the brevity of the saying, and its apparently proverbial character, it can scarcely be assigned to any form of Q, tho it certainly cannot be proved not to have been in that document.

AGAINST THE PHARISEES
(Mt xxiii, 13; Lk xi, 52)

It is possible to regard these rather as variants of the same saying than as workings over of the same source. Even in the divergences, however, some striking resemblances are to be noted. Matthew says κλείετε τὴν βασιλείαν; Luke says ἤρατε τὴν κλεῖδα. These words seem to betray a common literary source in the background. The idea conveyed by the two phrases is the same. Matthew says, "Ye shut up the kingdom of heaven before men"; Luke says, "Ye take away the key of knowledge" (of salvation, probably, as in Lk i, 77). The last part of the saying is still more unmistakably based upon an ultimate common source. Yet, as I have so often argued with reference to other and similar sections, to ascribe to either Matthew or Luke, working upon an identical source, the amount of re-working here involved, credits them with a degree of freedom in the treatment of Jesus' sayings which finds no parallel in their treatment of such sayings as they take them from the Gospel of Mark. We therefore assign the section to QMt and QLk. But such assignment cannot be insisted upon.

AGAINST THE PHARISEES
(Mt xxiii, 23–26; Lk xi, 39–42)

There is thruout this section a varying degree of verbal agreement. The sections are very differently placed, Matthew putting them among the Jerusalem sayings, Luke early in the ministry. What is conclusive evidence for some form of Q, indeed for the two recensions, is the translation variant in vss. 26 and 41.[1] The section is thus not merely assigned, but we may say is demonstrated to belong, to QMt and QLk.

A WOE UPON THE SCRIBES
(Mt xxiii, 29–31; Lk xi, 47–48)

There is so little verbal agreement here as to raise the question whether we have not merely two different traditions of the same saying. What inclines us to cling to the assignment to QMt and QLk is the fact that these words are preceded and followed in both Gospels by passages which have much more close verbal agreement with each other than is found in this section. The verses are assigned to Q by all five of the investigators quoted at the beginning of this chapter. But anyone who will compare the slight verbal agreement thruout these verses with the verbal identity shown in other passages assigned to Q will wonder why these scholars have not availed themselves of the hypothesis of the two recensions. For upon the basis of their treatment of other passages, both

---

[1] See the treatment of this passage on p. 124.

from Q and from Mark, the divergences in this passage are altogether too great to be assigned directly to Matthew or Luke.

"I SEND UNTO YOU PROPHETS"
(Mt xxiii, 34–36; Lk xi, 49–51)

The assignment of this section to simple Q, and the ascription of all divergences to one or the other of the evangelists, would be easier if it could be shown that either evangelist shows a uniform tendency in the divergences. But such is not the case. Luke seems more primary, and nearer to the source, when he quotes the words of the passage from "The Wisdom of God"; for no evangelist, finding the words ascribed to Jesus in his source, would take them away from him and ascribe them to anyone else. But Matthew, or his source, may merely have interpreted the words "The Wisdom of God" to refer to Jesus. Luke is later than Matthew, where he substitutes "apostles" for Matthew's "scribes"; but Matthew is secondary to Luke where he has σταυρώσετε, in apparent reminiscence of the death of Jesus. He is also secondary in his vs. 34, which seems to reflect the persecutions of the Christians. But Luke again is secondary in omitting Matthew's mistaken identification of Zachariah as the son of Barachiah. The use of verbs in the second person in Luke and in the third person in Matthew is accounted for by the quotation in the one Gospel and the direct address in the other. ἐπὶ τῆς γῆς and ἀπὸ καταβολῆς κόσμου may be translation variants. Careful comparison of the verbal similarities indicates unmistakably a common literary source lying in the background; but a source much worked over before reaching Matthew and Luke.

THE LAMENT OVER JERUSALEM
(Mt xxiii, 37–39; Lk xiii, 34–35)

Tho placed so differently by Matthew and Luke, this section has the greatest verbal agreement. Out of fifty-six words in Matthew and fifty-three in Luke, fifty are identical. Luke omits the repetition of one verb, omits "desolate" and substitutes two particles of his own for four of Matthew's. Harnack's explanation of Luke's omission of "desolate"[1] on the ground that the meaning is the same without it does not seem conclusive. It is better to assume that it was added by Matthew in deference to Jer xxii, 5. The wording of the section shows so little deviation between the two Gospels that it may be assigned simply to Q.

THE DAY OF THE SON OF MAN
(Mt xxiv, 26–27; Lk xvii, 23–24)

There is slight verbal resemblance here, but enough to indicate unmistakably a literary relationship. QMt and QLk are much more likely than simple Q.

THE BODY AND THE EAGLES
(Mt xxiv, 28; Lk xvii, 37)

In Matthew, but not in Luke, these words form the conclusion to the words just considered. The substitution of σῶμα for πτῶμα sounds like an oral variation; but it may be Luke's way of avoiding a word which he nowhere uses. The wording is otherwise so close as to warrant assignment to simple Q.

THE DAYS OF NOAH
(Mt xxiv, 37–39; Lk xvii, 26–27)

Luke, or his recension of Q, says here, as elsewhere, "the days of the Son of man," where Matthew says "the

---

[1] See his *Sayings of Jesus*, pp. 30–31.

parousia of the Son of man." The reason for this deviation is not obvious, unless the variation was in the source. We therefore assign the passage to the two recensions.

THE ONE TAKEN, THE OTHER LEFT
(Mt xxiv, 40–41; Lk xvii, 34–35)

In Matthew, but not in Luke, these words are immediately connected with those just discussed. Luke, or his source, wishes to indicate that the parousia may be in the night, and so adds the words $\nu\upsilon\kappa\tau\grave{\iota}$ and $\kappa\lambda\acute{\iota}\nu\eta s$. But the arrangement of the verses is in the same order in both Gospels, and there is strong similarity, especially in vss. 41 and 35. We consider assignment to QMt and QLk to account most nearly for all the facts.

THE WATCHING SERVANT
(Mt xxiv, 43–44; Lk xii, 39–40)

The verbal coincidence here is great. The last fourteen words are exactly alike in both Gospels, even to their order. It should be assigned to simple Q.

THE TRUE AND FALSE SERVANT
(Mt xxiv, 45–51; Lk xii, 42–46)

The connection of these sections with the one just considered is the same in both Gospels. The verbal agreement is equally striking. Out of one hundred and ten words in Matthew and one hundred and two in Luke, eighty-two are identical; twenty-six of these occur consecutively and with no deviation in order. The section may be assigned to Q.

RESULTS OF THE PRECEDING INVESTIGATION

This investigation yields about one hundred and ninety Q verses (in some instances only parts of verses) in Matthew, paralleled by about one hundred and eighty Q verses in Luke. The difference in the number of verses has no significance, being due chiefly to the verses not being similarly divided in the two Gospels. Of this total, ninety-eight in Matthew and ninety-four in Luke are ascribed simply to Q. This does not mean, as has been said before, that Matthew and Luke both had a document Q, and in addition Matthew had a document QMt and Luke another document QLk; but merely that Matthew and Luke had two recensions of Q, each of which had passed thru a history of its own, and had become in many ways differentiated from the other; and that in certain parts of each recension such differentiation had not occurred, so that these sections of the two recensions may still be referred to under the symbol Q. Of the two recensions, therefore, so far as these reappear in parallels in Matthew and Luke, about half in each differs so widely from the same half in the other that it is altogether unreasonable to attribute the difference to either or both of the evangelists.

If it be asked, why we should attempt to attribute to any form of Q this material which is too seriously dissimilar to have been drawn directly by the evangelists from an identical source—why we do not simply assign this to totally separate sources, and restrict Q to the sections which are practically identical in the two Gospels—the answer is: this material in the two gospels seems to betray not merely an oral but a literary affinity; it is of the same general character as that which is assigned directly to Q; and almost without exception, in one gospel or the other or in both, it is inextricably mingled with this.

Thruout this discussion the distinction between narrative material and sayings-material, and the difference in treatment accorded to these two kinds of material by Matthew and Luke, must be constantly borne in mind. The amount of literary divergence that may be fairly assigned to the initiative of Matthew or Luke in their use of a document of sayings is hard to define. But Sir John Hawkins is surely wrong when he says[1] that Matthew and Luke need not be expected to adhere more closely to Q than they do to Mark. For in the sayings of Jesus which they find in Mark, Matthew and Luke do generally adhere very closely. It is in the narrative portions of Mark that they permit themselves liberties. But there is little or no narrative in Q; the only certain instance of narrative being that of the healing of the centurion's son; and in this instance it is significant that the deviations between Matthew and Luke are in the narrative and not in the logian portions. Speaking of each document as a whole, it should be clear that Q would be followed with very much greater fidelity than Mark by both Matthew and Luke.

Now the translation variants are proof positive of two Greek translations of the original Aramaic Q, these two translations having been made from two texts of the original which betray some divergences or corruptions. Tho these two Greek translations were thus made from two Aramaic copies, nevertheless in about half of the matter which Matthew and Luke agree in taking from these translations no substantial differences had crept in; but half, also, shows deviations too great to be ascribed to Matthew and Luke. If all the matter common to Matthew and Luke were identical, or nearly so, no need would arise for QMt and QLk. If it were all as dissimilar as half of it is, no place would be left for Q of any sort.

[1] *Oxford Studies in the Synoptic Problem*, p. 109.

The distinction between Matthew's and Luke's recensions of Q best accounts alike for the agreements and the divergences.

In the preceding examination the number of Q (including QMt and QLk) verses ascribed to Matthew and Luke respectively is substantially the same as the number ascribed to them by Harnack and Hawkins in Tables II and III (pp. 110–11 and 116–17). This agreement merely indicates that Harnack and Hawkins have confined their Q material pretty closely to the sections which show the greatest verbal agreement. The difference between the position reached in these pages and that reached by Harnack and Hawkins is that the present writer feels that those two scholars cannot be justified in ascribing such wide divergences to the literary activity of the evangelists themselves, and that they have hampered themselves by not taking advantage of the fact of the recensions, as guaranteed to us by the translation variants.

CHAPTER III

Q IN THE SINGLE TRADITION OF MATTHEW (QMt)

Thus far, examination has been made of only such material as is somewhat closely duplicated in Matthew and Luke. Examination will now be made of the sayings that are found in Matthew, unduplicated in Luke, to see whether any of these may also be assigned, with any great probability, to Q. In this unduplicated material no data are at hand for distinguishing QMt from simple Q; but since QMt is the symbol for the copy of Q used by Matthew, that symbol will be employed here instead of Q.

The criteria for distinguishing Q material in Matthew unduplicated by Luke are the general character of the material, chiefly its eschatological use of the phrase "the kingdom of heaven," its Jewish coloring, its antipathy to the Pharisees, the absence of indications of Matthean invention, and the proximity to and connection with other material heretofore attributed to Q or QMt. This last item is not so important in Matthew, on account of his habit of transposing his Q material; yet within limits it is a valuable criterion.

Examination will be made of all passages in which there is reason to suspect the possible presence of Q material. This having been done in the case of the Gospel of Matthew, a similar examination will be made of the Gospel of Luke. The results of these two examinations will give us data for the comparison of Q as used by Matthew and Q as used by Luke. We shall then be able to say whether the differences between what we have called QMt and what we have called QLk are too great for the assumption that they are different recensions of the same ground-document. Matter already assigned to Q (or QMt or QLk) will not be examined again. As the sayings reported in each Gospel are examined, in cases where the material is rejected from QMt or QLk, suggestions will be made as to possible or probable sources.

TWO BEATITUDES
(Mt v, 4-5)

Many manuscripts invert the order of these beatitudes. Vs. 4a is a quotation from Ps xxxvii, 11. Vs. 5 sounds like a reminiscence of Ps cxxvi, 5, and Isa lxi, 2. The tendency to apply prophecy to Jesus is especially strong in Matthew; but whether this should be charged to him or his source remains to be determined. The משח of the Hebrew, or the ἔχρισεν of the Greek, of Isa lxi, 1, would forcibly suggest such application in this case. Of the Judaistic and the universalistic tendencies found side by side in Matthew it is probable that the Judaistic are earlier, and therefore that they belonged in the source; the universalistic, naturally assumed to be later, will be more easily attributed to Matthew. Aside from this it is hardly to be assumed that Matthew invented any beatitudes on his own account. From both these considerations it is reasonable to conclude that these two beatitudes were added to Q before it reached Matthew.

FOUR MORE BEATITUDES
(Mt v, 7-10)

For vs. 7 there is no close Old Testament exemplar, tho Joel ii, 13, has been suggested. The suggestion is the more plausible since the same verse would also have served as an indirect source of the next beatitude in vs. 8. There is no reason for crediting Matthew with the manufacture of either of these beatitudes. Vs. 8 may be reminiscent of Ps xxiv, 4; li, 10; lxxiii, 1, as well as of the verse in Joel. "They shall see God" is probably used here in an eschatological sense. An expression combining the ideas and in part the wording of vss. 8 and 9 is found in Heb xii, 14: Εἰρήνην διώκετε . . . . οὗ χωρὶς οὐδεὶς ὄψεται τὸν κύριον. If this is not a reminiscence of these beatitudes in Matthew, it at least embodies a similar tradition. The δικαιοσύνης of vs. 10 is peculiar to Matthew among the Gospels. From its Judaistic coloring it is to be ascribed to Matthew's Q rather than to the evangelist himself. If I Peter iii, 14, be allowed to be a direct reference to this beatitude, this will heighten the probability that all these beatitudes were added to Q before its use by Matthew. It is not impossible that Matthew found in Q only the beatitudes now standing in Luke, and that he added these others (also making correction in those now duplicated in Luke), not inventing these himself, but possibly taking them from an oral tradition, or from a separate written source. But this theory seems to the writer to be much more complicated and less probable than the one here advocated. It is quite out of the question that Luke should have found these six beatitudes in his Q and should have omitted them. Yet the beatitudes common to Matthew and Luke are by all scholars attributed to Q. Harnack is undoubtedly correct in saying, "The beatitudes certainly circulated in various recensions from the beginning."[1] The process of alteration and accretion would begin long before the days of Matthew.

[1] *Sayings of Jesus*, p. 52.

Q IN SINGLE TRADITION OF MATTHEW 169

"YE ARE THE LIGHT OF THE WORLD"
(Mt v, 14)

In the Johannine tradition this saying has become "I am the light of the world." Like the saying, "Ye are the salt of the earth" (in Mt v, 13), it emphasizes, as against Luke's version, the direct address of the beatitudes and the conjoined sayings to the disciples. It probably stood in Matthew's Q.

"LET YOUR LIGHT SHINE"
(Mt v, 16)

The intervening vs. 15 is found in Luke. With that verse omitted, the connection between vss. 14 and 16 is improved. I Peter ii, 12, is a reminiscence, or almost a direct quotation, of vs. 16. Of vss. 13a, 14, and 16 it should be observed that, while they are unduplicated in Luke, they change the character of all the words in their context from the character which those words have, so far as they are duplicated, in Luke; for they make of them no longer general remarks, but words of extremely earnest exhortation addressed directly to the disciples. It is extremely unlikely that Matthew should have found the sayings in Q as mere general remarks, and should himself have given them this character of pointed exhortation by inserting the words, "Ye are the salt of the earth," "Ye are the light of the world," etc. But it is equally improbable that Luke should have found these pointed words in his recension of Q, and should by their omission have degraded the sayings to the rank of mere general observations. The best way to save these sayings for Q is by the hypothesis of the recensions.

VARIOUS SAYINGS FROM THE SERMON ON THE MOUNT
(Mt v, 17, 19-24, 27-28)

Concerning the section v, 17-48, Hawkins says, "I would place this section by itself as one which we may regard as more likely to have formed part of Q than any other which is to be found in a single Gospel."[1] Yet it is to be noted that in the section of which Hawkins makes this statement there are eleven verses (vss. 18, 25, 26, 32, 39, 40, 42, 44-47) which are not "found in a single Gospel," but which have very close parallels in Luke, and would on this latter consideration be assigned to Q. This fact heightens the probability that the unduplicated verses should also be assigned to some form of that document. Only those verses are considered here which have no parallel in Luke.

Thruout these verses there is a strong Judaistic coloring. They may be compared in this respect with such other New Testament passages as Rom iii, 31; x, 4; Jas ii, 10; II Pet ii, 14. The words, "till heaven and earth pass away" at the beginning of vs. 18 do not quite agree with the words "until all things be fulfilled" at the end of the verse; the latter words have been suggested by Schmiedel as being a gloss. If, with the two verses that follow them, they be not such a gloss, they are, says Schmiedel,[2] not from the final editor, who does not care for Jewish legalism, but from some earlier editor. In other words, universally attributed as the section is to Q, these words were not in Luke's version of that document, and it is inconceivable that Matthew should have added them. They are part of the accretion that took place in Matthew's recension of Q before it reached Matthew. Harnack, however, main-

[1] *Oxford Studies*, p. 133.
[2] *Encyclopedia Biblica*, Vol. II, col. 1864.

tains that there is no inconsistency in attributing the words to Jesus himself. Vs. 20 illustrates the unchronological placing of the sayings, since it implies that the break with the pharisees has already occurred. In vss. 21 and 22 is the word ἔνοχος, occurring four times; Matthew uses it in one other passage where he has taken it from Mark, who uses it twice; but Luke consistently avoids it, both in his Gospel and in Acts. Unchronological in their setting are also the words in vss. 23–24; they were evidently spoken in Jerusalem, not in Galilee. They would not have been added from an oral tradition, much less invented, in times as late as those of the final editor of the Gospel.

A SAYING ABOUT OFFENSES
(Mt v, 29–30)

For this saying there is a doublet in Mt xviii, 8–9, taken from Mk ix, 43–48. Mark may in this passage also have been following Q. That this saying should have been absent from Luke's recension of Q, while present in that of both Matthew and Mark, and that it should also, as Dr. Stanton maintains, have been absent from Luke's copy of Mark, seems rather too much of a coincidence. But the saying is like several others which Luke omits because of their strong tincture of asceticism, or because the instructions in them might be understood in too literal a way. Whether it was or was not in Luke's recension of Q, its character and connection seem to indicate its presence in Matthew's recension of that document.

THE COMMANDMENT ABOUT DIVORCE
(Mt v, 31)

Like vss. 21, 27, 33, 38, and 43 of this same chapter, this verse quotes an Old Testament commandment, as introductory to the teaching of Jesus upon the subject of that command. Since much of the teaching of Jesus upon these items is duplicated in Luke, but this quotation of the Old Testament commandment is omitted by him each time, the quotation will be ascribed either to Matthew or his source. The fact that it is his source, and not the final editor (who for convenience is all along here called Matthew), who is responsible for the Judaistic coloring of the Gospel, the universalistic tendency being attributed to Matthew, inclines us to assign all these verses in quotation of the commandments to QMt.

ABOUT OATHS
(Mt v, 33–37)

This passage has also a strong Judaistic coloring. It is reminiscent of Ps xlviii, 3. Most students assign it simply to Q. If it stood in Luke's recension of that document, the same non-Jewish bias which is observable in many of his omissions of Marcan material would account for his omission of the saying. It is neither possible nor necessary to prove that these verses were not in Luke's recension. But considering their character and their context, it is much more likely that Matthew took them from his recension of Q than from any other source known to us.

THE SECOND MILE
(Mt v, 41)

This sounds like a secondary accretion. It adds little or nothing to the force of the injunction, and rather interrupts the connection between vss. 40 and 42. It may have been added by Matthew from some source of his own; but more probably stood in Matthew's Q.

Q IN SINGLE TRADITION OF MATTHEW

ANOTHER OLD TESTAMENT COMMANDMENT
(Mt v, 43)

In this verse and the five others which quote the commandments, the word ἐρρέθη occurs; it is not used by Mark or Luke, and by Matthew is used only in these verses. So far as this may be said to throw any light upon the origin of these verses, it would indicate their presence in Matthew's recension of Q, rather than their invention or addition by Matthew.

ABOUT ALMS-GIVING
(Mt vi, 1-4)

Dr. Robinson, in his *Study of the Gospels*,[1] maintains, quite correctly, that Matthew's chap. vi breaks the connection in his Sermon on the Mount. If it is omitted, the connection is not only better, but is the same as that of Luke's in his Sermon on the Plain. He also considers that Mt vi, 7-15, breaks the connection between the verses that immediately precede and immediately follow them. He therefore concludes that Mt vi, 1-5, 16-18, at one time had a separate existence of its own. This is not impossible. The disarrangement by the insertion of chap. vi is indeed obvious. Bacon, in his *Sermon on the Mount*, and Votaw, in his article under the same title in Hastings' *Dictionary of the Bible*, bring out the same composite character of the Sermon as Matthew has it. But much of this material which Matthew has inserted in his Sermon on the Mount is duplicated word for word in other connections in Luke, and so is uniformly accredited to Q. This creates a presumption that the rest of this interpolated material, especially where it is obviously homogeneous in character with the Q material generally,

[1] P. 78.

was taken by Matthew from his recension of Q. It is not contended that none of this material which Matthew has here inserted and which is nowhere duplicated in Luke was in Luke's recension; it is only contended that since Matthew's recension and Luke's recension are demonstrated to have been different from each other in certain passages, it is fair to press the argument from this difference to its reasonable limit, and assume that much if not most of this logian matter peculiar to Matthew stood before him in his source. In the case of the verses now before us, however, it seems extremely improbable that Luke with his interest in alms-giving (see Lk xi, 41; xii, 33) should have found them in his source and have omitted them.

ABOUT PRAYER

(Mt vi, 5–8)

This sounds like a "midrash" on the Lord's Prayer. There are several Matthean words in the passage. Μισθός is used ten times by Matthew as against once by Mark and thrice in Luke's Gospel. Βατταλογέω is found here only in the New Testament, and not in the Septuagint. Πολυλογία is found here only in the New Testament. Εἰσακούω is an infrequent word in the New Testament, being used only in this passage, in Luke's chap. i, once in Acts, and twice in the Epistles. Ἀποδίδωμι is used eighteen times by Matthew; seven of these uses are found in the section xviii, 25–34, and three in the unduplicated verses vi, 4, 6, 18. It is used once by Mark and eight times by Luke in his Gospel. These facts are hardly enough to establish any verdict as to the origin of the section now in question, tho they would rather look toward Matthew's derivation of it, with its corresponding sections vi, 1–4, and vi, 16–18, from some written source. Such being the case, Matthew's recension of Q will certainly fit the requirements better than any other known document.

ABOUT FASTING
(Mt vi, 16-18)

If the Lord's Prayer, which Luke gives in another and better connection, be omitted from Matthew's chap. vi, we shall have here three consecutive sections which have very striking literary resemblances; they are the sections on alms-giving, on prayer, and on fasting. That these should have found no echo in the Gospel of Luke, if they stood in his source, is strange; especially considering his peculiar interest in alms-giving and prayer. As to the literary affinities among these three sections, the use of μισθός, four times, has been noted. The phrase ἀπέχουσιν τὸν μισθὸν αὐτῶν occurs three times; the longer phrase ἐν τῷ κρυπτῷ, καὶ ὁ πατήρ σου ὁ βλέπων ἐν τῷ κρυπτῷ ἀποδώσει σοι, three times.[1] Quite without these recurrences of the same formulae, the form and sentiment of the three sections are so markedly the same as to suggest that they were originally consecutive, and that they have been taken from one written source. No more probable source can be suggested than QMt.

PEARLS BEFORE SWINE
(Mt vii, 6)

Schmiedel has suggested that this fragment may "indicate a time when the eucharist had been so long celebrated as materially to influence the general tradition of the doctrines of Jesus." A passage somewhat similar in tone is that occurring in the story of the Canaanitish

[1] Κρυφαίῳ is in vs. 18 substituted for κρυπτῷ used in 4 and 6.

woman: "it is not proper to take the bread of the children and give it to the dogs." Matthew takes this story from Mark; but, significantly, he has omitted one sentence of Mark's which tones down the Jewish particularism of the passage, "let the children first be fed." He also inserts in that story the sentence, not in Mark, "I am not sent except to the lost sheep of the house of Israel," which corresponds somewhat closely with this statement concerning the command of Jesus to his disciples, also peculiar to Matthew, "Into the way of the nations do not go, and into a city of the Samaritans do not enter; but go rather to the lost sheep of the house of Israel." It is only fair to admit that these instances, in which Matthew heightens, once by insertion and once by omission, the Jewish coloring in a story taken from Mark, tell against the theory generally advocated by the writer, that the Judaistic features of Matthew's Gospel are referable to his source, and the universalistic features to Matthew himself. But, on the other hand, this vs. 6 has no discernible connection in its present context, and no reason suggests itself for Matthew's insertion of it, except his desire to retain what was in his source. This source may have been a special one, perhaps even an oral one; but considering the Judaistic character of so many sayings attributed to Matthew's Q, that recension would also fit this saying.

THE FALSE PROPHETS
(Mt vii, 15)

The mention of "the" false prophets, as a class to be avoided, has a late sound. It is not found elsewhere in the Gospels except in the "little apocalypse" and in Luke vi, 26. It is not necessarily as late as Matthew, and may fairly be assigned to his recension of Q.

A SAYING ABOUT TREES
(Mt vii, 19)

In an earlier place this saying is attributed by both Matthew and Luke to John the Baptist. In that earlier connection it evidently was taken from Q. It probably did not occur twice in that document, but was inserted here by Matthew from memory, being suggested naturally by the context. It offers no new Q material.

"BY THEIR FRUITS"
(Mt vii, 20)

This verse is a repetition, with the particle ἄραγε prefixed, of vs. 16. Vs. 18 is also a repetition in the form of a declarative sentence of what is said in vs. 17 in the form of a question. The whole speech is considerably longer than the corresponding speech in Lk vi, 43–44. These repetitions and duplications suggest a good deal of reworking; but not the sort of re-working that would be done by Matthew, whose tendency is to condense instead of to expand. Vs. 20 may be a gloss, tho I am not aware of any manuscript authority against it. There is no new Q material here.

AN OFT-REPEATED FORMULA
(Mt vii, 28a)

This formula must be considered, as it is also found in five other places in Matthew (xi, 1; xiii, 53; xix, 1; xxvi, 1). The first six words of the formula are precisely alike in all five instances, καὶ ἐγένετο ὅτε ἐτέλεσεν ὁ Ἰησοῦς. In two instances these words are followed by the words τοὺς λόγους τούτους; in one instance by the words πάντας τοὺς λόγους τούτους; in another instance by the words τὰς παραβολὰς ταύτας. In these four instances the formula not only follows a group of sayings, but is followed by a narrative section; and so apparently marks the transition from one of Matthew's sources to another. In the fifth instance, however, the closing words of the formula are διατάσσων τοῖς δώδεκα μαθηταῖς αὐτοῦ; and in this instance the formula does not mark a transition from Q to Mark, but is followed as it is preceded by Q material. It is generally argued that since the formula does not occur in either Mark or Luke, and since the construction ἐγένετο ὅτε does not occur in Matthew outside of these five passages, but is found twenty-two times in Luke, the formula was each time taken by Matthew from his source. This source must have been Matthew's recension of Q, since the formula is always found with Q material. Considering Matthew's tendency to repeat himself, all that need be affirmed is that in at least one of the five instances Matthew did find the formula in Q. It certainly could not have occurred five times, or even three or four times, in Luke's source, and have been each time omitted by him.

THE CONCLUSION OF THE STORY OF THE CENTURION'S SERVANT
(Mt viii, 13)

Harnack thinks this verse of Matthew's and the corresponding verse in Luke (Lk vii, 10) were not in Q, tho the rest of the story was. But the deviation here is no greater than it is in the earlier part of the story, in the item of the messengers. Matthew has separated this conclusion of the story from the body of it by his insertion of Jesus' saying, "Many shall come from the east and west," which Luke gives in another context (Lk xiii, 28–29). Luke's conclusion evidently belongs with his version of the story, for it contains the reference to the messengers who do not appear in Matthew's version. Some manuscripts give the conclusion to the story in Matthew in words almost identical with Luke's. If this deviation in manuscripts suggests that the verse in Matthew may be a gloss, this suggestion may be held to be strengthened by the assumption that if Matthew himself had inserted this concluding verse he would hardly have cut it off from the rest of the story by the saying "Many shall come," etc. Chiefly on the ground of the alternative reading in ℵ, and the ease with which a gloss would be suggested to a scribe who had the Lucan narrative also before him, the writer inclines to the opinion that the verse is a later addition.

"I WILL HAVE MERCY AND NOT SACRIFICE"
(Mt ix, 13)

There is a duplicate of this quotation in Mt xii, 7. In each instance Matthew has inserted the quotation into a Marcan narrative. Considering the fact of this insertion in each case, and the absence of a duplicate in Luke, the verses may be ascribed to Matthew, perhaps upon the basis of an oral tradition.

THE HEALING OF TWO BLIND MEN
(Mt ix, 27–31)

There is a strong similarity between this story and the story of the healing of two blind men near Jericho (Mt xx, 29–34). In the latter case Matthew substitutes the two men for Bartimaeus in the story of Mark and Luke. The source is apparently a special one, perhaps an oral tradition influenced by Mk x, 46–52.

THE HEALING OF A DUMB MAN
(Mt ix, 32–34)

Vs. 34 is a doublet of Mt xii, 24; the latter is from Mk iii, 22, where Mark also appears to be following Q. Perhaps ix, 27–34, has been inserted at just this place, in order to warrant the statement of Jesus to John the Baptist that "the blind see and the deaf hear." It is hardly necessary to assign it to a special literary source.

INSTRUCTIONS TO THE DISCIPLES
(Mt x, 5–8)

These verses have a strong Judaistic coloring: "Into a way of the Gentiles do not go, and into a city of the Samaritans do not enter," etc. They also betray the expectation of the early coming of the parousia. These two items are inconsistent with the invention of these verses by Matthew. They must have arisen long before Matthew's time. Yet they are imbedded in Q material. No theory of their origin suits all these facts so well as that they are a portion of the Q material which was added to that document after its original compilation, and in the recension that was finally used by Matthew. It is interesting to observe that Matthew here makes Jesus teach his disciples (vs. 7) the same formula which he himself had learned from John the Baptist.

FURTHER INSTRUCTIONS TO THE DISCIPLES
(Mt x, 16b–25, 41–42)

Of the chapter in which this section occurs Mr. Streeter says that Matthew begins with Mark, adds some Q material parallel to Luke's Q material in the same connection, then Q material unparalleled, then Q material paralleled in other connections in Luke, then material from a totally different part of Mark.[1] The verses enumerated here are not paralleled in either Mark or Luke. They are not like the verses, for the most part, which Matthew and Luke agree in taking from Q; and they show marked difference in some respects from those which we have thus far assigned to Matthew's recension of Q. In his *Apostolic Age* Professor James Hardy Ropes[2] suggests that at least one purpose of the collection of Jesus' sayings was "to furnish a kind of handbook of missionary practice for those times." These verses, better almost than any other section out of the instructions to the disciples, answer this purpose. If they rest upon words of Jesus spoken at the time he sent out his disciples, they are at least colored by the needs of Christian missionaries who went out toward the end of the apostolic age. They betray the conviction that the time of the parousia is near. As coming from Jesus they contain a prediction so obviously unfulfilled as to make their later invention and ascription to him very difficult. On the other hand no words ascribed to him would by themselves more easily originate in the times of the early Christian missions. Considering their position here, and giving due weight to Professor Ropes's suggestion, it seems much more probable that they are taken by Matthew from some written source than from an oral tradition. If so, no better source can be posited than Matthew's recension of Q.

A SAYING ABOUT ELIJAH
(Mt xi, 14)

Like the reference to Elijah in Mk ix, 12, this verse sounds like a parenthesis. It adds nothing to the context, and rather interrupts than furthers the matter.

[1] *Oxford Studies in the Synoptic Problem*, p. 149.
[2] Pp. 40–42.

If not inserted by Matthew from some unknown, perhaps oral, source, it may perhaps best be considered as a gloss.

"HE THAT HATH EARS, LET HIM HEAR"
(Mt xi, 15)

This is a proverbial saying occurring seven times in the Gospels (eight times in the received text); three times in Matthew, twice each in Mark and Luke. It also occurs eight times in the Apocalypse. Each evangelist has a form of his own, to which he adheres thruout. The saying sounds here as if it were intended to drive home what has just been said about Elijah, and may with propriety be assigned to the same hand as the preceding verse.

THE OCCASION OF PRONOUNCING WOES UPON THE GALILEAN CITIES
(Mt xi, 20)

This verse is quoted here chiefly because it furnishes so excellent an illustration of the nature of the introductory formulae found in Matthew and Luke in conjunction with their Q material. Sometimes, as in the case of the Lord's Prayer, such an introduction is present in Luke and absent in Matthew. In the present instance Matthew alone has it. Yet few passages from Q disclose a closer verbal agreement with the corresponding passage in Luke than the passage to which this verse is an introduction. In all such instances as this the writer sees no difficulty in ascribing the introductions to the evangelist in whose pages they are found.

REASON ASSIGNED FOR THE PRONUNCIATION OF THE WOES
(Mt xi, 23b–24)

Following the woes, Matthew alone has this statement of the reasons for their being given. He has a doublet for vs. 24 in x, 15. As this latter is paralleled by Lk x, 12, it may in that context be assigned to Q; here it may be assigned either to Matthew or one of his early editors. There is at least no new Q material here.

"COME UNTO ME"
(Mt xi, 28-30)

It is impossible to suppose that this unusually fine utterance could have been in Luke's copy of Q and could have been omitted by him. Yet of the five scholars quoted in Table II (pp. 110-11), Wellhausen alone attributes it to Q. The others all attribute the preceding section to Q, but stop at vs. 27, where the parallelism between Matthew and Luke breaks off. This is necessary, of course, upon the assumption that nothing should be attributed to Q except what is thus paralleled. But if anything stood in Matthew's recension of Q that was not also in Luke's, certainly these verses stood there. Weiss's remarks concerning them indicate that he has no reason for assigning them, as he does, to a special source, except the fact that they do not appear in Luke. He says "Since these words are not in Luke we have no right to refer them to Q. This is not to say that they are the work of Matthew; they have been taken from another source, oral or written."[1] It has been pointed out by Montefiore that these verses are largely made up of quotations. "The last bit of vs. 29 comes from Jer xi, 7, and the rest is an adapted echo of Sirach li, 23 seq."[2] The parallel, however, as Montefiore also says, covers vss. 25-27 as well as those now under consideration. Loisy[3] argues that the words cannot safely be ascribed to Jesus, but

[1] *Schriften des Neuen Testaments*, I, 324.
[2] *The Synoptic Gospels*, I, 608.
[3] Quoted by Montefiore, I, 610.

adds, "It may be readily admitted that the evangelist found them in the collection of Logia."

A SAYING ABOUT THE LAW
(Mt xii, 5–7)

This saying occurs, not in the midst of Q material, but as an appendix to a discussion which Matthew and Luke both take from Mark. The passage seems to be well attested textually. Considering its context, and its relation to the material immediately preceding, it seems natural to assign the verses either to Matthew himself or to some early editor, rather than to seek a special source for them or to attribute them to Matthew's Q. Vs. 7 has already been considered in connection with ix, 13. If the ἀναιτίους in this latter verse were singular instead of plural it would certainly be taken as a reference to the condemnation and death of Jesus; indeed, it may naturally, tho not with so much assurance, be so taken as it stands.

AN OLD TESTAMENT QUOTATION
(Mt xii, 17–21)

This long quotation, occurring as it does in the midst of a Marcan narrative, may be ascribed either to Matthew or one of his sources; but there is no evidence that such quotations were part of Q.

"GENERATION OF VIPERS"
(Mt xii, 34a)

Γεννήματα ἐχιδνῶν is used once by Matthew and Luke in common (Mt iii, 7; Lk iii, 7) and twice by Matthew alone. The question in which it occurs here seems to render the statement in vss. 36–37 less justifiable. The repetition, not only of the one phrase, but of the idea, in the section might be taken to indicate that this half of a verse is an addition either by Matthew or by some later hand.

A SAYING ABOUT THE JUDGMENT
(Mt xii, 36-37)

If Matthew be credited with the insertion of vs. 34a, it is not unlikely that he added these verses also, as a corrective of the impression that might be drawn from the previous insertion. In character, however, the verses are similar enough to Q, and might be assigned to Matthew's recension.

AN INTERPRETATION OF THE SIGN OF JONAH
(Mt xii, 40)

This verse occurs in a passage concerning the demand for a sign, which Matthew and Luke have evidently taken from Q. Luke's form of the saying about Jonah is evidently the original one. Matthew's reference to the three days spent by Jesus "in the heart of the earth" is *post eventum*, and even so cannot be early. It may perhaps be taken for a gloss, or it may have been added by Matthew. It may equally well have been added by some editor of Q before that document fell into Matthew's hands; there is nothing to determine, except that the strong resemblance, almost amounting to identity, between Matthew and Luke in the rest of the passage may properly incline one toward the assumption of a late addition.

THE WEED IN THE FIELD
(Mt xiii, 24-30)

This parable, tho it has a Q sound in the first verse, is too long for any recension of that document. It is better assigned to a special source, oral or written. The allegorical character of the parable, with its elaborate interpretation in vss. 36–43, seems to indicate its comparatively late origin, and it may be based upon Mk iv, 26–29. At all events it should not be ascribed to Q.

THE PARABLES OF THE TREASURE, THE PEARL, THE FISH-NET, AND THE SCRIBE INSTRUCTED IN THE KINGDOM
(Mt xiii, 44–52)

In this chapter Matthew has eight parables.[1] The parables of the Sower and of the Mustard Seed he has taken from Mark. That of the Yeast he and Luke have taken from Q. That of the Weed in the Field has just been assigned to some special source. The four in vss. 44–52 we assign to Matthew's recension of Q. The grounds upon which this assignment is made are the following: the parables are extremely similar in form and content to those that admittedly come from Q, as the parable of the Yeast in this same chapter. They are so brief as to come under the category of "sayings" rather than of "parables" in the ordinary sense. They are, with one exception, without allegorical or other interpretation. These facts establish their general Q character. The parable of the Fish-Net, in vss. 47–50, contains an allegorical interpretation. Vs. 50 also contains the phrase ἐκεῖ ἔσται ὁ κλαυθμὸς καὶ ὁ βρυγμὸς τῶν ὀδόντων, which Matthew employs in five other connections. This phrase occurred at least once in Q (Mt viii, 12; Lk xiii, 28).

But in spite of a tendency toward repetition which may be observed in Matthew, it seems hardly fair to charge him with having inserted the phrase in the other five places where it occurs. It seems strange also that Matthew should record the parables of the Treasure, the

[1] Sometimes counted as only seven, the similitude in vs. 52 not being reckoned as a parable.

Pearl, and the Converted Scribe without interpretation, but should himself be responsible for the interpretation of the parable of the Fish-Net. It is much more likely that he found the interpretation, with the parable, in his source.

In these four parables obviously there are two items which most scholars would agree in calling secondary: the allegorical interpretation of the parable of the Fish-Net, and the entire parable of the Converted Scribe. Yet the parables of the Pearl and the Treasure are as primary as any utterances recorded of Jesus. The strong general similarity in form and content between these parables and those taken by Matthew and Luke from Q argues the probability of their presence in some form of that document. Their absence from the Gospel of Luke indicates their absence from the recension in his hands. And the presence in them of these secondary traits argues their addition to Q at some time after its original compilation. All these considerations make the assignment of these four little parables to QMt in a high degree probable.

PETER WALKING ON THE WATER
(Mt xiv, 28-31)

The presence of so much narrative material in this section argues at once against its derivation from any form of Q. It belongs to a cycle of Peter-sayings preserved in Matthew alone. The source appears to have been a special one, very probably oral.

"TO THE LOST SHEEP OF THE HOUSE OF ISRAEL"
(Mt xv, 22-24)

These verses are an insertion of Matthew's into the story of the Syrophoenician woman, which he has copied from Mark. It is worthy of note that thruout the entire story the verbal agreement is much more slight than is usual in narratives, especially such as contain sayings of Jesus, taken by Matthew from Mark. Luke has no parallel. Considering the very slight proportion of narrative, and the great preponderance of sayings-material, in the section, it would not be strange if it stood in Q. If it stood in Luke's recension, the attitude of Jesus toward non-Jewish peoples, as implied in the story, would be sufficient to account for Luke's omission of it. The sentiment of vs. 24, in particular, is extremely "primary." It could hardly have been invented and ascribed to Jesus after his time. Mark's words, "Let the children first be fed," tone down the excessively Jewish particularism of Matthew's account; even aside from these words, which are absent from Matthew, Matthew's entire version of the incident is more primary than Mark's. This may be, and has been, explained by saying that Mark's story has been worked over by an editor, subsequent to Matthew's use of his Gospel. But since Mark and Q have been shown to coincide in a certain amount of material, a simpler explanation is that they coincided in this story of the Syrophoenician woman; the more primitive character of Matthew's account is then explained by its dependence upon Q, which is older than Mark. It cannot be shown to have been absent from Luke's recension, and its presence there may be probable, but cannot be demonstrated. It is therefore assigned—but with some hesitation—to QMt.

A SUMMARY OF JESUS' HEALING WORK
(Mt xv, 29–31)

This little summary, like that in Mt iv, 23–25, would naturally be ascribed to Matthew. It might be regarded as a re-working of Mk vii, 31, and a substitute in general terms for the story which immediately follows that verse in Mark.¹ The use by Matthew of such a phrase as τὸν θεὸν 'Ισραήλ would be explained by the fact that the cures are represented as being worked outside of Jewish territory. With this explanation the verses may be ascribed to Matthew.

THE KEYS OF THE KINGDOM OF HEAVEN
(Mt xvi, 17–19)

This is another Peter-section inserted in a story taken from Mark. Luke has the story but not this insertion. The section apparently belongs to the same cycle of Peter-stories with the incident of the walking on the water, already considered. It should be ascribed to some special and undetermined source. The general character of this particular section would indicate its very late origin.

AN INSERTION IN THE STORY OF THE TRANSFIGURATION
(Mt xvii, 6–7)

No special source, other at least than oral tradition, is necessary to account for so slight an addition. Yet considering Matthew's general tendency to condense, rather than to expand, Mark's narratives, and the faithfulness with which he has transcribed the rest of this narrative, it may be easier to regard this insertion as a gloss.

"WHOSOEVER HUMBLES HIMSELF AS THIS LITTLE CHILD"
(Mt xviii, 4)

The verse immediately preceding this is found in Mark, but in another context, from where Matthew has evidently transposed it to this place. This vs. 4 is found

---

¹ So regarded, apparently, by J. Weiss in his *Schriften des Neuen Testaments*, I, 342.

in Matthew alone. A variant of it is found in Mt xxiii, 12. This latter is closely similar to, but not identical with, the saying twice given by Luke (Lk xiv, 11; xviii, 14). Considering his dislike for doublets, the fact that the saying occurs twice in Luke may naturally be taken to indicate its presence in both Mark and Q. But the verse under consideration here can be at most but a reminiscence of the saying which occurs twice in Luke and in Mt xxiii, 12. Considering the fact that Matthew is here obviously exercising his talent at combination, the verse should probably be ascribed to his editorial hand.

THE UNFORGIVING SERVANT
(Mt xviii, 23–35)

In spite of its reference to the kingdom of Heaven this parable is much too long for Q, and should be assigned to a special source.

ABOUT EUNUCHS
(Mt xix, 10–12)

This saying is appended to a discussion taken from Mark. Considering its loose connection in the context, it is perhaps safer to assume that it has been added from some oral authority.

THE LABORERS IN THE VINEYARD
(Mt xx, 1–16)

The parable is too long for Q, tho like the Q parables it has to do with the kingdom of God. The last verse is an apparently proverbial saying, for which Matthew has a doublet in xix, 30, and Luke a variant in Lk xiii, 30.

THE TWO SONS
(Mt xxi, 28-32)

Like the other matter in this vicinity peculiar to Matthew, and like the parables of this length thruout, this parable should be assigned to a special source.

THE WEDDING FEAST
(Mt xxii, 1-14)

J. Weiss assigns this parable, with Lk xiv, 16-24, to Q. But upon the principle we have been following the parable is too long for Q. While it is evidently the same parable as that told in Lk xiv, 16-24, there is clearly no literary connection between Matthew and Luke here. Both Wellhausen and Wernle assign it to Q; Harnack and Hawkins to a special source. This instance brings up the question of what degree of literary similarity must be present in order to warrant the assumption of literary connection. No words are identical here except such as had to be to enable two men to tell the same story.

AGAINST THE PHARISEES
(Mt xxiii, 2-3, 5, 8-10, 15-22)

Matthew here conflates his Q material with his Marcan material. The matter is partially duplicated in Luke's chap. xi. The similarities and the differences between the Matthean and Lucan versions are precisely such features as have led to the hypothesis of the two recensions. The verses should be assigned to QMt.

THE PARABLES OF THE TEN VIRGINS, THE TALENTS, THE JUDGMENT
(Mt xxv, 1-46)

The first two of these parables J. Weiss assigns to Q; presumably on the ground that parallels for them are found in Luke's chaps. xii and xix. But if Q be extended to include so many such long parables as these, it loses entirely its character as a collection of "sayings." Moreover, the parallelism between Matthew's and Luke's versions of these two parables is extremely slight. The subject-matter is the same, but there is no indication of dependence upon a common written source. The parable of the Judgment is peculiar to Matthew. It seems better to assign all three of these parables to a special source.

"TWELVE LEGIONS OF ANGELS"
(Mt xxvi, 52–54)

This is an insertion of Matthew's in the story which he has taken from Mark. There is no indication of Q in it.

We have now gone over all the logian sections of Matthew unparalleled in either Mark or Luke. We have found some of these that ought, in our judgment, to be assigned to Matthew's recension of Q. This assignment cannot claim to be anything more than a suggestion; in many instances, however, it may reach a very high degree of probability; and we have tried to restrict it to such instances. By saying that a certain section should be assigned to a "special source," it is not meant that this is one and the same source for all sections so assigned; but only that these sections cannot be assigned either to Matthew or to his recension of Q. In a few instances I have ventured to suggest an oral rather than a written source. Further comments will be made upon this analysis when a similar study has been made of the sections peculiar to the Gospel of Luke.

CHAPTER IV

Q IN THE SINGLE TRADITION OF LUKE (QLk)

The single tradition of Luke will now be examined with reference to possible Q material unparalleled in Matthew. Narrative material will not be considered. As Luke has omitted much more of Mark than Matthew has, and as he has a much larger amount of non-Marcan material which obviously bears no sign of having stood in any form of Q, it is natural to expect the additions to our total of Q matter to be much less in the single tradition of Luke than of Matthew.

THE PREACHING OF JOHN THE BAPTIST
(Lk iii, 10-14)

This section in Luke follows immediately the description of John's preaching which Luke and Matthew have taken from Q. It is a natural supposition that it stood in Luke's Q, tho not in Matthew's, just as the discussion between Jesus and John at the baptism stood in Matthew's but not in Luke's. But there is one thing which indicates either that it did not so stand, or that it has been worked over by Luke in a manner peculiar to him. That is the presence of dialogue. If this dialogue appeared only in those sayings of Jesus that appear in Luke but not in Matthew, and that are of a character to have come from any form of Q, we should pick out this item as a characteristic of the recension used by Luke. But dialogue is also a characteristic of many of the Lucan parables which could not under any hypothesis be attributed to Q. In spite of its general resemblance to the Q matter just preceding, it seems best, therefore, to attribute this little section to some peculiar Lucan source.

THE INITIAL PREACHING OF JESUS IN NAZARETH
(Lk iv, 16–30)

This is a complete re-working of Marcan material. In his *Synoptische Tafeln zu den drei älteren Evangelien*, J. Weiss attributes it to a special source. This assignment is correct, in the sense that there are sayings of Jesus in the section which Luke would certainly not manufacture, and which he must therefore have derived from some source. At all events there is no Q material in the passage.

THE CALL OF PETER
(Lk v, 1–11)

The same is to be said of this section as has just been said of iv, 16–30. It is a re-working of Mk i, 16–20. The latter part of vs. 10 has an especially genuine sound. Ζωγρῶν occurs here only in the Gospels. The dialogue characteristic of Luke appears here also. With the possible exception of the latter half of vs. 10, nothing in the section could be attributed to any form of Q.

THE WOES
(Lk vi, 24–26)

We have here the alternatives of supposing that Luke invented these woes, that he found them in some altogether different source and inserted them here in the midst of his Q material, or that they stood, with the beatitudes, in his recension of Q. Since the beatitudes themselves, without the woes, show such difference as to preclude Matthew's and Luke's having drawn them from an identical source, but since they seem, if anything, to have stood in Q, it seems natural to assign these woes of Luke's, as we have assigned the beatitudes peculiar to Matthew, to the recension used by him. The sympathy shown in the Gospel of Luke for the poor has usually been referred to Luke himself. It may just as well have been a characteristic of one or more of his sources.

THE RECEPTION OF JOHN'S PREACHING
(Lk vii, 29-30)

These two verses are inserted in the midst of Jesus' testimony to John the Baptist. They have the sound of a purely editorial insertion. On the other hand, if they were found elsewhere by Luke, his insertion of them in this place is accounted for by his desire to explain Jesus' saying about John. A possible hint of a source is found in the presence of δικαιόω. This verb is found in three other passages that are peculiar to Luke and that are evidently not from QLk. If not from Luke himself, these verses are from some special source. But they are only what might be expected from Luke himself in the way of editorial comment.

THE SINNER IN SIMON'S HOUSE
(Lk vii, 36-50)

Tho this narrative has considerable resemblance to that in Mk xiv, 3-9, and Mt xxvi, 6-13, the different placing of the story, and the differences in the story itself, far outweighing the resemblances, seem to indicate a special source for it. There is no reason to attribute it, or any saying in it, to Q.

A WOULD-BE FOLLOWER OF JESUS
(Lk ix, 60b–63)

This may either be attributed to Luke (or to some later scribe) as an amplification of the incident just related by both Matthew and Luke from Q, or may be assumed to have stood in Luke's recension of Q. The two facts, that such amplification would be quite unlike Luke, as his literary habits are revealed to us in his treatment of Mark, and that the saying about the man who has put his hand to the plow has an extremely original and geniune sound, lead us to the latter alternative.

THE RETURN OF THE SEVENTY
(Lk x, 17–20)

Tho the existence and mission of a separate band of seventy disciples be attributed to Luke, he would certainly never have manufactured these sayings that are connected with their return. The sayings may indeed be ascribed to a special source; and are so ascribed by those who allow nothing to Q except the paralleled material. But these sayings are extremely primary in character, especially vss. 18 and 20; and they are similar to much Q material. If in Luke's recension of Q the mission of the disciples was a mission of seventy instead of twelve, Luke will be relieved of the burden of personal responsibility for the creation of this mission of the seventy; he has then merely conflated the account of the mission of the seventy which he found in his recension of Q with the mission of the twelve which he found in Mark. It must be admitted that such conflation is contrary to Luke's habit. The alternatives to this hypothesis are, either that he invented the mission of the seventy himself, or that he had before him three accounts of the sending out of disciples, one by Mark and one in Q, and a third in some unknown source. This lends probability to the ascription of these sayings to QLk.

THE GREAT COMMANDMENT
(Lk x, 25-28)

Mark has a partial parallel to this section in Mk xii, 28-31, which Matthew takes from him (Mt xxii, 34-40). Luke's account is evidently not from Mark, however. Luke may have omitted the Marcan narrative because of this parallel of it in his own Gospel. The logian material in the section is of a primary character; the implication that one might inherit eternal life by merely keeping the commandments is not such as to have been later invented, and sounds particularly strange in Luke's Gospel. No source is more probable for it than QLk.

THE GOOD SAMARITAN
(Lk x, 29-37)

This parable is entirely too long to be ascribed to any form of Q. Its affinities with others of the long parables peculiar to Luke is such as to indicate for all of them a special source.

MARY AND MARTHA
(Lk x, 38-42)

Mr. Streeter[1] suggests a reason why this incident may have been omitted by Matthew even if it stood in Q. But I can see no reason for assuming it to have stood in the latter source. It has great affinity with much other Lucan material which should not be assigned to Q, and is apparently from a special source.

---

[1] *Oxford Studies*, p. 192.

THE PARABLE OF THE FRIEND ON A JOURNEY
(Lk xi, 5-8)

This parable is brief enough to have stood in Q. But it does not, apparently, relate to the kingdom of God, as the undoubted Q parables do. It is also similar in motive to other Lucan parables assigned to a special source.

THE MOTHER OF JESUS PRAISED
(Lk xi, 27-28)

Wellhausen considers this a variant of Lk viii, 19-21, which latter is taken from Mark (iii, 31-35). The parallelism is not very close, to say the least. While a case may be made out for the occurrence of this section in Q, as is apparently done by Mr. Streeter, it seems better to us to assign it to a special source of Luke's.

"IF THINE WHOLE BODY IS LIGHT"
(Lk xi, 36)

If this saying were genuine, it would naturally be assigned to QLk. But the text is not well attested, and it is perhaps better to regard it as a gloss.

THE PARABLE OF THE FOOLISH RICH MAN
(Lk xii, 13-21)

Wernle remarks concerning this section that anyone with a sense for *Herrenworte* will recognize at once that vss. 15 and 21 are from Luke and not from Jesus. Vs. 21 is omitted in some manuscripts. The parable is from a special source.

AN EXHORTATION TO WATCHFULNESS
(Lk xii, 35-38)

This might almost be considered as a variant of Matthew's parable of the Ten Virgins. It stands in close connection here with Q material. No more probable source can be suggested for it than Luke's recension of Q.

"TO WHOM MUCH IS GIVEN"
(Lk xii, 47–48)

This section, consisting entirely of sayings, and occurring between two blocks of Q material, is almost universally ascribed to a special source, simply because it is not paralleled in Matthew. But it is quite homogeneous with Q. It is, indeed, unlikely that Matthew would have omitted it if it had stood in his recension of Q; but no better source can be posited for it than QLk. Of fifteen occurrences of δέρω in the New Testament, eight are found in Luke's Gospel and in Acts. The three occurrences in Acts are not indicative, as they are accounted for by the subject-matter; the five in the Gospel are, except in this passage, paralleled in Matthew and Mark. While the word is therefore in a sense a "Lucan" word, there is nothing to indicate that it was not in the source Luke used.

"I CAME TO CAST FIRE UPON THE EARTH"
(Lk xii, 49–50)

These two verses have a very primary sound. The difficulty of them is much against their invention by Luke or anyone in his time. But if Luke derived them from any written source, they are exactly such sayings as would have found a place in his recension of Q.

THE GALILEANS SLAIN BY HEROD
(Lk xiii, 1–5)

This saying was evidently spoken in Jerusalem, but Luke has placed it during the journey thither. We may perhaps detect here the beginnings of a Jerusalem tradition.

THE PARABLE OF THE FIG TREE
(Lk xiii, 6-9)

Like the preceding, the parable is given as part of the conversation on the Samaritan journey. But it seems to be Luke's version of the story told by Mark of the cursing of the fig tree; and this latter Mark places in Jerusalem. This may be taken as another hint of the origin of this section in a Jerusalem tradition.

"GO TELL THAT FOX"
(Lk xiii, 31-33)

Mr. Streeter[1] remarks of this section that it is so "un-Lucan in its rough vigor that it is certainly original"; in other words, that it certainly stood in Luke's source. This source Mr. Streeter maintains is Q, not only for this brief section, but for the solid block of Lk ix, 51—xiii, 59 (with the possible exception of the two parables of the Good Samaritan, the Rich Fool, and perhaps the story of Martha). The passage, xiii, 1-17, he suggests may have been interpolated into Q before Q came to Luke.

The primary character of the section now under consideration cannot be doubted. The fact that Luke has apparently left his Q material by itself, instead of mingling it with his Marcan and other matter, would argue for Mr. Streeter's position. Yet Luke has not altogether followed this general rule of his; and he has made some very notable transpositions of Marcan material. This saying, also, is not quite like most of the sayings that are by common agreement to be ascribed to Q. It is neither a general rule of conduct, like the sayings in the Sermon on the Mount, nor has it to do with the kingdom of God, like the brief parables of Q. If

[1] *Oxford Studies*, p. 193.

Luke inserted it from another source, his reason for inserting it in just this place may have been the fact of its closing with the word "Jerusalem." Yet the lament over Jerusalem which immediately follows is evidently wrongly placed by Luke, in the midst of his Perean journey. We are inclined to assign these verses, tho with some uncertainty, to a special source. The words were apparently spoken neither on the Perean journey (assuming such a journey to have taken place) nor at its close in Jerusalem, but in Galilee.

THE HEALING OF THE DROPSICAL MAN
(Lk xiv, 1-6)

The only saying in this section is that paralleled in Lk xiii, 15-16, and duplicated in Mt xii, 11. The incident is somewhat similar to that recorded in Mk iii, 1-6; and it is noticeable that Matthew, in taking over that incident from Mark, inserts in the midst of it this saying of Jesus about the ox or ass falling into the pit on the Sabbath. If the saying occurred in Q, Matthew has thus taken it out of its original context and made it a part of a Marcan story; but he would hardly have done this if it already, in his copy of Q, constituted part of another and equally good story. In view of the general character of Q as a collection of "sayings," with as little mixture of incident as possible, it seems better to say that this saying about the ox or ass falling into the pit occurred once in Q, unconnected, and that Luke found it again in the story before us, in some other source.

ABOUT TAKING THE LESS HONORABLE SEATS AT TABLE
(Lk xiv, 7-11)

This saying may have been manufactured upon the basis of Mk xii, 39 ("they love the chief seats at feasts," etc). Vs. 11 is the oft-repeated formula discussed on p. 182. While this and the following section are not impossible for QLk, it seems better to assign them both to one of Luke's special sources.

WHOM TO INVITE TO A FEAST
(Lk xiv, 12–14)

This saying of Jesus seems out of place at a dinner to which he had been invited. The saying itself is not unlike Q. Observing that this saying and the two just preceding are placed by Luke at feasts given for Jesus, but that they contain sayings of Jesus either placed elsewhere by Matthew or not given by him at all, Mr. Streeter is inclined to assign the setting of these sayings in each case to Luke, and the sayings to Q. This would seem more justifiable if it were not plain that Luke had, besides his recension of Q and Mark, at least two or three other sources. One cannot be categorical on such a matter, and it is possible that this section with the two preceding should be assigned to QLk.

THE PARABLE OF THE DINNER AND THE INVITED GUESTS
(Lk xiv, 15–24)

This parable is generally regarded as parallel to Mt xxii, 1–10, and the two are assigned to Q. But while the two evangelists are evidently relating the same parable, there is so little verbal resemblance as to give no proof of a common literary source. Upon the assumption of such a source, the violence done to it by Matthew or Luke or both in its transcription is quite beyond belief. If the parable in either Gospel is assigned to Q, the one in the other should be otherwise assigned. It seems better to ascribe both of them to special sources. The two versions are about as unlike as they could well be, and still be versions of the same parable.

CONDITIONS OF DISCIPLESHIP
(Lk xiv, 28-35)

Here are four detached sayings, the first two similar in meaning. Vs. 28 sounds like a genuine logion, with vss. 29 and 30 added as an explanatory comment. The same may be said, respectively, of vss. 31 and 32. Vs. 33, tho beginning with οὕτως, does not seem to fit in this place. Vs. 34a is from Mark (ix, 50) or influenced by it. Considering the connections, it is probably best to assign the passage to QLk, with improvements by Luke.

THE LOST SHEEP
(Lk xv, 1-7)

Mr. Streeter suggests that Luke may have elaborated this parable out of the saying in Mt xviii, 12-13. Johannes Weiss, as indicated in his *Synoptische Tafeln zu den drei älteren Evangelien*, seems also to consider that while the parable as a whole is drawn from one of Luke's peculiar sources, there is a literary connection between vss. 4-7 and Matthew's saying. Considering the connection of the parable with the two that immediately follow, it seems better to assign all three to a common Lucan source.

THE LOST COIN AND THE PRODIGAL SON
(Lk xv, 8-32)

These parables may be assigned without comment to one of Luke's special sources.

THE UNJUST STEWARD
(Lk xvi, 1-12)

The composite character of this parable has been asserted by various writers. Schmiedel[1] suggests that

[1] *Encyclopedia Biblica*, col. 1864.

vss. 10–12 have been added by a later hand. If the parable stops with vs. 9, the meaning of it apparently is that one should give mammon away; the two following verses seem merely to inculcate honesty in business matters. Indeed, perhaps the parable should be considered as ending with vs. 7, and vs. 8 as probably an editorial comment upon it. In the latter case, the ὁ κύριος of vs. 8 refers to Jesus. This supposition requires the further one that the writer of vs. 9 has forgotten that vs. 8 is indirect discourse attributed to Jesus. Vs. 13 is from Q and is duplicated in Mt vi, 24. But there is no new Q material here.

A CRITICISM OF THE PHARISEES
(Lk xvi, 14–15)

The verses which immediately follow these are from Q. Streeter[1] inclines to assign vss. 14–15 to the same source. But if vss. 16–18 be omitted here and placed in some other connection, vss. 14–15 constitute an excellent introduction to the parable of the Rich Man and Lazarus which follows in vss. 19–31. In favor of Mr. Streeter's assignment is the fact that Q was apparently a collection of sayings neither topically nor otherwise arranged, and that the four sayings in vss. 15–18 are thus detached, Matthew having taken the three in vss. 16–18 and "worked them into appropriate contexts." Of vss. 14 and 15 about all that can be said is that the latter sounds like Q. Considering Matthew's fondness for everything that reflects upon the Pharisees, it seems likely that if vs. 15 stood in any form of Q it was in Luke's recension only.

[1] *Oxford Studies*, p. 201.

THE RICH MAN AND LAZARUS
(Lk xvi, 19–31)

This parable seems to show something of the same composite character as is found in that of the Unjust Steward, the first part having to do with rich and poor and the second part with believing and unbelieving. There is no Q material in it.

"UNPROFITABLE SERVANTS" AND THE HEALING OF THE TEN LEPERS
(Lk xvii, 7–10; xvii, 11–19)

The former of these two sections might conceivably have stood in Luke's recension of Q; the latter not in any recension. It is better to assign them both to a special source.

ABOUT THE COMING OF THE KINGDOM OF GOD
(Lk xvii, 20–21)

This little section certainly has a Q sound. If it stood in Matthew's recension, reasons may easily be given for his omission of it; he would not have understood the non-apocalyptic statement, "the kingdom of God is within [or among] you." But it cannot be proved, at least, that the section stood in Matthew's Q; therefore if it is assigned to Q at all it would better be assigned merely to Luke's recension.

Later than this in the Gospel of Luke there is nothing that needs to be examined for possible Q material. His single tradition from here on includes the parables of the Unjust Judge, and the Pharisee and the Publican in the Temple, the story of Zacchaeus, the lament over Jerusalem, the institution of the Lord's Supper, and a few sections in the story of the trial, the death, and the resurrection appearances of Jesus. Of these only one, the lament over Jerusalem, bears any resemblance to the Q material in general. Professor Burkitt suggests, indeed, that xxii, 15–16, 24–32, and 35–38, may be remnants of Q's account of the passion. We have seen no reason to suppose that there was such an account in Q. If there was, there are no signs by which it can be identified in this portion of Luke's narrative. It is better to assign all this material to a special source. The fact that Luke has no resurrection appearances in Galilee may perhaps be taken as confirmation of our hypothesis of a Jerusalem source in his hands.

MATTER PECULIAR TO MATTHEW OR TO LUKE

In the determination of Q material in the single traditions of Matthew and Luke on pp. 166–206, the writer has ventured occasionally to suggest a possible source for such material as is not assigned to any form of Q.

In addition to the sayings-material considered on pp. 166–92, Matthew has in his single tradition the following narratives: the birth and infancy sections, chaps. i, ii; the temple tax, xvii, 24–27; the children in the temple, xxi, 14–16; the death of Judas, xxvii, 3–10; the wife of Pilate, and Pilate and the crowd, xxvii, 19, 24–25; miracles at the death of Jesus, xxvii, 51–53; the watch at the grave, xxvii, 62–66; xxviii, 11–15; the angel rolling away the stone, xxviii, 2–3; the appearances of Jesus to the women, xxviii, 9–10; to the disciples, xxviii, 16–20.

In addition to the sayings and parables of the single tradition of Luke, considered on pp. 193–206, that tradition contains the following narratives: the birth of John the Baptist, the birth and infancy of Jesus, with the ancestry, chaps. i, ii, iii, 1–38; the miraculous draft of fishes, v, 4–9; the raising of the widow's son, vii, 11–17;

the ministering women, viii, 1–3; an event in a Samaritan village, ix, 51–56; the healing of the woman, xiii, 10–17;[1] the ten lepers, xvii, 11–19; Zacchaeus, xix, 2–10; the trial before Herod, xxiii, 6–12; the thief on the cross, xxiii, 39–43; the walk to Emmaus, xxiv, 13–35; the appearances of the risen Jesus, xxiv, 36–53.

Matthew's peculiar material is scattered thru his entire Gospel. He begins and ends with it. After he reaches the Passion, his peculiar material becomes unusually abundant. In the twenty-three chapters between the infancy and the passion, he has only seventeen insertions of peculiar material. In the three chapters that follow, he has nine. These latter are of a different sort. In the earlier part of his single tradition, sayings and parables predominate; here, except for the saying about the legion of angels, the peculiar material is all narrative.

Luke has likewise distributed his peculiar material thruout his gospel, and also begins and ends with it. But after his stories of the birth and childhood, he has, up to his chap. ix, five insertions of peculiar matter. Four of these are incidents, one is a speech of John the Baptist. With ix, 51, begins his great interpolation. In the less than ten chapters covered by this he has grouped twenty-five sections of his peculiar material. This matter has a prevailing character of its own. There are four narratives in it, three of them being healings. The other twenty-one sections consist of sayings and parables. If we consider the relative length of the sayings, the narratives, and parables of this section, we shall see that the whole is practically a parable section. With the coming of Jesus to Jerusalem, this material stops. From here

---

[1] The healing of a dropsical man (Lk xiv, 1–6), tho a narrative section, has been considered on p. 201, on account of the sayings in it.

on Luke has two brief sayings and one longer one, five sections of narrative, and no parable, in his single tradition.

Whether the source of Matthew's peculiar material was one or more than one, it suggests itself at once that the birth and infancy stories may have come from a place by themselves. They have, to a considerable extent, a vocabulary of their own. Constituting about one twenty-second of the total matter of Matthew's Gospel, they contain almost one-tenth of the occurrences of the characteristic words of that Gospel.[1] Even if the constantly recurring γεννάω of the genealogy be removed, the peculiar words occur with much more frequency in this birth and infancy section than in the rest of the Gospel. The force of this fact, however, is considerably weakened by the peculiar subject-matter of these chapters.

More decisive upon this matter is the general character of the birth and infancy sections, which is sharply distinguished from that of the body of the Gospel. This is not due to the presence of the marvelous in these early chapters, since that is found to some degree throughout, but to the presence of what may be more distinctly called the legendary element. In this characteristic it is like some of the material at the end of Matthew's Gospel. Let one compare the general character of the stories of the star and the magi, the slaughter of the innocents, and the flight into Egypt with the story of the opening of the graves and the awakening of the departed dead, and the angel rolling away the stone from the grave, and the question will suggest itself, whether Matthew may not have obtained all these stories from one source.

This suggestion might appear to be seconded by the fact that this material, which has such a striking family

[1] Hawkins, *Horae Synopticae*, p. 9.

resemblance, is not scattered thru the body of Matthew's work, but occurs, part of it before he has reached his junction with Mark and Luke, and the rest of it after he has parted from them. He not only begins and ends alone, but he begins and ends with material of a remarkably similar character. This is not enough, of course, to prove the unity of Matthew's source for the first and last parts of his single tradition; but it is enough to suggest it.

As to the source of the rest of Matthew's peculiar material, we cannot get beyond guesswork. Some of it has an extremely genuine sound; for example, the sayings appended to the Sabbath discussion, "The priests break the sabbath in the temple and are blameless," etc. (xii, 5–6); the saying about the angels of the little ones (xviii, 10); the parable of the Fish-Net, preserving so well the eschatological features of the preaching of Jesus (xiii, 47–50); the parable of the Two Sons (xxi, 28–31). The incident of the temple tax (xvii, 24–27) seems to go back for its origin to a time when the temple was still in existence, and, when it is relieved of the item of the coin in the fish's mouth (which may easily be a later addition to the story), seems to bear traces of undoubted genuineness.

The parable of the Laborers who received every man a penny (Mt xx, 1–16) seems likewise to indicate a time considerably later than that of Jesus; a time, namely, when those who had long waited for the parousia were asking whether those who had come in at the eleventh hour were to receive the rewards of the coming kingdom exactly as those who had "borne the burden and the heat of the day." That it was in such a time as this that Matthew wrote his Gospel may suggest the hypothesis that he has here worked over some genuine saying of Jesus, or received such a saying as it had been worked over by the waiting community, to suit the need of the times.

In much the same manner the story of the Wise and Foolish Virgins (xxv, 1–13) seems to come from a period when the church was commonly spoken of as the bride of Christ, or when Christ was awaited as the coming bridegroom of the church; this is not necessar.ly later than the times of Paul's letter to the Ephesians, and so may be much earlier than Matthew, but is certainly later than the time of Jesus.

The saying about eunuchs who have made themselves such for the kingdom of heaven has a harsh sound in the mouth of Jesus; and we wonder whether the circumstances of the expectation of the kingdom warranted such a statement at the time Jesus is said to have made it. We cannot but notice also, as Wernle has remarked, that the saying seems to be displaced in Matthew, coming in with extreme inappropriateness between Jesus' insistence upon the sacredness of marriage and his blessing of the children. It may bespeak the period of developing asceticism within the church. If it is not to be assigned to Jesus we cannot fix very closely the date of its origin.

On the whole, we must probably say that some parts of Matthew's tradition, outside of his infancy section and the stories of the wonders at the crucifixion, show indications of antiquity and genuineness, while others arouse our suspicions as to their coming from Jesus, or even from Matthew.

MATTER PECULIAR TO LUKE

As to whether the source of Luke's single tradition was one or many the statement in his prologue predisposes us toward the latter supposition. The difference between the infancy sections and the rest of Luke's peculiar material, as in the case of Matthew, is marked. Hawkins reckons one hundred and fifty-one words as characteristic of Luke. Of these, seventy-seven, or more than half, occur once or more in the first two chapters, while seventy-four of them are absent from these chapters. These first two chapters contain about one hundred and thirty-two verses, about one-ninth of the whole Gospel; yet one-half of the occurrences of Luke's peculiar words are found here.

A strong Hebraic character is observable in Luke's infancy sections, quite absent from his other peculiar material. In the twenty-one verses in i, 5–25, καί is used many times where Luke's habit elsewhere would lead us to expect the substitution of δέ. There are also many Hebraic phrases, such as πορευόμενοι ἐν πάσαις ταῖς ἐντολαῖς, προβεβηκότες ἐν ταῖς ἡμέραις, μέγας ἐνώπιον κυρίου, and the construction ἐγένετο, thrice used, as the formula introducing a paragraph. Luke's own hand may be seen in the introduction of δέ three times. One of these is in connection with εἶπεν, which is probably Luke's substitute for the historic present. The retention of so many Hebraistic and non-Lucan features probably justifies Jülicher's suggestion of a special (Hebraistic, Aramaic) written source for these infancy sections. A written and not an oral source is also indicated in Luke's table of ancestors,[1] especially in its awkward placing after the baptism. It is quite impossible that Luke is here drawing upon the same source as in his

---

[1] Unless this should be regarded as a gloss, which would not so well account for its awkward position. See Sanders, *Journal of Biblical Literature*, October, 1913.

great interpolation. Even more decisive in this direction than the vocabulary is the general character of the material.

Sanday is "especially glad to see the stress that is laid [in certain other essays in the same volume] on the homogeneity of the peculiar matter of Luke."[1] He does not expressly say that he includes here the infancy sections, or whether he refers merely to the great interpolation; in the absence of such a statement, it may be fair to assume the former. He adds, "I fully believe, myself, in its Jewish-Christian and Palestinian origin." But when he adds further, "I can altogether go along with the view that St. Luke probably collected this material during his two years' stay at Caesarea (Acts xxiv compared with xxi and xxvii, 1); I could even quite believe with Harnack, Mr. Streeter, and Dr. Bartlet that his chief informants were Philip the evangelist and his four daughters," he is open to the suspicion of being too much influenced by a desire to trace the tradition back to a definite and authentic source, even where the data do not warrant it. There is certainly no justification for referring the infancy stories to Philip and his four daughters (and perhaps, as suggested above, Dr. Sanday does not mean to do this).

Dr. Sanday further agrees with Dr. Bartlet "that the information derived in this way probably lay before St. Luke in writing. The interval between his stay in Caesarea and the publication of his Gospel could hardly have been less than some fifteen years and I doubt if the freshness, precision, and individual touches which characterize St. Luke could well have been preserved otherwise than by writing." If Dr. Sanday means that the writing was done by Luke during his stay in Caesarea,

---

[1] *Oxford Studies*, Introductory Essay, pp. xx-xxi.

from oral tradition given him by Philip and his daughters, we are left with the assumption that Luke kept this written material of his own for fifteen years (probably a good deal longer) before he incorporated it in his Gospel. This would agree well with the theory that Luke, as the traveling companion of Paul, kept a diary of events, which he preserved for a still longer period, until he finally incorporated it in his Book of Acts. Both these assumptions are strange upon the face of them; and for those who do not accept the same authorship for the "we sections" and the rest of Acts (as the present writer does not), and who also think the Gospel of Luke was not written till considerably more than fifteen years from the time of Luke's stay in Caesarea, and who do not identify the author of the Third Gospel with the traveling companion of Paul, Dr. Sanday's statement will not appear conclusive.

Outside of Luke's infancy sections (and the passion sections which will be considered in a succeeding paragraph) there is an apparent homogeneity in much of Luke's single tradition. Luke and Matthew start out in their attempt to tell the gospel story, each on his own independent line. They come together at the point where Mark has begun his story. Except for a few insertions and transpositions they stay together and with Mark up to Lk ix, 51. Here Luke inserts something more than nine chapters before he gets back again to Matthew and Mark.

In these more than nine chapters there are some sections which Matthew has in the earlier part of his Gospel, and little which Mark has;[1] but in these nine chapters Luke inserts most of the material peculiar to himself, and

[1] See pp. 8-9, 16-18.

by far the greater part of the nine chapters is made up exclusively of such material. From the end of Luke's infancy section to his great interpolation there are about one hundred and fourteen verses of exclusively Lucan material, but in this interpolation there are about one hundred and seventy verses. The suggestion of these facts, to the effect that Luke is here employing a source distinct from that which he has used in his infancy section, and that he is for the most part employing one source and not several, may be further favored by the fact that when he comes back to the story told in Mark (and Matthew) he takes that up, not where he left it, at Mk vi, 41, but at viii, 27; as if he had found it inconvenient to make his peculiar source here work in with the common tradition.[1]

DID LUKE'S GREAT INTERPOLATION ORIGINALLY EXIST AS A SEPARATE DOCUMENTARY SOURCE?

The material of Luke's "great interpolation," after the comparatively small amount of matter common to Luke and Matthew is subtracted from it, has a decided homogeneity of its own. It consists of nine sayings, one incident (the occurrence in the Samaritan village) which might with almost equal propriety be reckoned as a saying, three healings, all of which have the appearance of being introduced, not for the sake of the cure, but of the appended saying, and thirteen parables.

These thirteen parables have not only a striking similarity among themselves, but an equally striking *dis*similarity to those parables which Luke has in common with one or both of the other evangelists. Matthew's parables are usually brief sayings, beginning with the

---

[1] Holtzmann's suggestion that Luke omitted the Mark section because it ends with the second feeding of the multitude—implying the same sort of omission by mistake as is often made when two lines end with the same word—seems strangely insufficient.

phrase, "The kingdom of heaven is like," etc. The parables peculiar to Luke (there are fourteen in all and thirteen of them occur in this section) are stories rather than parables in the strict sense. Some of them are introduced by the brief formula, "And he said unto them," or "And he said to his disciples," etc. Others are given a more definite setting, like the story of the Good Samaritan, which is introduced as an answer to the question "Who is my neighbor?" However introduced, they usually contain a more or less elaborated conclusion, easily distinguished from the parable proper. Thus in the story of the Good Samaritan, Jesus asks the lawyer which of the three men he considers to have been neighbor to him who fell among the thieves. The lawyer makes his reply, and upon the basis of it Jesus dismisses him with a word of pointed advice. In the same manner the story of the Rich Fool is introduced as a rebuke to the man who asks Jesus to help him secure his portion of an estate, and closes with the reflection that whoever has the riches of this world but is not "rich toward God" is like this man. So the stories of the Lost Sheep and the Lost Coin are introduced with the statement that the Pharisees objected to Jesus' eating with "sinners," and close with the statement, "Likewise there is joy in the presence of the angels of God,"[1] etc.

At least one or two of these parables seem to be provided with more than one conclusion. The story of the Unjust Judge (xviii, 1–8) is introduced in vs. 1 as being spoken concerning the necessity of continued prayer. The story or parable itself then follows in vss. 2–5. Vss. 6–8a give the conclusion in the words of Jesus, beginning

[1] Why does Luke have *two* laments over Jerusalem, as well as two missions of the disciples, especially considering his apparent avoidance of duplicates?

with the words, "And the Lord said." Then Luke himself, in vs. 8b, adds, "But, when the Son of man cometh will he find the faith in the earth?"[1] The story of the Rich Man and Lazarus is introduced as a rebuke to the Pharisees (Lk xvi, 14–15), who loved riches and thot well of themselves. The parable as thus introduced and as answering to this purpose appropriately closes at vs. 25, where Abraham reminds the rich man that he had his good things and Lazarus his poverty upon the earth, but now their situations are reversed.[2] What follows in vss. 27–31, tho here given as a continuation of the same story, has nothing to do with the contrast between rich and poor, or with heartlessness and pity, but only with belief and unbelief.

It may be observed also that the insertion of here and there a few verses that are elsewhere paralleled in Matthew interrupts the otherwise good connection of Luke's peculiar account. Thus the story of the Rich Man and Lazarus is introduced, as just remarked, as a rebuke to the Pharisees, who loved money and "justified themselves in the sight of men." If it were allowed to follow immediately upon this, the setting would be appropriate. But between this introduction, which is peculiar to Luke, and the story itself, also peculiar to him, there are inserted three verses (xvi, 16–18) in regard to law and divorce, which quite break the connection. These interrupting verses, however, are not peculiar to Luke, but are found in Matthew also.

[1] This last, quite inappropriate alike in the mouth of Jesus and as a part of his parable, becomes, in the mouth of Luke, a pathetic commentary upon the difficulty of preserving the Christian faith while waiting for the long-delayed parousia.

[2] The soliloquy in the parables of Jesus is introduced by Luke alone. The dialogue, tho more frequent in Luke than in Matthew, is not restricted to him.

When all these facts are taken into account it is not surprising that the hypothesis has risen that the great interpolation, exclusive of the Q material contained in it, came from a special source.

But the unity of this source is much harder to demonstrate than is the unity of Q. A considerable amount of the material, aside from the Q material, in these sections is more or less closely duplicated by Matthew, and the Perean source or its equivalent in parts must therefore have been used by him also. Matthew's demonstrated faithfulness to his sources raises serious doubt as to whether he could have known this Perean source and have omitted so much of it. The assumption that he did so, and the assignment of the double tradition thruout this portion of Luke, would require also an entire rearrangement of Q. Burton accepts this requirement, and, instead of Q, goes back to the Logia as a special source of Matthew. The fact that some of this material in the so-called Perean section of Luke may easily be assigned to his own invention, and that in the larger part of it where he is not duplicated by Matthew his own hand can be clearly seen in additions and rearrangements, would seem to tell against the unity of the Perean source, or against the assumption of any Perean source properly so called, and common to Matthew and Luke. On the whole the hypothesis of a Perean source does not seem to the writer to have been substantiated.

OTHER POSSIBLE SOURCES FOR MATERIAL PECULIAR TO LUKE

Suggestion has been made in connection with a few of the passages considered on pp. 193–206 as to a possible Jerusalem source. Nothing can perhaps be said in support of such a hypothesis, except what is suggested in the analysis on those pages and lies upon the surface of the passages. Another possible clew to the determination of one of Luke's sources lies in the material that has to do particularly with women. Compare the raising of the widow's son and the speech of Jesus referring to the Old Testament widow; the ministering women, Mary and Martha, and the speech of the woman about the mother of Jesus. The writer does not consider this (or the preceding) to be anything more than a suggestion.

CONCLUSIONS REGARDING Q MATERIAL IN THE SINGLE TRADITIONS OF MATTHEW AND LUKE

The preceding investigations represent the recension of Q used by Matthew as containing about two hundred and sixty-seven verses, or parts of verses. Of these ninety-eight are so closely parallel to Luke as to be marked simply Q. Eighty-nine, paralleled in Luke, but with divergences such as to indicate a different wording in the source that lay before Matthew and Luke and eighty without any parallels in Luke, are assigned to QMt. The recension of Q used by Luke, according to our analysis, contained about two hundred and thirty-eight verses or parts of verses. Of these, ninety-four are closely enough paralleled in Matthew to be assigned simply to Q; eighty-one are paralleled in Matthew, but with such differences as to suggest different wording in the source; and sixty-three are peculiar to Luke.

It is not to be assumed that all of Q is reproduced in either Matthew or Luke. But from the treatment accorded to Mark by Matthew and Luke, respectively, it is to be expected that Matthew would omit less of the Q material that lay before him than would Luke; and this presumption is confirmed by the results obtained.

The examination of Luke's material indicates his command of a larger number of sources aside from Mark and Q than are apparent in Matthew, and this again agrees with Luke's statement in his preface. Luke's Gospel is longer than Matthew's, and approaches the limit apparently convenient in ancient documents.[1] This fact, together with the greater amount of material he wished to incorporate from other sources, would further account for Luke's greater omissions from his Q. Yet there is nothing to prove that Luke's Q, as it was certainly different in some of its contents, was not also briefer than Matthew's.

It is possible to limit Q strictly to the sections of Matthew and Luke in which the correspondences are extremely close, to leave the remainder of their double tradition to unidentified sources, and to make no claims for Q (QMt and QLk) in the single traditions of Matthew and Luke. This indeed is the procedure of most scholars. But it has the disadvantages of ignoring much material in the single traditions which is extremely similar to the Q material and often stands, in one or both Gospels, in closest connection with it, and of leaving without explanation the material which is nearly enough alike to require some common basis but not near enough alike to indicate the use of the same recension of the same document. The assumption of QMt and QLk, going back to two different translations, from different copies of the Aramaic original, and undergoing the process of alteration and accretion in different surroundings before falling into the hands of Matthew and Luke, best accounts for the agreements, the divergences, and the peculiar but strongly similar material.

[1] Sanday, *Oxford Studies*, pp. 25–26.

Thus far we may claim that the facts of two hundred and sixty-seven verses in one source against two hundred and thirty-eight in the other, ninety-eight in one extremely close in wording (with many verses absolutely identical) to ninety-four in the other, and eighty verses in one against sixty-three in the other, unduplicated, but strongly suggesting by form and content their relationship with the rest, do not throw any discredit upon the assumption of two recensions (translations) of one document, but are what would be expected. If the date for the original Q is to be set as early as the year 60, or even earlier, and its use by Matthew and Luke be put as late as 85 to 95, the divergences between Matthew's and Luke's recensions will be further justified.

CHAPTER V

REVIEW OF Q MATERIAL IN MATTHEW, LUKE, AND MARK

The accompanying tables of contents of Q material in Matthew, Luke, and Mark are prepared to facilitate comparison between the evangelists as to the amount and character of their Q material. They will help to determine whether QMt and QLk have enough in common, and of such a sort, as to entitle them still to be regarded as recensions of the same original. They will also help us toward a determination of the original order of Q. The division into sections is a somewhat arbitrary one, but has been made as nearly equal in Matthew and Luke as possible. Title and number are given to each section in each Gospel, to make the comparative study of contents and order more easy. Some slight differences may occasionally be detected between the assignments as they are made here, and as they were made in the examinations of the double and single traditions. These will be chiefly due to the necessity of taking the material here in sections instead of in detached verses and will not affect the results heretofore obtained.

CONSIDERATIONS FAVORING ANALYSIS OF Q INTO QMT AND QLK

In the subjoined tables of Q material in Matthew and in Luke the duplicated material is starred. The sections which are identical (or in a few cases not absolutely but practically so), or in which the deviations are so slight as easily to be ascribed to the editorial work of Matthew

TABLE IV
Contents of Q Material in Matthew

Sec.	Chap. Verse	Subject	Source
*1	iii, 7–10	Preaching of the Baptist...............	Q
*2	iii, 11–12	Messianic announcement of the Baptist	Q
*3	iv, 1–11	The temptation......................	Q
*4	v, 3	Blessed are the poor in spirit..........	QMt
5	v, 4	Blessed are the meek................	QMt
6	v, 5	Blessed are they that mourn..........	QMt
*7	v, 6	Blessed are they that hunger after righteousness......................	QMt
8	v, 7	Blessed are the merciful..............	QMt
9	v, 8	Blessed are the pure in heart.........	QMt
10	v, 9	Blessed are the peace-makers.........	QMt
*11	v, 10–12	Blessed are the persecuted............	QMt
*12	v, 13	Ye are the salt of the earth. If the salt, etc..............................	QMt
*13	v, 14–16	Light of the world. Candle and bushel.	QMt
*14	v, 17–20	Relation to the law. Except your righteousness, etc.......................	QMt
15	v, 21–22	Do not kill. Whoever is angry........	QMt
16	v, 23–24	If thou bring thy gift to the altar......	QMt
*17	v, 25–26	Agree with thine adversary...........	QMt
18	v, 27–28	On adultery and lustfulness...........	QMt
19	v, 29–30	If thine eye, hand, offend thee........	QMt
*20	v, 31–32	On divorce..........................	Q (Mk)
21	v, 33–37	On the taking of oaths...............	QMt
*22	v, 38–42	On revenge. Resist not..............	QMt
*23	v, 43–48	Love your enemies...................	QMt
24	vi, 1–4	On almsgiving.......................	QMt
25	vi, 5–8	On prayer: be not as the hypocrites are.	QMt
*26	vi, 9–13	The Lord's Prayer...................	QMt
*27	vi, 14–15	About forgiveness....................	QMt
28	vi, 16–18	On fasting: not as the hypocrites......	QMt
*29	vi, 19–21	About treasures not on the earth......	QMt
*30	vi, 22–23	The light of the body. If thine eye be single............................	Q
*31	vi, 24	About serving two masters............	Q
*32	vi, 25–34	About care..........................	Q
*33	vii, 1–2	About judging.......................	QMt
*34	vii, 3–5	The mote and the beam..............	Q
35	vii, 6	Pearls before swine...................	QMt
*36	vii, 7–11	Seeking and finding..................	Q
*37	vii, 12	The Golden Rule....................	Q
*38	vii, 13–14	The narrow gate.....................	QMt
39	vii, 15	Warnings against false prophets.......	QMt
*40	vii, 16–18	By their fruits ye shall know them.....	QMt
*41	vii, 21–23	Not everyone that saith, "Lord, Lord"..	QMt
*42	vii, 24–27	House on rock and sand..............	QMt
43	vii, 28a	And it came to pass when he had finished, etc..............................	QMt
*44	viii, 5–10	The centurion's servant healed........	QMt
*45	viii, 11–12	Many shall come from east and west....	QMt
*46	viii, 19–22	Two men who would follow Jesus......	Q
*47	ix, 37–38	The harvest is great, the laborers are few	Q
*48	x, 1	The commission of the twelve.........	Q (Mk)
49	x, 5–6	Not in way of gentiles. Lost sheep of Israel.............................	QMt
*50	x, 7	Preach the kingdom of heaven at hand .	QMt
51	x, 8	Heal sick, raise dead; freely ye have received..........................	QMt
*52	x, 9–10	Instruction as to what to take. Laborer and his food.......................	Q (Mk)
*53	x, 11–13	Conduct on the way. Greet the house..	Q (Mk)
*54	x, 14	Whoever does not receive you.........	Q (Mk)

Review of Q in Matthew, Luke, and Mark

TABLE IV—Continued

Sec.	Chap. Verse	Subject	Source
*55	x, 15–16	More tolerable for Sodom, I send you forth as sheep among wolves........	Q
*56	x, 19–20	Take no thot what ye shall answer.....	Q
*57	x, 24	The disciple not above his teacher......	Q
*58	x, 26–33	Fearless confession. Be not afraid of them; things hidden and revealed....	QMt
*59	x, 34–36	Division among relatives..............	QMt
*60	x, 37–39	Conditions of discipleship; saving and losing one's soul.....................	QMt
*61	x, 40–42	He that receiveth you.................	QMt
*62	xi, 2– 6	The question of the Baptist, and answer	Q
*63	xi, 7–10	Jesus' testimony to John. Law and prophets till John..................	Q
*64	xi, 21–23	Woes upon Galilean cities.............	Q
*65	xi, 25–27	Wise and prudent. All things are given unto me.........................	Q
66	xi, 28–30	Come unto me, all ye that labor......	QMt
67	xii, 5– 7	The priests blameless; mercy, not sacrifice.............................	QMt
*68	xii, 22–32	The Beelzebul controversy. Blasphemy	Q (Mk)
*69	xii, 24–35	A good man out of the good treasure of his heart.........................	Q
*70	xii, 39–40	The sign of Jonah....................	QMt
*71	xii, 41	The men of Nineveh..................	Q
*72	xii, 42	Queen of the South...................	Q
*73	xii, 43–45	About backsliding; "empty, swept"....	Q
*74	xiii, 12	Whoso has, to him shall be given......	Q (Mk)
*75	xiii, 16–17	Blessed are your eyes.................	QMt
*76	xiii, 31–32	Parable of the Mustard Seed..........	Q (Mk)
*77	xiii, 33	Parable of the Yeast.................	Q
78	xiii, 44	Parable of Treasure Hid in Field.......	QMt
79	xiii, 45–46	Parable of the Pearls.................	QMt
80	xiii, 47–48	Parable of the Fish-Net..............	QMt
81	xiii, 51–52	Pharisee instructed in the kingdom of heaven.............................	QMt
*82	xv, 14	Blind leading the blind...............	Q
*83	xvii, 20	Faith like a grain of mustard seed......	QMt
*84	xviii, 6– 7	About offenses.......................	Q (Mk)
85	xviii, 12–14	Parable of Lost Sheep................	QMt
*86	xix, 28	The apostles on twelve thrones........	QMt
*86a	xxii, 35–38	The great commandment.............	Q (Mk)
87	xxiii, 2– 3	Scribes and Pharisees in Moses' seat....	QMt
88	xxiii, 4	They bind heavy burdens.............	QMt
89	xxiii, 5	They broaden their phylacteries	QMt
90	xxiii, 8–10	Be not called rabbi...................	QMt
*91	xxiii, 13	Ye shut up the kingdom of heaven.....	QMt
*92	xxiii, 15–16	Woes upon Pharisees.................	QMt
*93	xxiii, 37–30	Lament over Jerusalem...............	QMt
*94	xxiv, 26–27	The day of the Son of man............	QMt
*95	xxiv, 28	Where the body is, there the eagles, etc..	Q
*96	xxiv, 37–39	The days of Noah....................	QMt
*97	xxiv, 40–41	The one taken, the other left..........	QMt
*98	xxiv, 42–44	The watching servant................	Q
*99	xxiv, 45–51	The true and false servants...........	Q

* The asterisk indicates Q material in Matthew duplicated in Luke.

TABLE V
Contents of Q Material in Luke

Sec.	Chap. Verse	Subject	Source
*1	iii, 7–9	Preaching of the Baptist................	Q
*2	iii, 16–17	Messianic announcement of the Baptist.	Q
*3	iv, 1–13	The temptation......................	Q
*4	vi, 20	Blessed are ye poor...................	QLk
*5	vi, 21	Blessed are ye that hunger............	QLk
*6	vi, 22–23	Blessed are ye when men hate you.....	QLk
7	vi, 24–26	Woes upon rich, full, laughing, popular..	QLk
*7a	vi, 31	The Golden Rule.....................	Q
*8	vi, 27–36	Love your enemies....................	QLk
*9	vi, 37–38	About judging........................	QLk
*10	vi, 39	Parable of the Blind Leading the Blind..	Q
*11	vi, 40	The disciple not above his teacher......	Q
*12	vi, 41–42	The mote and the beam...............	Q
*13	vi, 43–44	Tree known by its fruits..............	QLk
*14	vi, 45	A good man out of the good treasure of his heart............................	Q
*15	vi, 46	Why call ye me "Lord, Lord".........	QLk
*16	vi, 47–49	House with and without foundation.....	QLk
*17	vii, 1–2, 7–9	The centurion's servant healed.........	Q
*18	vii, 18, 22–23	Question of John the Baptist and answer	Q
*19	vii, 24–28, 31–35	Jesus' testimony to John..............	Q
*20	viii, 16	Candle and bed (bushel)..............	QLk
*21	viii, 17	Things hidden and revealed............	QLk
*22	viii, 18	Whoever has, to him shall be given.....	Q (Mk)
*23	ix, 1–2	The mission of the twelve.............	Q (Mk)
*24	ix, 5	Whoever shall not receive you.........	Q (Mk)
*25	ix, 57–60	Two men who would follow Jesus......	Q
26	ix, 61–62	A third; no man putteth his hand to the plow...............................	QLk
*27	x, 2	The harvest is great; the laborers are few................................	Q
*28	x, 3	I send you forth as lambs among wolves	Q
*29	x, 4 (ix, 3)	Instructions as to what to take........	Q (Mk)
*30	x, 5–7	Conduct on the way; greet the house. Laborer worthy of his hire.........	Q (Mk)
*31	x, 8–11	Whoever receives, or does not receive, you...............................	Q (Mk)
*32	x, 12	More tolerable for Sodom..............	Q
*33	x, 13–15	Woes upon Galilean cities.............	Q
*34	x, 16 (ix, 48)	He that heareth (receiveth) you........	QLk
35	x, 17–20	Satan falling from heaven, names written	QLk
*36	x, 21–22	Wise and prudent; all things are given unto me............................	Q
*37	x, 23–24	Blessed are the eyes that see what you see	QLk
*38	x, 25–28	The great commandment..............	Q (Mk)
*39	xi, 2–4	The Lord's Prayer....................	QLk
*40	xi, 9–13	Seeking and finding...................	Q
*41	xi, 17–23	Beelzebul controversy.................	Q (Mk)
*42	xi, 24–26	About backsliding; "empty, swept"....	Q
*43	xi, 29–30	The sign of Jonah....................	QLk
*44	xi, 31	Queen of the South...................	QLk
*45	xi, 32	The men of Nineveh..................	Q
*46	xi, 34–35	The light of the body. If thine eye be single.............................	Q
*47	xi, 39–52	Woes upon Pharisees. Take away the key of knowledge...................	QLk

REVIEW OF Q IN MATTHEW, LUKE, AND MARK 225

TABLE V—Continued

Sec.	Chap. Verse	Subject	Source
*48	xii, 4– 9	Fearless confession; be not afraid of them................................	QLk
*49	xii, 10	Blasphemy against Son of man (Beelzebul controversy)...................	Q (Mk)
*50	xii, 11–12	Take no thot what ye shall answer.....	QLk
*51	xii, 22–31	About care...........................	Q
52	xii, 32	Fear not, little flock.................	QLk
*53	xii, 33–34	About treasures, not on the earth......	QLk
54	xii, 35–38	About the necessity for watchfulness....	QLk
*55	xii, 39–40	The watching servant................	Q
*56	xii, 42–46	The true and false servants...........	Q
57	xii, 47–48	Beaten with few stripes or with many...	QLk
58	xii, 49–50	I came to cast fire; I have a baptism...	QLk
*59	xii, 51–53	Division among relatives..............	QLk
60	xii, 54–56	Signs of the time.....................	QLk
*61	xii, 57–59	Agree with thine adversary............	QLk
*62	xiii, 18–19	Parable of the Mustard Seed..........	Q (Mk)
*63	xiii, 20–21	Parable of the Yeast.................	Q
*64	xiii, 23–24	The narrow door (gate)..............	QLk
65	xiii, 25–27	When the door is shut................	QLk
*66	xiii, 28–29	Many from east and west.............	QLk
*67	xiii, 34–35	Lament over Jerusalem...............	Q
68	xiv, 7–11	About taking the chief seats at a feast..	QLk
69	xiv, 12–14	About whom to invite to a feast.......	QLk
*70	xiv, 26–27	Conditions of discipleship.............	QLk
71	xiv, 28–30	Man building a tower.................	QLk
72	xiv, 31–33	King going to war....................	QLk
*73	xiv, 34–35	Salt is good. If the salt has lost.......	(Mk)QLk
*73a	xvi, 13	About serving two masters............	Q
*74	xvi, 16	The law and prophets until John.......	Q
*75	xvi, 17	Relation to the law...................	QLk
*76	xvi, 18	Divorce.............................	Q (Mk)
*77	xvii, 1– 2	Offenses............................	Q (Mk)
*78	xvii, 3– 4	On forgiveness.......................	QLk
*79	xvii, 5– 6	Faith as a grain of mustard seed.......	QLk
80	xvii, 20–21	The kingdom cometh not with observation...............................	QLk
*81	xvii, 22–25	The day of the Son of man............	QLk
*82	xvii, 26–27	The days of Noah....................	QLk
83	xvii, 28–32	The days of Lot......................	QLk
*84	xvii, 33	Saving and losing one's soul..........	Q
*85	xvii, 34–35	Two in one bed (field)................	QLk
*86	xvii, 37	Where the body is, there the eagles, etc.	Q
87	xviii, 1– 8	The parable of the Unjust Judge.......	QLk
88	xxi, 34–35	The necessity for watchfulness and prayer.............................	QLk
89	xxii, 30	Eating and drinking in the kingdom of God; twelve thrones................	QLk

* The asterisk indicates Q material in Luke duplicated in Matthew.

or Luke, are marked Q. The sections unduplicated, or duplicated but with deviations too great to be assigned to Matthew or Luke working upon a similarly worded text, are marked QMt or QLk.

As to the generally homogeneous character of the sections marked Q, there will be no dispute. Since these are restricted to the passages showing the very closest parallelism, there can be no question about the propriety of assigning them to Q. The only question will be as to the assignment of any unduplicated material to any form of Q, and the assignment of the duplicated but not closely paralleled sections to QMt and QLk instead of simply to Q. Reasons have been given[1] for such assignments in each case. But a few sections may be taken as again illustrating the advantages of the QMt-QLk hypothesis.

PASSAGES CLOSELY SIMILAR, YET WITH DIVERGENCES TOO GREAT TO BE ACCOUNTED FOR UPON THE HYPOTHESIS OF AN UNDIFFERENTIATED Q

Sections 42 in Matthew and 16 in Luke contain the saying about the house on the rock and the sand (with and without foundations). These sections are universally ascribed to Q, both from their general similarity and from their position in each Gospel as the conclusion to the Sermon on the Mount (Plain). But the wording is very dissimilar. Only those words are alike which must necessarily be so if two men were using the same subject as an illustration; and this is true, not only of the wording, but of the thought. Those who assign the passage simply to Q are compelled to suppose that, Matthew representing the original text, Luke has observed that the correct antithesis is not between a house built on a rock and a house built on the sand, but between one built with a foundation and one built without one. So he says nothing about the soil, whether rock or sand, but says that in one case the man built upon the surface, and that in the other he digged deep and laid a good foundation. The amount of re-working, reinterpreting, and

[1] Pp. 129–206.

re-writing thus required of Luke is wholly unjustified by any treatment he has accorded to any of the sayings of Jesus in Mark. It is presumable that he exercised his editorial function on his recension of Q as he did upon the sayings-material in Mark. But it is much more natural to suppose that the story that lay before him in his source lay before him in a form considerably different from that which it had in Matthew's source. The assumption of the two recensions therefore has the advantage of preserving the section for Q, without the disadvantage of ascribing to Luke a wholly unwarrantable amount of re-working.

Sections 4–11 in Matthew and 4–6 in Luke contain their different versions of the beatitudes. Those who assign indiscriminately to Q all the verses contained in these sections have to assume that Luke omitted five of the beatitudes. No reason can be assigned for his doing so, and it is wholly improbable that he would have deliberately mutilated a passage so liturgically complete and impressive. The five omitted beatitudes are additions to the teachings of Jesus, manufactured on the basis of Old Testament exemplars. But if anything stood in Q, these five beatitudes stood there, only not in Luke's recension, but in Matthew's.

WITH MATTHEW'S Q BEFORE HIM, LUKE WOULD NOT HAVE OMITTED SO MUCH OF IT

Those who argue for Luke's omission of so much Q material which (according to their assumption) stood before him, allege as a precedent his omission of so much Marcan material, especially of the continuous section Mk vi, 45—viii, 21. It is held by many students that the copy of Mark used by Luke did not contain this section.[1] The writer does not see the necessity for this assumption as there are obvious reasons for Luke's omission of the section if it stood in his copy of Mark. It contains the doublet of the feeding of the four thousand. Luke avoids doublets as far as possible. It contains the story of the walking on the sea, a story similar in many respects to that of the storm at sea which Luke had already taken from Mark. The dispute about hand-washing and the things that defile would have no interest for Luke or his gentile readers. The story of the Canaanitish woman and her difficulties in securing help from Jesus, and the methods of healing the dumb man, would offend Luke's non-Jewish sympathies and his artistic sense. The discussion about leaven he would omit because he had a partial parallel from another source. In this whole section which Luke omits from Mark there are very few sayings of Jesus, and those of a character not to please or interest Luke. The omission of such a section, or of anything else that Luke omits from Mark, offers no precedent for the omissions he is alleged to have made from Q.

In the preceding table of contents for Q material in Matthew (pp. 222–23), there are twenty-nine sections for which Luke has no parallel. Five of these, the omitted beatitudes, have already been discussed. Of the remaining twenty-four there are a few which, it may be admitted, Luke might not have cared to include, even if they were in his Q. Such are the sections on oaths, on fasting, on the blamelessness of the priests, and on the Pharisee instructed in the kingdom of God—all of a strongly Jewish character. To these may be added

---

[1] So Wendling. Stanton also says Mark's connection is better with Mk vi, 45—vii, 23, omitted.

four other brief sections, all from Matthew's discourse against the Pharisees; especially, the reference to phylacteries, which would have no meaning for Luke's readers, and the injunction not to be called "Rabbi." The saying, "Give not that which is holy unto the dogs [heathen] nor cast your pearls before swine [unbelievers]," he would hardly have taken if it had stood in his source. But there are other sections which would particularly have delighted him, and which it is almost inconceivable that he should have read and omitted. Such are the sections on alms-giving (a favorite subject with Luke; see Lk xi, 41; xii, 33); on prayer (a subject which he mentions eighteen times against Matthew's ten, outside of this passage); the three little parables of the Treasure Hid in the Field, the Pearls, and the Fish-Net, and the beautiful saying, so fitted to Luke's universalistic purpose, "Come unto me."

Much less can any reason be assigned for Matthew's omission of the sixteen unduplicated sayings ascribed to QLk.[1] Matthew almost invariably shortens Mark's narratives, and sometimes omits a narrative section, but practically never omits a saying of Jesus given in Mark. The case of the third would-be follower of Jesus, with the particularly fine saying, "No man having put his hand to the plow"; the little parables of the Man Building a Tower and the King Going to War; the sayings, "I came to cast fire upon the earth," "I have a baptism to be baptized with," "Fear not, little flock," would attract Matthew as much as they did Luke, and with Matthew's almost slavish adherence to Mark in all Mark's sayings-material, no reason can be given for his omission of them.

[1] It should be said that most of those who argue for Luke's omission of so much Q material assign these sixteen sections to some special source of Luke's.

If it be asked why these unduplicated sections, which have been assigned to QMt and QLk, are not assigned simply to special and undetermined sources, the answer is that all these sections stand more or less closely connected with Q material, they are strongly similar to the other Q matter in form and idea, and equally different in form and feeling from the passages assigned to special sources. They consist, in both Matthew and Luke, of short parables of the undoubted Q type (cf. the Treasure Hid in the Field, the Pearls, the Fish-Net, the Unjust Judge) and of short sayings; whereas the special source or sources (whether of Matthew or Luke) consist of narratives (the opening chapters of both Gospels, the Peter-sections in Matthew, the death of Judas in Matthew, Jesus before Herod in Luke, the watch at the grave in Matthew, the Emmaus incident in Luke, and the peculiar matter of both Matthew and Luke in their accounts of the days in Jerusalem) and of story-parables like the Prodigal Son, the Lost Coin, the Good Samaritan, the Entrusted Money. These similarities in the material assigned to a special source or sources are not enough to prove the unity of that source for either Matthew or Luke, and are not so intended; but they are enough to distinguish the material so assigned from that assigned to QMt and QLk, and to establish the comparative homogeneity of this latter material in each case.

THE "SECONDARY TRAITS" ARE IN QMT AND QLK, NOT IN Q

The distinction between Q and QMt and QLk is further justified by the consideration of secondary traits. QMt and QLk represent deviations from, or additions to, an original Q. Since these deviations and additions would go back to a very early time, and even when comparatively late might embody an early tradition, the presence of primary traits in QMt and QLk need not surprise us.[1] Since Q cannot be proved to be earlier than 60–65, it may also easily contain secondary traits. But since QMt and QLk are in general later than Q, and presumably represent a later tradition, we should naturally expect to find in them a larger number of secondary characteristics.

In the material assigned to Q in Tables IV and V[2] the writer believes that not many unmistakably secondary traits appear. The messianic announcement of the Baptist is certainly primary as compared with Mark predicting Jesus as the fire-judge, contrary to the facts of his life. The temptation in Q is also primary as compared with Mark, with the exception of the conversation between Jesus and John in Matthew, which is obviously secondary and belongs to QMt. Of the sayings, only a few have a secondary sound. Such are especially those connected with the instructions to the twelve, which seem to embody some of the experiences, or bespeak some of the needs, of the early Christian itinerant preachers: "The laborer is worthy of his hire [or his keep]"; "I send you forth as sheep among wolves"; "The disciple is not above his master"; "The law and the prophets prophesied until John"; perhaps also Matthew's long beatitude, "Blessed are ye when men persecute you," etc.

But by far the most of the secondary traits, and the most unmistakable of them, are found in the additions to and deviations from the Q tradition *in QMt and QLk*. Such are the additional beatitudes supplied by Matthew's Q and made up of Old Testament quotations; the insertion

[1] See especially Matthew's "Go not into any way of the gentiles," which might be assigned to Q, with obvious reasons for Luke's omission.

[2] Pp. 222–25.

into the temptation story, in QMt, of the protest of John the Baptist and the answer of Jesus; the warning against false prophets in Matthew; the speech about those who say "Lord, Lord"; the prediction of division among relatives (seemingly answering the condition in which the early church found itself); the many coming from the east and the west (written in the days of the expanding church); the sign of Jonah interpreted (in Matthew) as referring to the resurrection; the parable of the Fish-Net with its eschatological interpretation; the saying about the twelve apostles on twelve thrones; and the various sections interpolated, apparently from QMt and QLk, into Mark's apocalypse.

Closer analysis of particular sections tends to corroborate this impression of secondary traits as coming not from Q but from the recensions. For example, the sayings about the light and the bushel and about the salt that had lost its savor appear to have stood in Q. But from his own recension of Q, Matthew prefixed to the saying what Luke did not find in his recension, "Ye are the light of the world," "Ye are the salt of the earth," two sayings which seem to reflect the exalted estimate of the apostles in the sub-apostolic age. The Lord's Prayer probably stood in the original Q much as it is in Luke; Matthew's amplifications, found in his source, have the liturgical and ecclesiastical coloring that betray the later time.

So, further, Luke's parable of the Unjust Judge, with its generally Q sound, but with its pathetic question appended (from Luke's recension), "Nevertheless, when the Son of man cometh, shall he find the faith on the earth?" bespeaks the times of persecution when the survival of the new faith looked problematical. Matthew's "Cast not your pearls before swine," "The Pharisee instructed in the kingdom of heaven," "The scribes and Pharisees in Moses' seat," all from QMt, and Luke's "Rejoice that your names are written in heaven," his saying about discerning the signs of the time (of the parousia), his "kingdom cometh not with observation," and his twice repeated injunction to watchfulness, all from QLk, certainly have a secondary sound. The presence of so many secondary traits in QMt and QLk does not prove that the passages so assigned might not be assigned to S or some other special or undefined source; but many if not all of them being passages ordinarily assigned simply to Q, the large number of secondary traits in them does tend to substantiate, in an unlooked-for manner, the assumption of the two recensions.

CHAPTER VI

DID MARK ALSO USE Q?

In the introduction to his *Beginnings of Gospel History*, Bacon remarks that the "dependence of Mark upon Q can be demonstrated." Wellhausen says that "independence [between Mark and Q] is not to be thot of." Streeter, in *Oxford Studies*, has made the most recent and thoro study of the relation of Mark and Q, and some of his results have already been utilized and acknowledged. Even Dr. Sanday, in the introduction to *Oxford Studies*, confesses himself an unwilling convert to the theory that Mark was acquainted with, and made some use of, Q. Wellhausen alone, so far as I know, maintains the apparently untenable position that Q is later than Mark, and that where the two overlap, Q has used Mark instead of Mark using Q. His acceptance of this position is partially explained by the fact that he makes no distinction between the original Q and the recensions of it in the hands of Matthew and Luke; he also allows to Q much material (e.g., the conversation between John and Jesus at the baptism) which other scholars, without the hypothesis of QMt and QLk, ascribe to the hand of Matthew or Luke. Harnack and Wernle maintain the priority of Q to Mark. Wernle concedes some small use of Q by Mark, and Harnack thinks Mark was at least "acquainted with" Q.

The discrimination between QMt and QLk and the original Q makes unnecessary a good deal of the work that has heretofore been done toward determining the primary and secondary traits in Mark and Q respectively.

Assuming that Mark used either the original Q, or as near to the original of that document as we can yet get, the recensions used by Matthew and Luke would be perhaps thirty, certainly twenty, years later than that used by Mark. In the fifty or more verses of Mark that appear to have stood also in Q, there is nothing that can be shown to be later than the year 70 (the date generally assigned to Mark). There is nothing to suggest that the author had witnessed the destruction of Jerusalem, or the events immediately leading up to it. The presence of the same material in Mark and Q is demonstrated by the agreements of Matthew and Luke against Mark, or by the deviations of the one or the other of them from the Marcan form of a saying, in such way as not to admit of explanation except by the assumption of two sources (Mark and Q) in the hands of Matthew and Luke. In other words, if Mark did use Q, but if he used the same text of it as was used by Matthew and Luke, and if the three followed Q with equal faithfulness, in all such instances Q would fail to appear, since both Matthew and Luke would appear to be following only Mark. It is therefore where there are deviations of either Matthew or Luke from Mark in sections where the other follows Mark closely, or where there are agreements of Matthew and Luke against Mark in sayings-material, that the presence of Q behind Mark can be detected.

Upon the hypothesis of Q without QMt or QLk, the argument by which the use of Q by Mark, as against the use of Mark by Q, was proven, consisted of picking out the primary and secondary traits in Mark and Q respectively, and of showing that the primary traits were in Q and the secondary in Mark. But this was very difficult to do, so long as, e.g., the Peter incidents peculiar to Matthew, or the conversation during the baptism, were attributed to Q. For these were indisputably secondary. If the priority of Mark was to be maintained, all such traits had to be removed from Q and assigned to the evangelist or to some special source.

Upon the theory now advocated by the writer, these secondary traits are practically all assigned, not to the original Q, but to QMt or QLk.[1] But if Mark used any form of Q, it was not QMt or QLk, but some much simpler, more primary, and doubtless less extended, form. The presence of secondary traits in QMt and QLk therefore does nothing toward proving the secondary character of Q in its original form, or in such an early form as would have been used by Mark. Since nothing can be found in Q which is either demonstrably or probably later than the date of Mark, the assumption that Mark used Q may be permitted to stand; and with the removal of the secondary traits to the recensions, it does not require the minute analysis which earlier hypotheses made necessary, since there are no longer any indications militating against Mark's use of Q. What now remains therefore is to determine as nearly as possible what material stood in Mark and Q.

WHAT MATERIAL DID MARK TAKE FROM Q?

In the attempt to determine what material Mark has taken from Q, an effort will also be made to decide whether Matthew and Luke took the same material directly from Q, or indirectly from Q thru Mark. The verses which one or both of them appear to have taken directly from Q (tho these verses stand also in Mark) will be added to the number of verses already attributed to Q (or QMt and QLk). We shall thus have before us

[1] See analyses on pp. 230–33.

the largest possible sum-total of Q material. The tables of contents already made out for the Q material, as it now stands in Matthew and Luke respectively,[1] will throw further light upon the propriety or impropriety of regarding QMt and QLk as recensions of one original document. The same tables will serve to indicate the probable order of Q, and the investigation now following will then be used to determine what acquaintance, if any, Mark had with Q, and what use, if any, he made of that document.

THE MESSIANIC ANNOUNCEMENT OF THE BAPTIST
(Mk i, 7–8)

Matthew and Luke are close to Mark in their wording here, but agree against him in putting his verses in reverse order and in the addition of καὶ πυρί. They then each add a verse (Mt iii, 12; Lk iii, 17) which has already been assigned to Q. In each Gospel this verse develops the idea introduced by the καὶ πυρί. The order of Matthew and Luke is here necessarily, and apparently originally, different from that of Mark, since the relative clause which begins the additional matter of Matthew and Luke depends upon the order of sentences in these two Gospels and will not fit Mark's arrangement. In spite therefore of the close agreement of Matthew's vs. 11 and Luke's vs. 16 with Mark, these verses must be assigned to Q. In other words, it is probable that here Matthew and Luke are depending directly upon Q, and not merely indirectly upon him thru Mark.

THE BAPTISM OF JESUS
(Mk i, 9–11)

This section is added to Q by many critics, on the ground of its position between the preaching of the Baptist and the temptation of Jesus, both related in Q.

[1] Pp. 222–35.

The agreements between Matthew and Luke against Mark are not, however, frequent or important enough by themselves to suggest this assignment. On the other hand, the addition in Matthew of the conversation between Jesus and John points to a source in that respect different from that of either Mark or Luke. Matthew also represents the voice from heaven as directed to the crowd, and not to Jesus alone, as do Mark and Luke. In both these deviations Matthew has an apparently later tradition, and has preferred to follow his recension of Q. Either Luke's recension here agreed substantially with Mark's, or else Luke has followed Mark more closely than Q.

THE TEMPTATION OF JESUS
(Mk i, 12–13)

The very brief account in Mark is followed in Matthew and Luke by nine and eleven verses respectively, which have been already assigned to Q. The question here is whether Matthew and Luke followed Mark in the first two verses of their narratives, and after that forsook him for Q, or whether they followed Q thruout. Matthew and Luke agree in substituting διάβολος for Mark's σατανᾶς, in the omission of the clause "and was with the wild beasts," and in placing the temptation in the period of hunger following the forty days' fast. They apparently followed Q rather than Mark, but each introduced some changes out of deference to the latter. Mark's account is similar enough to that of Matthew and Luke to be a brief extract from Q.

THE BEELZEBUL CONTROVERSY
(Mk iii, 20–29)

This Marcan section is duplicated in Mt xii, 24–32, and Lk xi, 15–23; xii, 10. Of these Matthean and Lucan accounts, Mt xii, 26–28, and Lk xi, 18–20, are practically identical, but not paralleled in Mark. In xii, 29, Matthew follows Mk iii, 27, almost word for word. At the same place Luke forsakes Mark and deviates widely, tho agreeing closely with Matthew in the three preceding verses. Matthew's xii, 30, and Luke's xi, 23, are again unparalleled in Mark, and are evidently from Q. Matthew's vs. 31 again goes back to Mark's vs. 28, but is influenced by his own Q material in the following verses. The derivation of Mark from Q in this passage is rendered doubly sure by the facts that the verses seriously interrupt the connection in Mark, and that the passage here consecutive in Matthew and Mark is separated in Luke. Matthew is a conflation of Mark and Q. Luke is apparently Q thruout. Matthew's Marcan and Q material being mixed, it is impossible to tell whether Matthew's Q was here identical with Luke's or not. Out of this section there should be added to Q the passages Mt xii, 25, and Lk xi, 17, 21.

FIVE DETACHED SAYINGS
(Mk iv, 21–25)

Such detached sayings, unconnected with Mark's narrative, create at once a presumption of their having been taken from Q. Luke has the first saying (about the lamp) in two places (viii, 16; xi, 33), indicating that he found it both in Mark and Q. He also has a duplicate for the second saying, while the fifth is repeated twice in both Matthew and Luke. Mk iv, 23, is the proverbial saying used twice in both Mark and Luke and three times in Matthew. There is thus only one of Mark's sayings (iv, 24) which is not given twice by Matthew or Luke or both. An additional indication of the occurrence of these verses in Q, and Mark's derivation of them from that source, is the fact that they are part of a section in Mark which seriously interrupts his narrative, interposing a private conversation of Jesus with his disciples between the teaching in the boat and the storm on the lake. The verses are also given by Matthew in four different chapters, and by Luke in two, and by both in different order from each other and from Mark. All five of these Marcan verses, therefore, and their parallels in Matthew and Luke, should be assigned to Q.

THE PARABLE OF THE MUSTARD SEED
(Mk iv, 30–32)

This parable has a strong resemblance to those already assigned to Q. Matthew's connection is the same as Mark's; Luke's is different. Luke agrees with Mark in beginning with a question, tho he omits the second half of the double question in Mark. Matthew follows Mark, or is strongly influenced by him in Mt xiii, 32. Matthew and Luke agree against Mark in the words ὃν λαβὼν ἄνθρωπος. According to a suggestion of Wellhausen's, ἔβαλεν εἰς κῆπον and ἔσπειρεν ἐν τῷ ἀγρῷ may be translation variants. In the conclusion Matthew and Luke agree much more closely with each other than with Mark. Except for the influence of Mark at the beginning, Luke seems to be following Q, while Matthew's parable is a conflation of Q and Mark. If Mark here rests upon Q, then Matthew is conflating a parable which Mark drew from Q with the same parable as he (Matthew) found it in his recension of Q. Complicated as this may seem, Mark's parable is too closely similar to Luke's to have had any but a Q origin. To Q in Luke should be added Lk xiii, 18–19; and to Q in Matthew, Mt xiii, 31–32.

THE SENDING OUT OF THE TWELVE
(Mk vi, 7–11)

This passage is to be compared with Mt x, 1, 7–8, 9–16, and Lk ix, 1–5; x, 1, 3, 4–7, 9–12 (with considerable rearrangement of order in the verses). The Marcan material, as it reappears in both Matthew and Luke, is mixed with much other material from Q. Luke's addition of a mission of seventy and his division of this Marcan material between that mission and the mission of the twelve add to the confusion. Matthew (x, 14) and Luke (ix, 5) agree in six words against Mark. In the verb ἐκτινάξετε, Matthew (x, 14) follows Mark against Luke. Matthew and Luke agree against Mark in saying μήτε ῥάβδον instead of εἰ μὴ ῥάβδον. In those parts of Matthew's and Luke's narratives that are not paralleled in Mark there is probably an oral tradition mingled with the Q material. Mark's version might cbe onsidered an excerpt, rather than a copy, of Q. To Q in Matthew may be added Mt x, 1, 9, 10ab, 14; and to Q in Luke, Lk ix, 1, 3, 5; x, 4, 10.

A SIGN REFUSED
(Mk viii, 12)

On the ground of Matthew's having doublets for this saying (Mt xii, 39; xvi, 4) and Luke a parallel to it (Lk xi, 29), it may without further consideration be assigned to Q. The agreement of Matthew and Luke, and the agreement of Matthew's doublets, in adding "Except the sign of Jonah," may be taken to indicate the difference here between Mark's Q and the later recensions.

"WHOSOEVER WILL FOLLOW ME"
(Mk viii, 34–35)

Matthew has doublets for this saying in x, 38–39; xvi, 24–25; Luke in ix, 23–24; xiv, 27; xvii, 33. Matthew and Luke copy the Marcan version with unusual fidelity thru about forty words. They agree against him in saying εἴ τις for Mark's ὅστις, in the substitution of a form (tho not the same form) of the verb ἔρχομαι for ἀκολουθεῖν, and in the employment of a subjunctive in place of an indicative of the verb ἀπόλλυμι. Luke adds the phrase "day by day." Considering the remarkably close verbal agreement as well as the agreement in order, there can be no doubt that Matthew in xvi, 24–25, and Luke in ix, 23–24, are following Mark; their agreements against him may be explained partly by a desire to correct his style, and partly by assimilation. The resemblances between the other member of the doublet in each case, and the saying as here reported in Mark (i.e., between Mt x, 38–39; Lk xiv, 27; xvii, 33, and Mk viii, 34–35), are sufficiently close to suggest, if not to prove, that Mark's saying was derived by him from Q. Since these verses have already been assigned to Q in the examination of the double tradition, they yield no new Q material here.

"WHOEVER IS ASHAMED OF ME"
(Mk viii, 38)

Matthew has a parallel of this saying, and Luke has doublets for it (Mt x, 33; Lk ix, 26; xii, 9). The verse may be assigned to Q.

ABOUT OFFENSES
(Mk ix, 42–48)

Matthew here follows Mark rather closely, except that he adds "Woe to the world because of offenses," and conflates Mark's two sayings about the hand and the foot into one. Matthew has doublets for Mk ix, 43, 45–47, in Mt v, 29–30, and xviii, 8–9. Luke has avoided the doublet, but has a parallel to Mark's verses in Lk xvii, 1–2. The section may be assigned to Mark and Q.

ABOUT SALT
(Mk ix, 49–50)

The little saying in vs. 49 is unduplicated in either of the other Gospels. If any source be suggested for it, nothing more likely than Q could be suggested. If the saying be assigned to Q, it will be the only Q saying in Mark not taken over by either Matthew or Luke. Luke agrees in xiv, 34, with Mark as against Matthew (v, 13), and with Matthew against Mark in $\mu\omega\rho\alpha\nu\theta\hat{\eta}$, but shows the influence of Mark again in $\dot{\alpha}\rho\tau\upsilon\theta\dot{\eta}\sigma\epsilon\tau\alpha\iota$. Either Mark follows Q very loosely, perhaps from memory, or Matthew and Luke have a different recension.

ABOUT DIVORCE
(Mk x, 11–12)

Matthew has doublets for this saying (Mt v, 32; xix, 9). In the latter occurrence of the saying in Matthew, the connection is the same as that of Mark's. It is omitted in that instance by Luke, presumably because it is part of a controversy with the Pharisees. But doubt is thrown upon the presence of the saying in Q by the fact that it occurs twice in Mark also, and may have been taken from him by Matthew in both instances.

THE FIRST WHO SHALL BE LAST
(Mk x, 31)

This saying is paralleled in Luke (xiii, 30) and has doublets in Matthew (xix, 30; xx, 16). It apparently stood in both Mark and Q.

TRUE GREATNESS
(Mk x, 43–44)

There are doublets for this saying in Mt xx, 26–27, and xxiii, 11, and in Lk xxii, 26; ix, 48. It probably stood in both Mark and Q, but this again cannot be proved, since Mark also has the saying twice (ix, 35).

ABOUT FAITH
(Mk xi, 23)

There is a parallel for this saying in Lk xvii, 6, and there are doublets for it in Mt xvii, 20, and xxi, 21. It stood in Mark and Q.

AGAINST THE PHARISEES
(Mk xii, 38–40)

This section is listed by Mr. Streeter as from Q, because it "looks like a reminiscence from a long denunciation in Q." This is probably correct, but the doublets to establish it are lacking.

THE HOLY SPIRIT SPEAKING IN THE DISCIPLES
(Mk xiii, 11)

This saying is paralleled in Mt x, 19, and has doublets in Lk xii, 11–12, and xxi, 14–15.

OTHER MARCAN PASSAGES CONSIDERED, BUT REJECTED

In addition to the passages assigned to Q in the preceding investigation, several are suggested by Streeter and Wernle. Streeter suggests Mk xiii, 15–16; but the doublets in Luke are apparently taken in both instances from Mark. Streeter thinks that xiii, 28–32, "has a

DID MARK ALSO USE Q? 245

genuine sound"; but there is nothing more specific to prove its presence in Q. Streeter's suggestion that Mk i, 2–3, is from Q seems unjustifiable. Vs. 3 is an Old Testament quotation which Matthew, Mark, and Luke all have in common. If it stood originally in Mark and is not to be regarded as a later addition, there is no occasion for the assumption of Q. Vs. 2 could hardly have stood in its present place when Matthew and Luke used Mark. It occurs in another connection in Matthew and Luke (Mt xi, 10; Lk vii, 27), and was probably copied from there into its present place by a later hand.

Wernle's additions to the above Q material in Mark do not seem to be justified. Some of them, e.g., Mk xi, 14, rest upon making doublets (in this case Mt xxi, 19, and vii, 7–8) where the wording is not close enough to warrant them. Others rest upon the general character of the sayings. The latter is a tempting criterion, and in Matthew and Luke, who demonstrably make such extensive use of Q, it is more justifiable and has been used to some extent in the preceding analyses. But in Mark, where Q is so sparingly and loosely used, it cannot be safely employed aside from other indications, especially the occurrence of doublets.

The writer believes that the matter listed in the above tabulation is about all that can at present safely be assigned to Q in Mark. It yields us, as new Q material in Matthew, sixteen verses, and as new Q material in Luke, seventeen. This would bring the totals for Q material in Matthew and Luke up to two hundred and eighty-three in Matthew and to two hundred and fifty-five in Luke.[1] The number of verses in Mark which can be traced to Q are about fifty. All but sixteen of these

[1] See the reckoning made without inclusion of Marcan Q on pp. 162, 218.

verses in Matthew and all but seventeen in Luke had already been assigned to Q. Only one stands in Mark alone.

TABLE VI

CONTENTS FOR Q MATERIAL IN MARK

Sec.	Chap. Verse	Subject	Source
1	i, 7– 8	Messianic announcement of the Baptist..	Q
2	i, 12–13	The temptation......................	Q
3	iii, 22–29	The Beelzebul controversy	Q
4	iv, 21	The light and the bushel..............	Q
5	iv, 22	Things hidden and revealed...........	Q
6	iv, 24	With what measure (about judging)....	Q
7	iv, 25	Whoever has, to him shall be given.....	Q
8	iv, 30–32	Parable of the Mustard Seed..........	Q
9	vi, 7–11	Mission of the twelve, what to take, conduct by the way, if any place does not receive you.......................	Q
10	viii, 12	A sign refused	Q
11	viii, 34, 38	Conditions of discipleship.............	Q
12	ix, 42	About offenses.......................	Q
13	ix, 49–50	Salt is good. If the salt has lost, etc. ..	Q
14	x, 11–12	About divorce.......................	Q
15	x, 31	First last and last first.................	Q
16	x, 43–44	Whoso would be great among you......	Q
17	xi, 23	About faith..........................	Q
18	xii, 38–40	Against Pharisaism...................	Q
19	xiii, 11	Take no thot what ye shall say........	Q

The above content being made out for the material common to Mark and Q, the use of Q by Mark may be permitted to rest upon its general probability, there being nothing to contradict it or to substantiate the opposite hypothesis. How closely Mark used Q, whether actually copying certain passages from him, or merely recalling what he had read or heard read from Q, cannot be determined, since what stood in the text of Q used by Mark is only an inference from what stood in the recensions used by Matthew and Luke.

DO THE VOCABULARY AND STYLE OF MARK AND Q, RESPECTIVELY, THROW ANY LIGHT UPON THEIR LITERARY RELATIONSHIP?

The inquiry might perhaps be carried a step farther by a comparison of the vocabularies of Mark and Q.

DID MARK ALSO USE Q? 247

Hawkins, between the first and second editions of his *Horae Synopticae*, made a second and more diligent search for linguistic peculiarities in Q, and declares himself unable to find any. Harnack, on the contrary, believes he finds some such.

Sentences in Q, according to Harnack, are generally connected by καί, δέ being used but seldom. The same is true of Mark. But this only indicates the comparative nearness of both Mark and Q to the Semitic. The same may be said of the preponderance of simple verbs in distinction from compound in both Mark and Q. Ἐάν is used twice as frequently as εἰ; Mark also appears to use the former thirty-six times and the latter but fifteen. This fact seems to have more significance by reason of the other, that Luke uses one word thirty-two and the other thirty-three times. Matthew, however, uses ἐάν exactly twice as often as εἰ. When we remember that all we have of Q is contained in Matthew and Luke, and only a small portion of it in Mark, these facts do seem to indicate a preference for ἐάν over εἰ as between Mark and Q on the one side and Luke on the other, but between Mark and Q on the one side and Matthew on the other no such contrast appears. Mark and Q are here no nearer to each other, or very little, than either of them is to Matthew.

The particle τε is never found in Q.[1] It occurs five times in Mt and seven times in Lk, and but once in Mk. Ὡς in temporal clauses seems to be absent; it is also absent from Matthew, while Luke uses it nineteen times and Mark but once. Clauses with γίνομαι, frequent in Matthew and Luke, are absent from Q; they also occur in Mark; but their absence from Q may be due simply

[1] Still according to Harnack.

to Q's lack of historical matter. Παρά and σύν are absent; the first is used about evenly by Mark and Matthew, and more frequently by Luke; the second, three times by Matthew, five times by Mark, and twenty-four times by Luke.

CONCLUSION AS TO MARK'S DEPENDENCE UPON Q

These facts do not all point in the same direction. They seem sometimes to indicate a linguistic affinity between Q and Mark, but this affinity usually extends to Matthew also. What seems to be proved by them is that Mark and Q and Matthew all stand nearer to the Semitic than does Luke. But this is only the obverse of the statement that Luke is the best Grecist. It throws no light upon the literary relation of Mark and Q. Such literary relation, in fact, cannot in the strict sense be "proved." It can only be rendered probable, tho perhaps extremely probable, by the unlikelihood that Mark and Q should have fifty verses in common without any literary relationship. Such relationship being assumed, the dependence is on the side of Mark.

CHAPTER VII

THE ORIGINAL ORDER OF Q

The following tables are intended to throw light upon the probable original order of Q. They will also facilitate comparison of the Q material in the two tables of contents given on pp. 222–25. The section numbers at the left are those in the tables for Matthew and Luke respectively on those pages. Table VII gives the sections in the order in which they come in Matthew, with the numbers of the corresponding sections as they occur in Luke; Table VIII, the sections as they come in Luke, with numbers of corresponding sections in Matthew. Unduplicated sections are not listed.

Since Matthew shows everywhere a tendency to group his material into discourses, it is *a priori* probable that the original order of the Q material is to be sought in Luke and not in Matthew. Given this tendency to combine, reasons are obvious for Matthew's combining, in his Sermon on the Mount, much matter that Luke has scattered thru his Gospel. But if the Q material originally stood in such continuous discourses, no motive can be assigned for Luke's breaking up these discourses and scattering their material thru so many chapters. The assumption that Matthew has combined, in his Sermon on the Mount, material which originally was separated as it still is in Luke, is corroborated by an analysis of that Sermon, which shows it to be anything but a unity. Much of the material which Matthew has combined into this Sermon has no duplicate in Luke. There is no means of telling where in Matthew's Q this unduplicated material stood. But the fact that the duplicated matter has been brot forward by Matthew from later

TABLE VII

Mt	Lk	Mt	Lk	Mt	Lk	Mt	Lk	Mt	Lk
Sec.	Sec.	Sec.	Sec.	Sec.	Sec.	Sec.	Sec.	Sec.	Sec.
1 =	1	30 =	46	50 =	23	63 =	19	83 =	79
2 =	2	31 =	73	52 =	29	63 =	74	84 =	77
3 =	3	32 =	51	53 =	30	64 =	33	86 =	89
4 =	4	33 =	9	54 =	24	65 =	36	86 =	38
7 =	5	34 =	12	54 =	31	68 =	41	91 =	47
11 =	6	36 =	40	55 =	32	68 =	49	92 =	47
12 =	73	37 =	7	55 =	28	69 =	14	93 =	67
13 =	20	36 =	64	56 =	50	70 =	43	94 =	81
14 =	75	40 =	13	57 =	11	71 =	45	95 =	86
17 =	61	41 =	15	58 =	48	72 =	44	96 =	82
20 =	76	42 =	16	58 =	21	73 =	42	97 =	92
22 =	8	44 =	17	59 =	59	74 =	22	98 =	55
23 =	8	45 =	66	60 =	70	75 =	37	99 =	56
26 =	39	46 =	25	60 =	84	76 =	62		
27 =	78	47 =	27	61 =	34	77 =	63		
29 =	53	48 =	23	62 =	18	82 =	10		

TABLE VIII

Lk	Mt	Lk	Mt	Lk	Mt	Lk	Mt	Lk	Mt
Sec.	Sec.	Sec.	Sec.	Sec.	Sec.	Sec.	Sec.	Sec.	Sec.
1 =	1	16 =	42	33 =	64	49 =	68	74 =	63
2 =	2	17 =	44	34 =	61	50 =	56	75 =	14
3 =	3	18 =	62	36 =	65	51 =	32	76 =	20
4 =	4	19 =	63	37 =	75	53 =	29	77 =	84
5 =	7	20 =	13	38 =	86	55 =	98	78 =	27
6 =	11	21 =	58	39 =	26	56 =	99	79 =	82
7a =	37	22 =	74	40 =	36	59 =	59	81 =	94
8 =	22	23 =	48	41 =	68	61 =	17	82 =	96
8 =	23	24 =	54	42 =	73	62 =	76	84 =	60
9 =	33	25 =	46	43 =	70	63 =	77	85 =	17
10 =	82	27 =	47	44 =	72	64 =	38	86 =	15
11 =	57	28 =	55	45 =	71	66 =	45	89 =	86
12 =	34	29 =	52	46 =	30	67 =	93		
13 =	40	30 =	53	47 =	91	70 =	60		
14 =	69	31 =	54	47 =	92	73 =	12		
15 =	41	32 =	55	48 =	58	73a =	31		

chapters in Luke would give the presumption that such of the unduplicated material as has no necessary unity where it stands also stood in QMt, not at the beginning where it now is, but later; and this is also what we should expect.

Taking the hint that Luke's order probably represents the original order of the Q material, we find this supposition confirmed by the present arrangement. In spite of Matthew's transpositions, the sections in Luke and Matthew, as grouped in Table IX, still stand in the same *relative* order.

TABLE IX

Lk	Mt	
1	1	The preaching of the Baptist
2	2	The messianic announcement of the Baptist
3	3	The temptation
4	4	Blessed are the poor
5	7	Blessed are ye that hunger
6	11	Blessed are ye when men hate you
8	23	Love your enemies
13	40	Tree known by its fruits
15	41	Why call ye me "Lord, Lord"?
16	42	House on rock and sand (with and without foundation)
17	44	The centurion's servant healed
18	62	Question of John the Baptist, and Jesus' answer
19	63	Jesus' testimony to John
25	46	Two men who would follow Jesus
27	47	The harvest is great, the laborers are few
29	52	Instructions to disciples as to what to take on journey
30	53	Conduct on the way; greet the house
31	54	Whoever receives you, receives you not
32	55	More tolerable for Sodom
47	91	Woes upon the Pharisees
47	92	Ye shut up the kingdom of heaven (take away the key of knowledge)
55	98	The watching servant
56	99	The true and false servants
62	76	Parable of the Mustard Seed
63	77	Parable of the Yeast
81	94	The day of the Son of man
82	96	The days of Noah

Each of these groups—one of seven sections, two of four, and six of two sections each—probably stood, within itself, in the same order as that in which we now find it in Matthew and Luke.

The sections grouped in Table X have suffered such slight transpositions as to make it probable that each of the groups constituted a continuous passage, probably in the order preserved by Luke.

TABLE X

Lk Mt	
21 = 58	Things hidden and revealed
23 = 48	The mission of the twelve
24 = 54	Whoever shall not receive you
25 = 46	Two men who would follow Jesus
27 = 47	The harvest is great, the laborers are few
28 = 55	I send you forth as lambs among wolves
29 = 52	Instructions as to what to take on journey
30 = 53	Greet the house
31 = 54	Whoever receives you
32 = 55	More tolerable for Sodom
33 = 63	Woes upon Galilean cities
34 = 61	He that receiveth you receiveth me
36 = 65	Wise and prudent; all things are given unto me of my Father
41 = 68	The Beelzebul controversy
42 = 73	About backsliding, "empty, swept and garnished"
43 = 70	The sign of Jonah
44 = 72	Queen of the South
45 = 71	The men of Nineveh
49 = 68	Blasphemy against the Son of man
48 = 58	Fearless confession; be not afraid of them
50 = 56	Take no thot what ye shall answer
51 = 32	About care
53 = 29	About treasures, not on the earth
81 = 94	The day of the Son of man
82 = 96	The days of Noah
85 = 97	The one taken, the other left
86 = 95	Where the body is, there the eagles will be gathered

There is one other item, which I owe to Mr. Streeter,[1] that strongly supports the assumption that Luke has preserved the Q material in its most nearly original form. That is, that Luke allows himself much less liberty in the rearrangement of Mark's order than does Matthew. The best single testimony to his faithfulness to Mark's order is seen in the fact that where he makes his great omission from Mk (Mk vi, 45—viii, 26), beginning at that point his great interpolation (Lk ix, 51—xviii, 14), he does not, after returning to Mark, go back and pick up any single item that he has omitted. Detached sayings, some brief, and some, like the Beelzebul controversy, of considerable length, which he places in a different connection from that in which Mark gives them, can uniformly be shown to have stood in Q as well as in Mark,[2] and Luke follows Q's order with Q's wording. In the earlier part of his narrative, Luke does permit himself some little freedom in deviating from Mark's order; notably in the imprisonment of John the Baptist, the call of the first disciples, and the rejection at Nazareth (in each case, apparently, at the expense of some anachronism). Except for these instances his transpositions of Marcan material are slight, and usually amount rather to its rearrangement within a single section than to a genuine change of order in the structure. An exception to this rule is his passion narrative, where his use of Mark is greatly influenced by his special source.

Q was apparently a collection of sayings, without chronological framework or data of any sort. But to the sayings of Jesus there was prefixed a slight account of the preaching of John the Baptist. This will not seem

[1] *Oxford Studies*, p. 146.
[2] See pp. 234–46 for material in Mark and Q.

strange when it is remembered that Q was a Palestinian document, and that the cult of John the Baptist long survived the origin of Christianity. What is not so easy to explain is Q's apparent inclusion of one narrative, the story of the centurion's servant. It also contained an account of the sending out of the twelve, but apparently no reference to the passion. The absence of narratives, or of any chronological hints, would make its rearrangement easy; perhaps it suffered some derangement at the hands of those who added the sections peculiar to Matthew's and Luke's recensions (as it did at the hands of Matthew himself), and who are responsible for some of the deviations between the two. As Mr. Streeter suggests, if Mark were lost, we could not, from Matthew and Luke, be sure either of Mark's content or his order. No more can we of Q. About all that can be said is that the strong probability is that Luke more nearly than Matthew reproduces that order.

CHAPTER VIII

SUMMARY AND CONCLUSIONS

The positions reached in this study may be gathered up in a few brief statements:

1. Matthew and Luke depend for the structure of their Gospels, and for practically all of their narrative material, upon Mark.

2. In the order of Marcan material, Matthew and Luke have made such changes as were desirable from the use to which they wished to put this matter. Matthew has made fewer omissions, Luke fewer transpositions.

3. The changes which Matthew and Luke have made in the substance or wording of the Marcan material, including their omissions from it, may be accounted for by a desire to produce a better literary form, to avoid statements that offended the growing sentiment of the church, and to adapt their own narrative to their own public. Some changes must go unaccounted for.

4. The hypothesis of a more primitive form of Mark in the hands of Matthew and Luke is not demanded by the facts. Matthew and Luke used substantially our Mark.

5. Matthew and Luke also used a document Q, whose content, within limits, is well agreed upon.

6. Various facts, especially translation variants, require the assumption that this Q was originally an Aramaic document, used by Matthew and Luke respectively, in

two Greek translations that went back to two different Aramaic texts.[1]

7. This furnishes the clue for the analysis of Q into QMt and QLk, and for the assignment to these two recensions of Q of much material which has hitherto been assigned to unknown sources.

8. Mark has some literary dependence upon Q; but the Q which he knew was an earlier form than those in the hands of Matthew and Luke.

9. The original order of Q is best seen in the order of the Q material preserved in Luke.

---

[1] A note by Professor Sanders says, quite correctly, that "The general agreement in translation words requires that one of these translations should have preceeded and influenced the other."

INDEXES

INDEXES

I. PASSAGES CITED

MARK:

i, 7–8, p. 237.
i, 9–11, pp. 37, 237–38.
i, 12–13, p. 238.
i, 16–20, 21–28, pp. 38, 95.
i, 29–31, pp. 38.
i, 32, p. 100.
i, 32–34, p. 39.
i, 35–38, pp. 39–40.
i, 40–45, p. 41.
ii, 1–12, pp. 41–42.
ii, 9–10, p. 93.
ii, 13–22, p. 42.
ii, 23–28, p. 43.
ii, 25–26, p. 94.
iii, 1–19, pp. 44–45.
iii, 7–8, p. 101.
iii, 20–30, pp. 45, 72–73.
iii, 20–29, pp. 238–39.
iii, 31—iv, 12, p. 45.
iv, 1–33, p. 77.
iv, 13–20, p. 46.
iv, 21–25, p. 47.
iv, 24–25, p. 239.
iv, 30–32, pp. 47, 240.
iv, 35–41, pp. 47–48.
v, 1–20, pp. 48–49.
v, 21–43, pp. 49–50, 72.
vi, 1–6, p. 51.
vi, 6–13, pp. 51–52.
vi, 7–11, p. 241.
vi, 14–16, pp. 52–53.
vi, 17–29, pp. 53–54.
vi, 30–44, pp. 54–55.
vi, 45–52, pp. 55–56.
vi, 45—viii, 26, pp. 92–93.
vi, 53–56, p. 56.
vii, 1–23, pp. 56–57.
vii, 24–30, p. 57.
vii, 32–37, p. 74.
viii, 1–21, p. 57.
viii, 12, p. 241.
viii, 22–26, p. 74.
viii, 27–33, p. 58.
viii, 34–35, pp. 241–42.
viii, 34—ix, 1, pp. 58–59.
viii, 38, p. 242.
ix, 2–13, 59.
ix, 11–13, p. 73.
ix, 14–32, pp. 60–61.
ix, 33–48, p. 61.
ix, 42–48, p. 242.
ix, 49–50, p. 243.
x, 11–12, pp. 61, 243.
x, 13–45, p. 62.
x, 29, pp. 101–2.
x, 31, p. 243.
x, 43–44, p. 244.
x, 46–52, p. 63.
xi, 1–11, p. 63.
xi, 12–14, p. 64.
xi, 20–25, p. 64.
xi, 23, p. 244.

MARK—*continued*

xii, i–12, p. 65.
xii, 3, pp. 102–3.
xii, 18–27, p. 65.
xii, 28–40, p. 66.
xii, 38–40, p. 244.
xiii, 9–20, p. 66.
xiii, 11, p. 244.
xiii, 24–32, p. 67.
xiv, 1, p. 103.
xiv, 3–9, 73.
xiv, 12, pp. 104–5.
xiv, 22–25, p. 68.
xiv, 25, p. 73.
xiv, 28, p. 73.
xiv, 32–54, p. 68.
xiv, 58, p. 73.
xiv, 66–72, p. 69.
xv, 21–32, p. 69.
xv, 42, p. 105.

MATTHEW:

iii, 7–10, p. 129.
iii, 11–12, p. 130.
iii, 13–17, p. 37.
iv, 3–11, pp. 130–31.
iv, 18–22, pp. 38, 95–96.
iv, 25, p. 101.
v, 3, p. 131.
v, 4–5, p. 167.
v, 5–6, p. 132.
v, 7–10, pp. 167–68.
v, 11–13, pp. 132–33.
v, 14, p. 169.
v, 15, pp. 47, 133–34.
v, 16, p. 169.
v, 17, 19–24, 27–28, pp. 170–71.
v, 18, p. 135.
v, 25–26, p. 135.
v, 29–30, p. 171.
v, 31, pp. 171–72.
v, 31–32, p. 61.
v, 33–37, p. 172.
v, 39–40, pp. 135–36.
v, 41, p. 172.
v, 43, p. 173.
v, 44–48, pp. 135–36.
vi, 1–4, pp. 173–74.
vi, 5–8, p. 174.
vi, 9–13, p. 136.
vi, 16–18, p. 175.
vi, 19–23, p. 137.
vi, 24–33, p. 138.
vii, 1–5, p. 139.
vii, 6, pp. 175–76.
vii, 7–11, pp. 139–40.
vii, 12–14, p. 140.
vii, 15, p. 176.
vii, 16–18, p. 141.
vii, 19–20, p. 177.
vii, 21–23, pp. 141–42.

MATTHEW—continued
vii, 24–27, p. 143.
vii, 28, pp. 177–78.
vii, 28–29, p. 38.
viii, 1–4, p. 41.
viii, 5–10, pp. 143–45.
viii, 11–12, pp. 145–46.
viii, 13, pp. 178–79.
viii, 14–15, pp. 38–39.
viii, 16, p. 100.
viii, 16–17, p. 39.
viii, 19–22, p. 146.
ix, 1–8, p. 41.
ix, 5–6, pp. 93–94.
ix, 9–13, p. 42.
ix, 13, p. 179.
ix, 14–17, p. 42.
ix, 18–26, pp. 49–50.
ix, 27–31, p. 179.
ix, 32–34, p. 180.
ix, 35, pp. 51–52.
ix, 37–38, p. 146.
x, 2–4, pp. 44–45.
x, 5–8, p. 180.
x, 10–13, pp. 146–47.
x, 15, p. 147.
x, 16, p. 148.
x, 16–25, pp. 180–81.
x, 19–20, p. 148.
x, 24–25, p. 148.
x, 26–33, pp. 149–50.
x, 34–36, p. 150.
x, 37–39, pp. 150–51.
x, 40, p. 151.
x, 41–42, pp. 180–81.
xi, 2–27, p. 152.
xi, 14, p. 181.
xi, 15, p. 182.
xi, 20, p. 182.
xi, 23–24, pp. 182–83.
xi, 28–30, p. 183.
xii, 1–8, p. 43.
xii, 3–4, p. 94.
xii, 5–7, p. 184.
xii, 9–21, p. 44.
xii, 17–21, p. 184.
xii, 22–37, p. 45.
xii, 27–28, p. 153.
xii, 30, p. 153.
xii, 34, p. 184.
xii, 36–37, p. 185.
xii, 38–42, p. 153.
xii, 40, p. 185.
xii, 43–45, p. 154.
xiii, 16–33, p. 154.
xiii, 18–23, p. 46.
xiii, 24–30, p. 185.
xiii, 44–52, pp. 186–87.
xiii, 53–58, p. 51.
xiv, 1–2, pp. 52–53.
xiv, 3–12, pp. 53–54.
xiv, 13–21, pp. 54–55.
xiv, 22–33, pp. 55–56.
xiv, 28–31, p. 187.
xiv, 34–36, p. 56.
xv, 1–20, p. 56.
xv, 14, p. 155.
xv, 21–28, p. 57.
xv, 22–24, pp. 187–88.
xv, 29–31, pp. 188–89.

MATTHEW—continued
xv, 32–39, p. 57.
xvi, 1–12, p. 57.
xvi, 13–23, p. 58.
xvi, 17–19, p. 189.
xvi, 24–28, pp. 58–59.
xvii, 1–8, p. 59.
xvii, 6–7, p. 189.
xvii, 9–13, p. 59.
xvii, 14–23, p. 60.
xviii, 1–5, p. 61.
xviii, 4, pp. 189–90.
xviii, 6–9, p. 61.
xviii, 7, p. 156.
xviii, 12–14, p. 156.
xviii, 21–22, p. 157.
xviii, 23–35, p. 190.
xix, 10–12, p. 190.
xix, 13–15, p. 62.
xix, 16–30, p. 62.
xix, 28, p. 157.
xix, 29, p. 101.
xx, 1–16, p. 190.
xx, 17–28, p. 62.
xx, 29–34, p. 63.
xxi, 1–11, p. 63.
xxi, 18–27, p. 64.
xxi, 33–46, p. 65.
xxi, 28–32, p. 191.
xxi, 35, p. 102.
xxii, 1–14, p. 191.
xxii, 34–40, p. 66.
xxii, 41–46, p. 66.
xxiii, 2–3, p. 191.
xxiii, 4, pp. 157–58.
xxiii, 5, 8–10, p. 191.
xxiii, 12–13, p. 158.
xxiii, 15–22, p. 191.
xxiii, 23–26, p. 159.
xxiii, 29–31, p. 159.
xxiii, 34–36, p. 160.
xxiii, 37–39, p. 161.
xxiv, 9–22, p. 66.
xxiv, 26–28, p. 161.
xxiv, 34–36, p. 67.
xxiv, 37–39, pp. 161–62.
xxiv, 40–41, p. 162.
xxiv, 43–51, p. 162.
xxv, 1–46, pp. 191–92.
xxvi, 2, p. 103.
xxvi, 17, p. 104.
xxvi, 26–29, p. 68.
xxvi, 36–58, p. 68.
xxvi, 52–54, p. 192.
xxvi, 67–68, pp. 104–5.
xxvi, 69–75, p. 69.
xxvii, 32–44, p. 69.
xxvii, 57, p. 105.

LUKE:
iii, 7–9, p. 129.
iii, 10–14, p. 193.
iii, 16–17, p. 130.
iii, 21–22, p. 37.
iv, 3–13, p. 130.
iv, 16–30, pp. 51, 194.
iv, 31–39, p. 38.
iv, 40, p. 100.

INDEXES 261

LUKE—continued

iv, 40–43, p. 39.
v, 1–11, pp. 38, 40.
v, 12–26, p. 41.
v, 23–24, pp. 93–94.
v, 27–39, p. 42.
vi, 1–5, p. 43.
vi, 3–4, p. 94.
vi, 6–19, p. 44.
vi, 17, p. 101.
vi, 20, p. 131.
vi, 21, p. 132.
vi, 22–23, pp. 132–33.
vi, 24–26, pp. 194–95.
vi, 27–30, 32–36, p. 135.
vi, 31, p. 140.
vi, 37–38, p. 139.
vi, 38, p. 47.
vi, 39, p. 155.
vi, 40, p. 148.
vi, 43–44, p. 141.
vi, 47–49, p. 143.
vii, 1–9, pp. 143–45.
vii, 18–35, p. 152.
vii, 29–30, p. 195.
vii, 36–50, p. 195.
vii, 41–42, p. 139.
viii, 4–10, p. 45.
viii, 11–15, p. 46.
viii, 16–18, p. 47.
viii, 19–21, p. 45.
viii, 22–25, p. 47.
viii, 26–39, pp. 48–49.
viii, 40–56, pp. 49–50.
ix, 1–6, pp. 51–52.
ix, 7–9, pp. 52–53.
ix, 10–17, pp. 54–55.
ix, 18–22, p. 58.
ix, 23–27, p. 58–59.
ix, 28–36, p. 59.
ix, 37–45, p. 60.
ix, 46–50, p. 61.
ix, 57–60, p. 146.
ix, 60–63, p. 196.
x, 2, p. 146.
x, 3, p. 148.
x, 5–8, p. 147.
x, 12, p. 147.
x, 13–15, p. 152.
x, 16, p. 151.
x, 17–20, p. 196.
x, 21–22, p. 152.
x, 23–24, p. 154.
x, 25–28, pp. 66, 197.
x, 29–37, p. 197.
x, 38–42, p. 197.
xi, 2–4, pp. 136–37.
xi, 5–8, p. 198.
xi, 9–13, pp. 139–40.
xi, 14–23, p. 45.
xi, 19–20, p. 153.
xi, 23, p. 153.
xi, 24–26, p. 154.
xi, 27–28, p. 198.
xi, 29–32, p. 153.
xi, 33, pp. 133–34.
xi, 34–35, pp. 137–38.
xi, 36, p. 198.
xi, 39–42, p. 159.
xi, 47–48, p. 159.

LUKE—continued

xi, 49–51, p. 160.
xii, 2–9, p. 149.
xii, 11–12, p. 148.
xii, 13–21, p. 198.
xii, 22–31, p. 138.
xii, 33–34, p. 137.
xii, 35–38, p. 198.
xii, 39–40, p. 162.
xii, 42–46, p. 162.
xii, 47–50, p. 199.
xii, 51–53, p. 150.
xii, 58–59, p. 135.
xiii, 1–5, p. 199.
xiii, 6–9, p. 200.
xiii, 18–19, p. 47.
xiii, 20–21, p. 154.
xiii, 23–24, p. 140.
xiii, 26–27, pp. 141–42.
xiii, 28–29, pp. 145–46.
xiii, 31–33, pp. 200–201.
xiii, 34–35, p. 161.
xiv, 1–6, p. 201.
xiv, 7–11, pp. 201–2.
xiv, 11, p. 158.
xiv, 12–24, p. 202.
xiv, 26–27, pp. 150–51.
xiv, 28–35, p. 203.
xiv, 34, p. 133.
xv, 1–7, p. 203.
xv, 4–7, p. 156.
xv, 8–32, p. 203.
xvi, 18, p. 61.
xvi, 1–12, pp. 203–4.
xvi, 14–15, p. 204.
xvi, 17, p. 135.
xvi, 19–31, p. 205.
xvii, 1, p. 156.
xvii, 1–2, p. 61.
xvii, 4, p. 157.
xvii, 6, p. 155.
xvii, 7–19, p. 205.
xvii, 9–13, p. 59.
xvii, 20–21, pp. 205–6.
xvii, 23–24, 26–27, p. 161.
xvii, 26–27, p. 161.
xvii, 33, pp. 150–51.
xvii, 34–35, p. 162.
xvii, 37, p. 161.
xviii, 15–17, p. 62.
xviii, 18–30, p. 62.
xviii, 29, p. 101.
xviii, 31–34, p. 62.
xviii, 35–43, p. 63.
xix, 28–38, p. 63.
xx, 1–8, p. 64.
xx, 9–19, p. 65.
xx, 10, p. 102.
xx, 27–40, p. 65.
xx, 45–47, p. 66.
xxi, 12–24, pp. 66–67.
xxi, 32–33, p. 67.
xxii, 1, pp. 103–4.
xxii, 7, p. 104.
xxii, 15–20, p. 68.
xxii, 28–30, p. 157.
xxii, 39–55, p. 68.
xxii, 56–62, p. 69.
xxiii, 26–43, p. 69.
xxiii, 54, pp. 105–6.

II. GENERAL INDEX

Abbott, E. A., 90.
Angels, twelve legions of, 192.
Arrest of Jesus, 68.
Assimilation, 91, 92, 242.
Authority of Jesus questioned, 64–65.

Bacon, B. W., 65, 108, 173, 234.
Bartimeus, 63.
Bartlet, J. V., 60, 108, 212.
Beatitudes, 131–32.
Beelzebul controversy, 238–39.
Birt, 36.
Blessing of the children, 62.
Blind leaders, 155.
Brotherhood of Jesus, 45.
Burkitt, F. C., 109, 112, 206.
Burton, 144, 217.

Calling of the first disciples, 38.
Canaanitish woman, 57.
Care, 138.
Centurion's son, 143–45, 178–79.
Changes of Matthew and Luke in Marcan narratives, chap. iv.
Changes of Matthew and Luke in Marcan order, Table I, 24–27.
"Come unto me," 183.
Conflation, 191, 240.
Crucifixion, 69.

Danger of riches, 62.
Dependence of Luke upon Matthew, 98, 99.
Dependence of Matthew upon Luke impossible, 98.
Detached sayings, 47.
Disciples, instructions to, 146–51, 180–81.
Disciples, mission of, 51–52
Disciples, return of, 54–55.
Discipleship, demands of, 58.
Distress, predictions of, 66–67.
Doublets, 190, 239, 241–45.

Elijah, 59.
Entry into Jerusalem, 63–64.
Epileptic boy, 60.
Evil husbandmen, 65.

Feeding of the five thousand, 54–55.
Feeding of the four thousand, 57.
Fig tree cursed, 64.

Gadarene demoniac, 48, 49.
Genealogies, 98.
Gennesaret, 56.
Gethsemane, 68.
Golden Rule, 140.
Goodspeed, E. J., 72.
Great Commandment, 66, 197.
Great Omission of Luke, 35, 92, 93.

Harnack, Adolf, 37, 110, 111, 112, 114, 115.
—, On content of Q, 108–19 *passim*, 126, 142, 165, 178, 191, 212, 234, 247.

Hawkins, Sir John, VI, 9, 15, 16, 33, 58, 67, 70, 84, 85, 110, 111, 112, 114.
— on content of Q, 108–19 *passim*, 164, 165, 170, 191, 208, 211, 247.
Healings in the evening, 39.
Herod, judgment concerning Jesus, 52–53.
Historic present in Mark, 85.
Holtzmann, J. H., 214.
Huck, Adolph, v.

Infancy section: in Luke, 211; in Matthew, 208.

Jairus' daughter, 49–50.
Jerusalem, lament over, 161.
Jerusalem narrative, 10.
Jerusalem tradition, 199–200.
John the Baptist: death of, 53; preaching of, 129; preaching of, in Luke, 193.
Jonah, 153, 185.
Judaistic features in Matthew, 167, 168, 170, 172, 176, 180, 188.
Jülicher, Adolf, 73, 125, 144, 211.

Kingdom of Heaven, eschatalogical meaning of, 166.

Last Supper, 68.
Leper healed, 41.
Logia, 97.
Loisy, A., 73, 183.
Lord's Prayer, 136–37.
Lost Sheep, parable of, 156.
Luke's Great Interpolation, 8–9.
Luke's Great Omission, 7, 8, 227–228.
Luke: matter peculiar to, 207, 210–18; single tradition of, 206–7; source peculiar to, 217–18.

Mark: his use of Q, 234–48; framework of, in Matthew and Luke, 3–13; words peculiar to, 85–87.
Matthew, matter peculiar to, 207–10; not a source for Luke, Robinson Smith's argument on, 100–107; single tradition of, 206; tendency to condensation, 189; messianic proclamation of, 130.
Montefiore, C. G., 183.
Motives of Matthew and Luke, 70, 71.
Mustard Seed, parable of, 47.

Narrow gate, parable of, 140.
Nazareth, preaching in, 51.

Offences, 61.
Omission of Marcan material by both Matthew and Luke, 30, 31.
Omissions of Luke, 32–36.
Order, deviations in, chap. ii.
Order of narratives of the Synoptics, chap. ii.
Oxford Studies, vi.

Parable of the Sower, 45; interpretation of, 46; of Treasure, Pearl, Fish-net, Converted Scribe, 186–87.
Parables peculiar to Luke, 197, 198, 200, 202, 203, 205.
Parables, purpose of, 45.
Paralytic healed, 41.
Parousia, 67, 180.
Passion narrative, 12, 13.
Perean source, 214–17.
Peter: calling of, 40, 194; confession of messiahship, 58; denial of, 69.
Peter's mother-in-law, 38.
Petrine strand in Mark, 75–76, 83–84.
Pharisaic accusation, 45.
Pharisees, 66, 153, 158, 159, 204.
Prediction of sufferings, 58, 60, 62.
Primary and secondary elements in Mark: according to von Soden, 74–77; according to Wendling, 74–87.
Primary and secondary traits, 187, 188; in Mark and Q, 235; in Luke, 200; priority of, 3–16.

Q: existence and content of, 108–20; analysis of, by Wellhausen, Wernle, Weiss, Hawkins, and Harnack, 112; distribution of, in Matthew, 112–13; Mark, overlapping of, 114; general agreement as to nucleus in Matthew, 114–15; in Luke, content according to Wellhausen, Wernle, Weiss, Hawkins, and Harnack, 116–19; distribution of in Luke, 119; necessity for further extension of, 120; originally an Aramaic document, 123–25; translation variance, 124, 125; analysis into QMt; and QLk, 126–65; in single tradition of Luke, 193–220; in single tradition of Matthew, 166–92; original order of, 249–54.
QMt, QLk: meaning of the symbols, 127; advantages of the hypothesis, 219, 221–33.

Resistance and non-resistance, 135–36.
Retirement of Jesus, 39.
Ropes, J. H., 181.
Rördam, T. S., 72.

Sadducees, 65.
Sanday, W., 89, 212–13, 219, 234.
Sanders, H. A., 98.
Schmeidel, Paul, 46, 67, 73, 135, 139, 170, 175, 203.
Seats in the Kingdom, 62.
Secondary traits in Q, QMt, and QLk, 230–33.
Seeking and finding, 139.
Sermon on the Mount, sayings from, 133–43; 167–78.
Seventy, return of the, 196.
Sign demanded, 57.

Smith, Robinson, 100, 107 *passim*, 173.
Soden, von, H. H., 74–84 *passim*.
Special source of Luke, 197, 201, 202, 203; meaning of, 192.
Stanton, V. H., 112, 171, 228.
Storm on the lake, 47.
Streeter, H. B., 114, 131, 180, 197, 198, 200, 202, 203, 204, 212, 234, 244, 253, 254.
Strife: about rank, 61; among relatives, 150.
Summary and conclusions, 255–56.
Synagogue at Capernaum, 38.

Tables: I, order of Marcan material in Matthew and Luke, 24–27; II, Q material in Matthew according to five scholars, 110, 111; III, Q material in Luke according to five scholars, 116–17; IV, Q material in Matthew, 222–23; V, Q material in Luke, 224–25; VI, Q material in Mark, 246; VII and VIII, on relative order of Q matter in Matthew and Luke, 250; IX, sections in Q material in their order in Matthew and Luke, 251; X, sections in Q material, slightly rearranged in order, 252.
Temptation, 130; in Mark and Q, 238.
Things that defile, 56–57.
Transfiguration, 59.
Translation variants, 240.
Transposition: in Luke, 70; in Mark, 72–74.
Tree and fruits, 141.
Twelve: calling of the 44; mission of, in Mark and Q, 241.
Two foundations, 143.

Unknown exorcist, 32, 61.
Ur-Marcus, 72, 88–93.

Verbal resemblance illustrated, 93–96.
Vocabulary in Mark and Q, 246–48.
Votaw, C. W., 173.

Widow's mite, 32.
Walk thru the corn, 43.
Walking on the sea, 55.
Weiss, B., 108.
Weiss, J., 46, 110, 111, 112.
— on content of Q, 108–10 *passim*, 134, 191, 194.
Wellhausen, J., 37, 55, 73, 110, 111, 112, 115.
— on content of Q, 108–19 *passim*, 133, 150, 183, 191, 198, 234, 240.
Wendling, E., 74–87, 228.
Wernle, Paul, vi, 32, 37, 65, 110, 111, 115.
— on content of Q, 108–19 *passim*, 191, 198, 210, 234, 244, 245.
Westcott and Hort, 69.
Withered hand, 44.

Yeast, a saying about, 57.

THE MACMILLAN COMPANY
64-66 FIFTH AVENUE :: :: :: NEW YORK

University of Michigan Studies

HUMANISTIC SERIES

General Editors: FRANCIS W. KELSEY and HENRY A. SANDERS

Size, 22.7×15.2 cm. 8°. Bound in cloth

VOL. I. ROMAN HISTORICAL SOURCES AND INSTITUTIONS. Edited by Professor Henry A. Sanders, University of Michigan. Pp. viii+402. $2.50 net.

CONTENTS

1. THE MYTH ABOUT TARPEIA: Professor Henry A. Sanders.
2. THE MOVEMENTS OF THE CHORUS CHANTING THE CARMEN SAECULARE: Professor Walter Dennison, Swarthmore College.
3. STUDIES IN THE LIVES OF ROMAN EMPRESSES, JULIA MAMAEA: Professor Mary Gilmore Williams, Mt. Holyoke College.
4. THE ATTITUDE OF DIO CASSIUS TOWARD EPIGRAPHIC SOURCES: Professor Duane Reed Stuart, Princeton University.
5. THE LOST EPITOME OF LIVY: Professor Henry A. Sanders.
6. THE PRINCIPALES OF THE EARLY EMPIRE: Professor Joseph H. Drake, University of Michigan.
7. CENTURIONS AS SUBSTITUTE COMMANDERS OF AUXILIARY CORPS: Professor George H. Allen, University of Cincinnati.

VOL. II. WORD-FORMATION IN PROVENÇAL. By Professor Edward L. Adams, University of Michigan. Pp. xvii+607. $4.00 net.

VOL. III. LATIN PHILOLOGY. Edited by Professor Clarence Linton Meader, University of Michigan. Pp. viii+290. $2.00 net.

Parts Sold Separately in Paper Covers:

Part I. THE USAGE OF IDEM, IPSE AND WORDS OF RELATED MEANING. By Clarence L. Meader. Pp. 1-112. $0.75.

Part II. A STUDY IN LATIN ABSTRACT SUBSTANTIVES. By Professor Manson A. Stewart, Yankton College. Pp. 113-78. $0.40.

Part III. THE USE OF THE ADJECTIVE AS A SUBSTANTIVE IN THE DE RERUM NATURA OF LUCRETIUS. By Dr. Frederick T. Swan. Pp. 179-214. $0.40.

Part IV. AUTOBIOGRAPHIC ELEMENTS IN LATIN INSCRIPTIONS. By Professor Henry H. Armstrong, Drury College. Pp. 215-86. $0.40.

University of Michigan Studies — *Continued*

Vol. IV. Roman History and Mythology. Edited by Professor Henry A. Sanders. Pp. viii+427. $2.50 net.

    Parts Sold Separately in Paper Covers:

    Part I. Studies in the Life of Heliogabalus. By Dr. Orma Fitch Butler, University of Michigan. Pp. 1–169. $1.25 net.

    Part II. The Myth of Hercules at Rome. By Professor John G. Winter, University of Michigan. Pp. 171–273. $0.50 net.

    Part III. Roman Law Studies in Livy. By Professor Alvin E. Evans, Washington State College. Pp. 275–354. $0.40 net.

    Part IV. Reminiscences of Ennius in Silius Italicus. By Dr. Loura B. Woodruff. Pp. 355–424. $0.40 net.

Vol. V. Sources of the Synoptic Gospels. By Rev. Dr. Carl S. Patton, First Congregational Church, Columbus, Ohio. Pp. xiii+263. $1.30 net.

Size, 28 × 19 cm. 4°.

Vol. VI. Athenian Lekythoi with Outline Drawing in Glaze Varnish on a White Ground. By Arthur Fairbanks, Director of the Museum of Fine Arts, Boston. With 15 plates, and 57 illustrations in the text. Pp. x+371. Bound in cloth. $4.00 net.

Vol. VII. Athenian Lekythoi with Outline Drawing in Dull Color on a White Ground, and an Appendix: Additional Lekythoi with Outline Drawing in Glaze Varnish on a White Ground. By Arthur Fairbanks. With 41 plates. Pp. x+275. Bound in cloth. $3.50 net.

Vol. VIII. The Old Testament Manuscripts in the Freer Collection. By Professor Henry A. Sanders, University of Michigan.

    Part I. The Washington Manuscript of Deuteronomy and Joshua. With 3 folding plates of pages of the Manuscript in facsimile. Pp. vi+104. Paper covers. $1.00.

    Part II. The Washington Manuscript of the Psalms. (*In Press.*)

Vol. IX. The New Testament Manuscripts in the Freer Collection. By Professor Henry A. Sanders, University of Michigan.

    Part I. The Washington Manuscript of the Four Gospels. With 5 plates. Pp. viii+247. Paper covers. $2.00.

    Part II. The Washington Fragments of the Epistles of Paul. (*In Preparation.*)

University of Michigan Studies — *Continued*

VOL. X. THE COPTIC MANUSCRIPTS IN THE FREER COLLECTION. By Professor William H. Worrell, Hartford Seminary Foundation. (*In Preparation.*)

VOL. XI. CONTRIBUTIONS TO THE HISTORY OF SCIENCE. (*In Press.*)

    Part I. ROBERT OF CHESTER'S LATIN TRANSLATION OF THE ALGEBRA OF AL-KHOWARIZMI. With an Introduction, Critical Notes, and an English Version. By Professor Louis C. Karpinski, University of Michigan. With 4 plates showing pages of manuscripts in facsimile, and 25 diagrams in the text. (*In Press.*)

    Part II. THE PRODROMUS OF NICHOLAS STENO'S LATIN DISSERTATION ON A SOLID BODY ENCLOSED BY NATURAL PROCESS WITHIN A SOLID. Translated into English by Professor John G. Winter, University of Michigan. With a Foreword by Professor William H. Hobbs. (*In Press.*)

VOL. XII. STUDIES IN EAST CHRISTIAN AND ROMAN ART.

    Part I. EAST CHRISTIAN PAINTINGS IN THE FREER COLLECTION. By Professor Charles R. Morey, Princeton University. With 13 plates (10 colored) and 34 illustrations in the text. Pp. xii+87. Bound in cloth. $2.50.

    Part II. A GOLD TREASURE OF THE LATE ROMAN PERIOD FROM EGYPT. By Professor Walter Dennison, Swarthmore College. (*In Press.*)

VOL. XIII. DOCUMENTS FROM THE CAIRO GENIZAH IN THE FREER COLLECTION. Text, with Translation and an Introduction by Professor Richard Gottheil, Columbia University. (*In Preparation.*)

SCIENTIFIC SERIES

Size 28×18.5 cm. 4°. Bound in cloth

Vol. I. THE CIRCULATION AND SLEEP. By Professor John F. Shepard, University of Michigan. Pp. x+83, with an Atlas of 83 plates, bound Separately. Text and Atlas, $3.00 net.

VOL. II. STUDIES ON DIVERGENT SERIES AND SUMMABILITY. By Professor Walter B. Ford, University of Michigan. (*In Preparation.*)

University of Michigan Publications

University of Michigan Publications

HUMANISTIC PAPERS

Size, 22.7 × 15.2 cm. 8°. Bound in cloth

LATIN AND GREEK IN AMERICAN EDUCATION, WITH SYMPOSIA ON THE VALUE OF HUMANISTIC STUDIES. Edited by Francis W. Kelsey. Pp. x+396. $1.50.

CONTENTS

THE PRESENT POSITION OF LATIN AND GREEK, THE VALUE OF LATIN AND GREEK AS EDUCATIONAL INSTRUMENTS, THE NATURE OF CULTURE STUDIES.

SYMPOSIA ON THE VALUE OF HUMANISTIC, PARTICULARLY CLASSICAL, STUDIES AS A PREPARATION FOR THE STUDY OF MEDICINE, ENGINEERING, LAW, AND THEOLOGY.

SYMPOSIA ON THE VALUE OF HUMANISTIC, PARTICULARLY CLASSICAL, STUDIES AS A TRAINING FOR MEN OF AFFAIRS; ON THE CLASSICS AND THE NEW EDUCATION; AND ON THE DOCTRINE OF FORMAL DISCIPLINE IN THE LIGHT OF CONTEMPORARY PSYCHOLOGY.

THE MACMILLAN COMPANY
PUBLISHERS   64–66 FIFTH AVENUE   NEW YORK

THE MACMILLAN COMPANY
64-66 FIFTH AVENUE :: :: :: NEW YORK

Handbooks of Archaeology and Antiquities

Edited by PERCY GARDNER, of the University of Oxford, and FRANCIS W. KELSEY, of the University of Michigan.

The Principles of Greek Art

By PERCY GARDNER, Litt.D., Lincoln and Merton Professor of Classical Archaeology, University of Oxford.

Makes clear the artistic and psychological principles underlying Greek art, especially sculpture, which is treated as a characteristic manifestation of the Greek spirit, a development parallel to that of Greek literature and religion. While there are many handbooks of Greek archaeology, this volume holds a unique place.

Illustrated, cloth, $2.25; postpaid, $2.46

Greek Architecture

By ALLAN MARQUAND, Ph.D., L.H.D., Professor of Art and Archaeology in Princeton University.

Professor Marquand, in this interesting and scholarly volume, passes from the materials of construction to the architectural forms and decorations of the buildings of Greece, and, lastly, to its monuments. Nearly four hundred illustrations assist the reader in a clear understanding of the subject.

Cloth, $2.25; postpaid, $2.45

Greek Sculpture

By ERNEST A. GARDNER, M.A., Professor of Archaeology in University College, London.

A comprehensive outline of our present knowledge of Greek sculpture, distinguishing the different schools and periods, and showing the development of each. This volume, fully illustrated, fills an important gap and is widely used as a textbook.

Cloth, $2.50; postpaid, $2.67

Greek Constitutional History

By A. H. J. GREENIDGE, M.A., Late Lecturer in Hertford College and Brasenose College, Oxford.

Most authors in writing of Greek History emphasize the structure of the constitutions; Mr. Greenidge lays particular stress upon the workings of these constitutions. With this purpose ever in view, he treats of the development of Greek public law, distinguishing the different types of states as they appear.

Cloth, $1.25; postpaid, $1.35

THE MACMILLAN COMPANY
64-66 FIFTH AVENUE :: :: :: NEW YORK

Greek and Roman Coins

By G. F. HILL, M.A., of the Department of Coins and Medals in the British Museum.

All the information needed by the beginner in numismatics, or for ordinary reference, is here presented. The condensation necessary to bring the material within the size of the present volume has in no way interfered with its clearness or readableness.

Cloth, $2.25; postpaid, $2.38

Greek Athletic Sports and Festivals

By E. NORMAN GARDINER, M.A., Sometime Classical Exhibitor of Christ Church College, Oxford.

With over two hundred illustrations from contemporary art, and bright descriptive text, this work proves of equal interest to the general reader and to the student of the past. Many of the problems with which it deals—the place of physical training, games, athletics, in daily and national life—will be found as real at the present time as they were in the far-off days of Greece.

Cloth, $2.50; postpaid, $2.66

Athens and Its Monuments

·By CHARLES HEALD WELLER, University of Iowa.

This book embodies the results of many years of study and of direct observation during different periods of residence in Athens. It presents in concise and readable form a description of the ancient city in the light of the most recent investigations. It is profusely illustrated with half-tones and line engravings.

$4.00 net; postpaid, $4.25

The Destruction of Ancient Rome

By RODOLFO LANCIANI, D.C.L., Oxf. d; LL.D., Harvard; Professor of Ancient Topography in the Unive sity of Rome.

Rome, the fate of her buildings and masterpieces of art, is the subject of this profusely illustrated volume. Professor Lanciani gives us vivid pictures of the Eternal City at the close of the different periods of history.

Cloth, $1.50; postpaid, $1.63

THE MACMILLAN COMPANY
64-66 FIFTH AVENUE :: :: :: NEW YORK

Roman Festivals

By W. WARDE FOWLER, M.A., Fellow and Sub-Rector of Lincoln College, Oxford.

This book covers in a concise form almost all phases of the public worship of the Roman state, as well as certain ceremonies which, strictly speaking, lay outside that public worship. It will be found very useful to students of Roman literature and history as well as to students of anthropology and the history of religion.

Cloth, $1.25; postpaid, $1.37

Roman Public Life

By A. H. J. GREENIDGE, M.A., Late Lecturer in Hertford College and Brasenose College, Oxford.

The growth of the Roman constitution and its working during the developed Republic and the Principate is the subject which Mr. Greenidge here set for himself. All important aspects of public life, municipal and provincial, are treated so as to reveal the political genius of the Romans in connection with the chief problems of administration.

Cloth, $2.50; postpaid, $2.63

Monuments of the Early Church

By WALTER LOWRIE, M.A., Rector of St. Paul's Church, Rome.

Nearly two hundred photographs and drawings of the most representative monumental remains of Christian antiquity, accompanied by detailed expositions, make this volume replete with interest for the general reader and at the same time useful as a handbook for the student of Christian archaeology in all its branches.

Cloth, $1.25; postpaid, $1.39

Monuments of Christian Rome

By ARTHUR L. FROTHINGHAM, Ph.D., formerly Professor of Archaeology and Ancient History in Princeton University.

"The plan of the volume is simple and admirable. The first part comprises a historical sketch; the second, a classification of the monuments."—*The Outlook*.

Profusely illustrated. *Cloth, $2.25; postpaid, $2.43*

www.ingramcontent.com/pod-product-compliance
Lightning Source LLC
Chambersburg PA
CBHW021137230426
43667CB00005B/159